Spiritual Tarot

Other Avon Trade Paperbacks by
**Signe E. Echols, M.S.,
Robert Mueller, Ph.D., and
Sandra A. Thomson**

THE LOVERS' TAROT

Spiritual Tarot

SEVENTY-EIGHT PATHS TO PERSONAL DEVELOPMENT

SIGNE E. ECHOLS, M.S., ROBERT MUELLER, Ph.D., and SANDRA A. THOMSON

AVON BOOKS ◆ NEW YORK

VISIT OUR WEBSITE AT
http://AvonBooks.com

AVON BOOKS
A division of
The Hearst Corporation
1350 Avenue of the Americas
New York, New York 10019

Copyright © 1996 by Signe E. Echols, Robert E. Mueller, and Sandra A. Thomson, Ed.D.
Published by arrangement with the authors
Library of Congress Catalog Card Number: 95-50112
ISBN: 0-380-78206-5

Library of Congress Cataloging in Publication Data:

Spiritual tarot : 78 paths to personal development / Signe E. Echols, Robert Mueller and Sandra Thomson.
    p.   cm.
  Includes bibliographical references and index.
  1. Tarot.   I. Echols, Signe E.   II. Mueller, Robert E. (Robert Eugene) III. Thomson, Sandra A.
 BF1879.T2S68   1996   95-50112
 133.3'2424—dc20   CIP

First Avon Books Trade Printing: July 1996

AVON TRADEMARK REG. U.S. PAT. OFF. AND IN OTHER COUNTRIES, MARCA REGISTRADA, HECHO EN U.S.A.

Printed in the U.S.A.

OPM   10 9 8 7 6 5 4 3

We must learn to offer the world a way of approach
that honors both the ego's desire to be holy
and the soul's true delight
at getting to be
all-too-human.

—Jacquelyn Small

To Georgia Lambert and Roger Weir.
Beloved teachers on the sacred path.

☀ Acknowledgments

Our debt to all the authors listed in the bibliography and to the extended community of Tarot teachers and workers will become more and more evident as you progress through the book.

Special thanks to Mary K. Greer for permission to use information regarding her innovative Tarot reading styles and for reading and improving on a preliminary copy of Chapter 15. Any errors in depicting her reading styles remain ours.

Certainly we have to acknowledge Tuna, our Tarot cat, who never failed in her duty to remind us when it was time for love breaks. She also signified her satisfaction with each page of the manuscript by sleeping on it, and expressed her dissatisfaction with the attention we gave the work by plopping herself down in the middle of pages we were proofreading.

☀ Contents

PART 1—LEARNING THE BASICS

PART 3—LEARNING THE CARDS: THE MINOR ARCANA

PART 4—MAPPING IT ALL OUT

PART 5—READING THE MAP

PART 6—SAMPLE JOURNEYS

PART ONE

✸ ✸ ✸

LEARNING THE BASICS

1 ☀ What Is the Tarot?

Welcome to the world of Tarot, where every human characteristic and personality trait is portrayed in a deck of 78 cards.

Will you find yourself there? You bet. Will you find your friend, lover, or mate? No doubt about it. A flip of the wrist, a few cards laid out in a specific pattern, and an entirely new perspective is available to you.

Will you be able to "read" the cards for others and catch a glimpse of their futures? Well, that *is* the traditional focus for the Tarot, and many people unfamiliar with the cards do think of them *only* as fortune-telling devices. However, we think that there are much better uses for the Tarot.

While we'd all like to have a peek at what's in store for us, *Spiritual Tarot: Seventy-Eight Paths to Personal Development* emphasizes two approaches to Tarot card reading that we believe are the most beneficial for the modern person: (1) reading to gain new insights on life issues or events, and (2) reading to stimulate and enhance self-exploration and understanding.

We like to think of the Tarot as a highly sophisticated, interactive "picture book" of life experiences, a finely tuned communication system, employing symbolism, mythology, and universal motifs unrestricted by time, culture, and semantics. It speaks a special language. To hear what it has to say, you'll need to attend to cards' visual images and listen with your heart.

What you'll learn may intrigue or delight you, reassure you or confirm your suspicions, but one thing is certain. Your experience with the Tarot will bear little resemblance to those commonly seen in novels and movies—which is where many of us get our first impressions of Tarot cards and what they can do.

Although author Martha Smilgis *(Fame's Peril)* intends to have a true-to-life psychic Tarot reader in her next mystery novel,[1] and the royal family in science fiction novelist Roger Zelazny's popular "Amber" series employs a modified Tarot deck to communicate with absent family members, fiction writers most often use Tarot cards to deliver warnings. Dire predictions of imminent danger heighten suspense and move the story along. Unfortunately, they also completely distort the real purpose, power, and potential of the cards.

For instance, in Al Guthrie's *Murder by Tarot*, a fortune-teller draws the Death card and tries to hide it from the heroine.

"Uh-oh," the reader is supposed to think. "Something horrible is going to happen to her."

We, on the other hand, don't see it that way. Since the *growth* meaning of the Death card is transition—the relinquishing of old ideas and attitudes to make way for new experiences or behaviors—we think that the heroine is about to make some internal changes. The Death card says that a lot of inner work is needed or has occurred.

Similarly, before the fictional James Qwilleran leaves for Scotland, one of the characters in Lilian Jackson Braun's *The Cat Who Went Into the Closet* does a Tarot reading for him and draws what is apparently the Nine of Pentacles from the Rider-Waite deck (one of the decks we use in this book).

The Tarot reader's interpretation—beware of fraud or treachery—is meant to clue us in to what's coming, only *we* understand the Nine of Pentacles to speak of *success*, enjoying the fruits of your labor, perhaps egotistically, and the need to draw upon inner feminine wisdom to help you accomplish the tasks in front of you.

If we were doing the reading, we would have said to Qwilleran, "Get smart here, fella. It's time to change your style of thinking. Use a little more intuition."

Now, hearing that wouldn't have hurt him and actually might have helped, but it's just not the sort of thing you see in fiction. Fictional Tarot readers foretell events with pinpoint accuracy in mere seconds because the plots of movies and books have to move quickly to keep their audience interested. Who is going to sit through a scene in which the hero has to spend fifteen minutes or more listening to a Tarot reader explain how an upcoming battle with his archenemy will bring up certain relationship issues and the potential for improved self-worth?

When you're the subject of a reading, however, and its objective is to generate insight and personal development, you *will want* to take the time to understand every nuance of the reading. You may even want to keep a record of your responses to mark your progress and serve as an inspiration for further Tarot work.

The basic principles and uses of the Tarot are easy to learn, and that's what this book is all about. You don't need to be psychic or specially gifted in any way. As you venture with us into new areas, our instructions will lead you to new awareness. What's more, your Tarot reader will be the person who is most concerned about you: YOURSELF.

In the introduction to our first Tarot book, *The Lovers' Tarot*, Peter Balin, author of *The Flight of Feathered Serpent* and creator of its accompanying Xultun deck, wrote, "There is no better way to enter into the process of self-understanding than through the Tarot."[2] We wholeheartedly agree.

The insights you'll obtain from your very first reading will surprise you, and your confidence will grow with each additional reading you do. Through it all, you will be in the driver's seat. *You* will decide whether or not, and when, to act on your new Tarot insights. In fact, you will be actively involved from start to finish. The Tarot "works" by evoking responses from you. It triggers *your* memories, feelings, or mental associations, and as a result, you expand your awareness of what's going on in particular situations or areas of your life.

If it is true, as philosopher William Irwin Thompson suggests, that we do not live in reality but rather in our habituated perceptions and illusions,[3] then the Tarot provides an opportunity to change our lives for the better by viewing our personal reality differently.

The Tarot works for you according to where you are with respect to your own needs and insight. The more you use the Tarot cards and the more you grow (as a result of your involvement with them or any other system for personal development), the more profound and complex your readings become.

At a given time, your desires and "hang-ups" will limit what you are able to attend to in a card and how you understand its meaning. But as you change, you will begin to see different things in the cards or understand a particular card differently. What you learn from the Tarot next year, or twenty years from now, will be a far cry from what you learned from the cards during your first reading—or could learn from today's.

Now, what about those newspaper and television advertisements that promise you'll find your soul mate, great wealth, or solutions to all your problems by calling a beautiful, exotic Tarot card reader at a pricey 900 number? We don't even have to lay out the cards to tell you that the one thing you'll definitely hear is how much of your present wealth to transfer into their bank account. The one to three dollars per minute that some 900 numbers charge adds up quickly when it takes *at least* thirty minutes to do an adequate reading or an hour to do a thorough one. And who knows what kind of advice you're going to get for your money?

There are greedy opportunists in every field of human endeavor. Don't let that dissuade you. Indeed, it's a good reason to learn the cards yourself and get your own answers. So take a deep breath, and like Alice, step through the looking glass and into the world of the Tarot, where you just might find a great deal more than you've ever dreamt.

2 ☀ What the Tarot Offers

Overview

The Tarot deck contains 78 cards: 22 Major Arcana or "great mysteries" and 56 Minor Arcana or "lesser mysteries." In using the Tarot for divination, the 22 Major Arcana are usually thought of as representing our reactions to or feelings about life experiences over which we have no control. As guides to inner development, they depict universal forces within us that are attempting to express to, or through, us. Our higher self may be bringing them to our attention, as we progress in our spiritual journey toward wholeness.

The 56 Minor Arcana cards are divided into four suits: Pentacles, Cups, Swords, Wands. Each suit has 14 cards ranging from Ace to Ten, plus four court cards—Page, Knight, Queen, and King.

When working with the Tarot for personal growth, the 16 court cards of the Minor Arcana—a Page, Knight, Queen, and King for each suit—represent various stages of personal or spiritual maturity. The remaining 40 cards depict personal experiences, gifts, and challenges in the areas "governed" by each suit: Pentacles for physical/sensual activities, Swords for logic and intellect, Cups for feelings, and Wands for spirituality/intuition.

Tarot historian Stuart Kaplan likens each of the four Minor Arcana suits in the Rider-Waite deck to a family story told backward from the King to the Ace.[1] Kaplan understands Pentacles to tell the story of "a wealthy family and the temptations and alternatives afforded them by the luxuries of wealth."

The Swords "family story" expresses the violent feelings of grief, revenge, capture, rescue, more grief and desire for revenge that a

7

sister experiences after her Knight/brother, and later her Page/lover, are killed.

According to Kaplan, Cups tell the story of "the paths to happiness and the search of two brothers for companionship." The Wands/Rods story is that of a family divided between traditional and modern ways. They discover that harmony and progress are best attained when the old and new work together.

In their most spiritual sense each minor suit represents one of the letters of the Tetragrammaton,[2] the fourfold division of the Divine name, as expressed in four Hebrew letters: Yod, Heh, Vau, Heh. The letters of the Tetragrammaton have been variously translated as YHWH, JHVH, and IHVH, pronounced Yahweh or Jehovah. As the one spiritual Godhead descends into matter, it separates into four discrete parts, each corresponding to a Minor Arcana suit. This symbolizes that an active aspect of God is in each of the four Minor Arcana suits.

Incidentally, these four Tarot suits became the four suits of our modern-day playing cards. Wands became clubs; Cups became hearts. Swords are now spades, and Pentacles are the suit of diamonds. The only Major Arcana card to make the transition was The Fool, a trickster figure who became—what else?—the Joker, a shape changer who can be any other card in some games or a wild card in others.

Symbols and Archetypes in the Tarot

Whether Major or Minor, each card conveys information through its scene or activity, its characters, their interaction, and the stance or attitude that seems to be depicted (passive/aggressive; friendly/hostile; aloof/close).

A variety of symbols are imbedded in each picture. They also affect our perception and activate our inner self. Symbols allow us to express facets of our experience and personality in an artistic presentation that is beyond language, but readily recognized by the unconscious. They bring together ideas that are not necessarily linked by logic. We may not be able to articulate them, yet we "know" their meaning intellectually and in our hearts.

This is what the art of the Tarot scenes and the "art" of a Tarot reading offer us. Although flat and two-dimensional themselves, the cards depict forces that have been active in everyone's life at some time or another. You "read" a card by comparing its scenes and symbols to events, interactions, conflicts, and accomplishments in your life. Does the activity on a card resemble the communication in your relationship? Does an authority figure on a given card refer to your boss or a parent, or the authority position you presently hold?

Through regular use, and by attending to the Tarot's symbolism, you can learn many wondrous things about yourself, including the role archetypal motifs play in your personal development.

Swiss psychiatrist C. G. Jung spent a lifetime developing his concept of archetypes (**ark**-eh-types), the *universal* qualities or patterns of energies operating within each of us. According to Jungian analyst and Episcopal priest John Sanford, they are the "essential building blocks of the personality." The central archetype—the unifying and organizing force at the core of our personality pushing us toward wholeness—is what Jung calls the Self. Some Jungians equate it with the soul.[3]

Two other frequently referred to archetypes are:

- the *anima*, which Jung originally considered the ultimate feminine principle embodied in such feminine aspects of the male personality as caring, responsiveness, and the facility for relationships. Jung revised his definition several times, and later came to regard the anima as the personified image of a man's soul.

  He said there were four basic images of the anima: Eve, Helen of Troy, Mary, and Sophia, the female God-wisdom aspect. In dreams she may appear as an unknown, but extremely significant or noticeable, woman, and tends to show up when a man has failed to acknowledge his feminine side.

- the *animus*, Jung's term for the masculine life principle as it appears in a female, which reflects a woman's capacity for courage, intellect, and spirituality. Appearing in her dreams as an unknown but extremely significant or noticeable male, the animus's presence suggests that the woman has failed to acknowledge her masculine side and its emphasis on autonomy, separation, principles/rights, and hierarchy.

These and other qualities, principles, or patterns of instinctual behavior determine our basic functioning as human beings. Although ancient, they are still alive in our psyches, allowing us to locate ourselves in myth and other symbology. They form the basis of religions, mythologies, legends, and fairy tales. As such, they are always culturally defined and expressed, even though their concept is universal.

Something that is archetypal is "typical" for all human beings,[4] and when taken all together, archetypes comprise a reservoir of knowledge that Jung called the *collective unconscious*.[5] Although we can all tap into the collective unconscious, its archetypal patterns can only be seen or expressed in outward images, artwork, and dreams. For Jung, the Tarot was just such a set of archetypal images, and their archetypal motifs may be one of the reasons the Tarot continues to intrigue people. It connects with those deep inner energies within that we can't easily describe, but nevertheless recognize as a part of ourselves.

The Tarot's Place in Daily Life

Tarot cards can enhance your daily life by offering you insight into a current situation. They tell you which forces are demanding recognition, which are being expressed, and which need to be considered within a given situation. They suggest the opportunities available to you and the tasks or tests required for personal development. They provide a visual encyclopedia of your inner state of being at any given time.

When you're experiencing strong emotions, use the cards to determine what "buttons are being pushed" and why. When a situation seems to be out of control, ask the cards, "Why is this happening?" They will shed light on your inner struggle and show you how to grow from your experience.

When you are having a difficult time, or facing an unpleasant situation, select a Major Arcana card with the attributes you think would help you handle the situation more effectively. Ask yourself, "What would The Hierophant (or Strength or Justice) do in this situation?" Then, to quote Captain Picard of the "Star Trek: The Next Generation" television series, "make it so." Act as you think the person in that card would act. If you think it would help play your "role," wear the same colors as your role model.

Meditating on the Cards

In addition to laying out the cards for a reading, you can select Major Arcana cards—either from your readings or because they appeal to you—and meditate on the role you think they or their archetypal energy play in your life.

In fact, one of the best and most common ways to understand a card's meaning is to meditate on it, and attend to whatever thoughts about it come into your mind. You can also mentally converse with the cards. Ask them questions about their meaning or intent. Wait for the answer. Your inner wisdom regarding the card will come through in their response. Ask a card to show you how its message applies to specific things that are happening in your life today.

Focus on each card separately over the course of a week. What symbols on the card seem to stand out to you? How might they apply to your own life? Wear the major colors of the card for that week, or place them in strategic places around your home to remind you of your Tarot work.

What memories do the images on the card evoke? If those memories are unpleasant, look to other symbols on the card for a more balanced perception of your experiences. Perhaps something about this card will stir you to resolve unpleasant past experiences and move forward.

Adopt the position of the figure(s) in a card. How would you feel if you sat or stood this way? What thoughts come into your mind as you do? What would you want around you? How would you feel if you looked around and saw the other images that are on the card?

Now walk, move, or even dance the way you think the figure in the card would. How does it feel? What insight does it give you about your inner Hierophant, say, or whatever card you're working on?

Consider those cards that you don't like—for all of us some cards are more appealing than others. What's happening there? Try to determine what in the card makes you feel uneasy, frightened, angry, or whatever you are feeling. Does the person or action depicted in the card resemble present or past experiences or present or past relationships? How do you think the events in this card were a part of your life, or are you afraid they may become a part of it?

The images that evoke strong negative feelings could represent an unacknowledged aspect of yourself. For instance, if you think the Queen of one of the suits is rigid and you don't take to her as well as you do to the other three Queens, where might that attitude exist in you? Have there been times when you felt or behaved like that Queen? What was happening? It takes courage to confront this issue, but could there be just a bit of that rigid, difficult-to-warm-up-to Queen in you? Even if you wish it weren't so, you've probably suspected it might be.

Don't worry. We have all felt that way, and our feelings usually tipped us off to some inner business that needed to be finished. This is likely to be true for you, too.

Unfinished business is an attitude or experience from your past that continues to actively influence your life today. Even though its origin may be buried deep in your unconscious, you still have some emotional investment in it. Jungian analysts refer to the unacknowledged and often unrecognized aspects of ourselves as the "shadow." Efforts to uncover and understand it are called "shadow work."

Shadow Work and the Tarot

Our personal shadows are the facets of ourselves that we came to believe were improper or unacceptable and subsequently disowned. Poet Robert Bly calls them the "long bag we drag behind us" and says they came into being when we, as infants "trailing clouds of glory," discovered that our parents wanted, instead, *nice* boys or girls.[6] Our shadows grew as our parents put certain restrictions on us ("You can't hit your little brother") or taught us various societal prohibitions ("You can't spit at the table"). Later our teachers, and other authority figures, added to them. We all have them.

No one reaches adulthood or acquires socialized behavior, self-confidence, and a strong ego without creating a shadow. The trick is to recognize and acknowledge its existence and learn from its various appearances. When you hit an impasse in your life or feel emotionally blocked, you need to turn to the shadow to see what you're holding in check, what you don't want to face. Reowning it releases a tremendous amount of creative energy and frees us to make choices once again.

There is, in fact, no access to the disowned aspects of ourselves except through the shadow; no move toward wholeness until we assimilate the knowledge of their always-underlying presence; and no harmony until we own up to our shadow impulses instead of attributing certain undesirable characteristics to people other than ourselves.

Each Tarot card has its shadow aspect, although it is rarely mentioned in traditional definitions. Some writers give you a glimpse of it in their interpretation of what the card means when it appears upside down. Others have dealt with shadow aspects by lumping all of them into one or two cards, usually The Devil and The Tower.[7] In literature, from fairy tales to classic film scripts, a similar shortcut is taken. By including one or two ominous figures—Dr. Jekyll's Mr. Hyde, Darth Vader in the "Star Wars" movies—and having them act out all existing shadow expressions, the storytellers remind us that we all have a shadow aspect. Unfortunately, that doesn't help us understand how the shadow works in our own inner being. In growth work, our shadow traits are identified and acknowledged bit by bit. And the Tarot cards that are the least appealing to you personally or make you the most uncomfortable contain a bit or two.

Those cards, no matter how many positive values some New Age Tarot readers may attribute to them, are tapping into some aspect of your personal shadow and offering you an opportunity to see and learn from it.

Keeping a Tarot Journal

With any type of growth work, it's a good idea to keep a log or journal of your experiences and insights. Tarot work is no exception. Enlarge and reproduce the Tarot journal pages in the Appendix to record your readings and interpretations. Each Tarot reading is only one episode or step in your journey toward wholeness, a process Jungian analysts call individuation.[8] Keeping track of your readings over a period of time allows you to monitor your inner development, including plateaus or temporary regressions to an earlier state.

If you are seeing some of the same cards in the same position(s) a year from now, maybe there's a message there that you've been ignoring. Maybe now, by noticing it, you can begin a new phase of your self-development. Or you may think your life is going nowhere, only to review a series of readings over time and see that your inner life is moving right along.

Whenever you or another reader interpret the cards and the positions in which they are found, you will need to ask yourself, "Does this make sense? Does this fit with what I know is happening? Does it clarify or broaden my understanding by bringing in something new to consider?" Sometimes it's tough to tell.

You are striving to understand the forces at work within you as they are expressed through the symbols of the Tarot. Patience may be required. Honor *all* information you receive, whether or not you immediately grasp it. Do not summarily dismiss it. Instead adopt an attitude of respectful regard, and if the cards seem like they don't apply to your situation or make sense, you can create a second reading to ask for clarification, or enter the original spread in your Tarot log and review it in connection with later readings. The puzzle pieces may not fall into place immediately, but after several days, weeks, or months, they will.

3 ❂ Choosing a Deck and Using It

Overview

No one knows when the first Tarot deck was created, although there are a number of intriguing stories about its origin. One of the most enduring gives the ancient Egyptians credit for developing the Tarot. Another suggests that the cards were inspired by the Egyptians, but painted by Gypsies who carried the Tarot decks and knowledge with them on their travels.

The late Manly P. Hall, founder of The Philosophical Research Society of Los Angeles, wrote of another belief—that the cards came to Southern Europe from India by way of Arabia, thanks to the efforts of the Knights Templars from Saracens, or another mystical Syrian sect. To conceal their true meaning, they were introduced in Europe as a gaming device.[1]

As wonderfully fanciful, endearing, and romantic as these and other legends are, the Tarot's actual beginnings are buried in obscurity and likely to stay there. However, the first *known* deck was painted in Italy during the fifteenth century, and since then, the production of Tarot decks has been continuous. Today there are "many hundreds" of them, according to Stuart Kaplan, president of U.S. Games, one of the leading distributors of Tarot cards.[2] More are designed every year, with each emphasizing its own special theme or symbolism.

Choosing Your Deck

To work with the Tarot is to identify with and live the symbolic life. The cards capture your cultural heritage, personal beliefs, and personal knowledge. They mirror your attitudes and ideals. Therefore, the deck you choose to work with must speak to you symbolically. It should stir you and satisfy you. Its images and colors should touch something deep within you.

In this book we have chosen to work with and compare three decks. The Rider-Waite deck, designed by Arthur Edward Waite, drawn and painted by Pamela Colman Smith, is one of the most popular in existence, and is readily obtainable from almost any shop that carries Tarot books. It was the first in modern times to portray a person or action on every card, and became the model[3] for many subsequent decks, including some that continued to use "pips" (designs without figures) for the Minor Arcana cards.[4]

The Aquarian and Morgan-Greer decks are offshoots of the Rider-Waite. Without distorting its intent, they portray situations in quite different moods that may appeal to readers who find the Rider-Waite too formal or dated. We think that exploring these subtle differences will add to your understanding of the cards' meanings.

The imagery on the Aquarian deck, designed by David Palladini, is less medieval, and more stylized, than that of the Rider-Waite. We think its cards often depict with more accuracy the inner struggles we experience as we attempt to grow.

Some people like the Aquarian deck's more humanized depiction of persons, and its art deco colors and designs. Others think the Aquarian characters appear too solemn or that the colors are too dark ("Has everyone just returned from a funeral?" someone asked us). Those people may be drawn to the softer, gentler—possibly more feminine—figures of the Morgan-Greer.

The Morgan-Greer deck, created by Bill F. Greer under the direction of Lloyd Morgan, purports to modify the Rider-Waite imagery according to the ideas of Paul Foster Case, the founder of Builders of the Adytum (BOTA), a modern mystery school located in Los Angeles. It is not clear to us from comparing the decks how this is so.

For some, the lack of borders around the Morgan-Greer cards evokes a feeling of expansiveness and lack of limitation, which appeals to them. As one person said after comparing the three decks, "You have to climb into the Aquarian and the Rider-Waite. They wait for you to approach. The Morgan-Greer draws you in."

Chances are that you will eventually select *one* of these three—or a totally different deck—as your favorite, and work exclusively with that deck. That's as it should be.

Your readings will evoke richer responses for you if you work with a deck that appeals to you, a deck with scenes that seem to speak to you more than others—a deck you're comfortable holding, turning over in your hands, viewing.

The *size* of one deck may feel better in your hands than another or be more convenient in certain situations. The Rider-Waite deck comes in four sizes. We like to carry a smaller size with us for readings elsewhere, but when reading at our offices, use a larger deck.

A deck's shape may affect how you feel about it as well. Some people enjoy the round cards of the Motherpeace deck, which celebrates the female experience. Evoking quite a different mood are the round cards of Michelle Leavitt's Tarot of the Cloisters, which are in the style of thirteenth-century stained-glass windows.

Certain colors may appeal to you more than others. Some people find the colors of the Rider-Waite deck too bold, for example, and respond more favorably to Mary Hanson-Roberts's softer coloring of the same scenes for the Universal Waite deck.

In addition to your emotional responses to a deck's predominant colors, you might want to consider what those colors symbolize. Each separate color has its own symbolism. Orange, for instance, frequently stands for spirituality and mental activity, while brown expresses our basic earthly nature and potential for growth. Thus, the predominance of these colors in the Aquarian deck makes it a natural for stimulating increased consciousness and grounded spiritual development.

If stylized figures or drawings don't appeal to you, consider James Wanless and Ken Knutson's Voyager Tarot. Some people believe they can find more meaning in its modern collages. Others find it too busy and distracting.

If you're attracted to modern scenes, Carol Bridges's Medicine Woman Tarot may appeal to you. When you need an irreverent jolt out of a rut, or a surprising perspective, try Morgan Robbins and Darshan Chorpash's Morgan Robbins Tarot. We guarantee you won't look at your situation the same way after using it.

If a particular philosophy appeals to you, then there are decks related to witchcraft, American Indian teachings, and Celtic or Druidic approaches. If you have an interest in Mayan art and symbols or the mythologies of various cultures, those decks exist too. Delve further and you'll find decks with flowers, herbs, and even one with scenes from *Alice's Adventures in Wonderland* and *Through the Looking*

Glass. Don't take our word for it; explore the various decks. Hold them in your hands, respond to their scenes and colors. Eventually you'll find the right one, or ones, for you.

Trust your intuition on this. It's your inner self telling you which unique combination of scenes, characters, colors, designs, sizes, shapes, and symbols is the easiest for you to connect with at this time. When a deck sparks your interest, the chances are that your higher self is suggesting that you need to delve more deeply into the concepts emphasized by that deck. However, after you have worked with that specific deck for a while, you may discover that another deck interests you. That new interest may be your inner self telling you that you've gotten all you can out of your first deck. You've grown out of it, and it's time to pay attention to other aspects of yourself, which will be stimulated by the new deck. Listen to yourself. Don't stay with the Rider-Waite or any other deck just because that's the one you learned on. If it still suits you years later, fine, stick with it. If it doesn't—if you aren't getting as much out of your readings as you used to—find another deck

Someday you might even be inspired to create your own deck, one that addresses *your* unique needs or special interests more thoroughly than existing versions. That's what artist and author Peter Balin did when he borrowed from Mayan and Aztec cultures to design the Xultun deck. That's also how Vicki Noble and Karen Vogel came up with the Motherpeace deck.

You can also select one deck to meditate with, and a totally different one to use for readings. We sometimes like to meditate on the Major Arcana cards from Dutch artist Nicolaas C. J. van Beek's beautiful, limited-edition Kashmir deck, which is based on a combination of Tibetan Buddhism and traditional Tarot symbolisms. Because the deck doesn't have Minor Arcana cards, it is inappropriate to use for many readings. However, we don't recommend meditating on cards from a second deck until you are quite familiar with the deck you're going to use for your readings and inner growth. To get the most out of that deck, you will want to study its cards thoroughly, meditate on them, and actually use the deck for some time.

Rather than spending that time memorizing what someone else thinks particular cards mean, we'd like you to get the "feel" of the cards and allow your inner self to respond to them.

That's why the one recommendation we do make is that you select a deck in which all 78 cards have scenes depicted on them. The message of the card is clearer, and you will be able to connect with a particular scene—or more readily recall how you felt when you were engaged in similar activities than you would if there were only three wands or four pentacles on the face of the card.

Reading Rituals

There are many opinions about how to take care of your cards, how to store them, and whom to let handle them. Some readers have a deck they use for themselves and a second deck they use when reading for others.

Steven Culbert, author of *Reveal the Secrets of the Sacred Rose,* regards most of these rituals as worthless superstitions[5] that distract you from your own response to the cards. *We* think it's important for you to draw your own conclusions and do what feels right for you.

Your Tarot deck is a picture book of essential human characteristics, a catalog of *seed ideas.*[6] You open that book to do individual readings that illuminate your life in particular, transforming the cards into richly detailed, personal snapshots. So the question is, how would you treat a treasured photograph album or scrapbook that documents all of your life experiences? That's how you want to treat your Tarot cards.

Although we have seen readers use old, ragged, dirty cards (and can only hope that this "familiarity" gives them a sense of comfort and security), our preference is to be gentle with our cards and to keep them clean and undamaged. We feel better when we use cards that have a nice appearance.

By taking care of our cards and handling them gently with clean hands, we are also symbolically honoring our inner archetypes. We are tending to and showing respect for vital aspects of ourselves. And this conveys to our higher self that we will handle with care the feelings and ideas our cards will evoke in us today.

In addition, removing our cards from their wooden containers and cloth wrappings or cloth bags and carefully shuffling them creates a mood for us. We shift into a different state of consciousness, a different awareness. Our actions say that these cards are special and the soon-to-follow reading is an important occasion. We reestablish that feeling and focus every time we engage in that simple "ritual."

If you need additional actions to set your emotional scene, then by all means use them. Lay out your cards on a special cloth reserved for your readings. Light some candles or incense. Place inspiring items near you; set the lights exactly right. Or sit facing a particular direction. Energy is traditionally considered to flow from north to south and east to west. Most authorities suggest the reader should face the direction from which the flow comes, i.e., east or north.[7] One of the best and easiest "little rituals" is simply shuffling your cards for a few minutes before each reading. It breaks up the energy of a previous reading and infuses new energy as you focus on your question.

As you do these things (or others that appeal to you), you become mentally prepared for an important experience. And that's what any ritual is about. By creating a particular mood, attitude, or set of conditions and engaging in the appropriate actions, you convey to your higher self that you are ready to proceed. You have established harmony with the gods or the circumstances of outer nature and metaphorically balanced your inner nature as well.

Priming the Pump

There may be periods in your life when you want to do a reading every day or even several different layouts in a single day. At other times you won't pick up the cards at all. There is no right or wrong time to work with them. Trust your own needs. When you do decide to seek input from the cards, take some time to thoroughly review the situation you want to know more about.

The Tarot works best when you "prime" your inner pump. So before a reading, carefully consider what's been happening within and around you. Maybe a recent experience has evoked some bewildering feelings. Or maybe last night's dream seems important, even monumental, but its actual meaning for your life remains perplexing.

Try listing the components of a troubling situation. What's occurring? What isn't? Reread your list and make notations about any questionable motivations you or someone else might have. You might want to review your last two or three Tarot readings, as well.

You'll need all this information in your psyche in order to carefully formulate a question. Here's how—and why.

When little Alice asked the Cheshire Cat which way she ought to go, the Cat replied that as long as she didn't care *where* she went, it didn't matter which *way* she went. In our best Cheshire Cat imitation, we, in turn, ask you, "If you don't know where you're going, how will you know when you have arrived?"

Translated into Tarot language, this explains why you will need to formulate a question for your Tarot readings: in order to know where to look for clues to your answer. All Tarot readings begin with the formulation of a specific question. The question focuses your attention and defines the parameters of your reading. It gives you direction, and lets you know when you've arrived.

When cosmic mythologies and fairy tales distinguish between divine and worldly realms, a bridge, ladder, or stairway usually connects the two, and is frequently guarded by a being with extraordinary abilities.

We think a Tarot reading also bridges the distance between the known and the unknown. A carefully formulated question and stimulating cards connect you to the ideas, memories, intuition, and other inner resources for finding your answer.

The Question Stimulates Transformation

Since you purchased and are reading our book, chances are that you want more out of a Tarot reading than vague suggestions that "a change is about to occur in your life" or "your future will be bright." To get more, you'll need to ask the right questions; questions that will not only cover such matters as whether the time is ripe to change jobs or start a relationship, but also delve into personal and spiritual elements of those issues.

In her book *Women Who Run with the Wolves*, author and Jungian analyst Clarissa Pinkola Estés writes that the central act of transformation in fairy tales, psychotherapy, and in achieving personal wholeness is asking the proper question. It is the key to the secret doors of the psyche that lead to awareness and healing. In legends of the Holy Grail, for example, if the knight on his quest fails to ask the right question of the Fisher King, keeper of the Grail Castle, then the Grail Castle disappears, the Fisher King remains wounded, and the knight's journey continues. The Grail quest is a metaphor for our own personal growth experience. It parallels the life journey each of us has to take and the obstacles and successes we encounter along the way. Thus, by posing the proper question prior to a Tarot reading, we open the door that leads to valuable insights about some aspect of our personal quest.

Concentrating on your question as you shuffle and cut the cards influences the arrangement of the cards. As a result, you draw the cards you need in the proper order to provide information to answer your question. Some Tarot teachers might say that asking the right question creates resonating energy in both your psyche and the greater

**Jill incorrectly wants the Tarot
to predict her future.**

**Susan creates a question
that asks for insight.**

**Figure 1
Formulating Questions**

universe, making it possible for you to draw those cards that give you the information you need.

Although you may think this sounds a little far-fetched, research is accumulating to show that concentrated thought can affect the growth of seeds, even laboratory-damaged ones, and the healing of patients.[8] It can even skew numbers generated by a microelectronic random-events generator.[9] So why not the ordering of Tarot cards?

The more thoughtfully you construct your question, the more likely it is that you will draw cards that tap into and clarify subtle issues in your mind. They will help you to see the issue in a different light and to make your decision with a more encompassing perspective.

Write your question several times until it is just the way you want it. Then begin to lay out your cards in the spread of your choice. The six we discuss in this book (and will teach you to use in Chapter 14) are summarized below:

(1) The *Cross of Awareness* layout (see Figure 4, Chapter 14) uses the basic form of the traditional Celtic Cross layout, with modernized names for the 10 positions to indicate more accurately the information we think they impart.

We believe the Cross of Awareness is the most effective layout, and the one that gives you the most complete information on an issue. However, it takes time to lay out 10 cards and understand them, and even though we'd *like* to say you should never put a time limit on your inner work, we know there will be occasions when your time will be limited.

(2) The *Micro-Cross* layout (see Figure 5, Chapter 14) gives you a short, quick fix on where you are with regard to some project, situation, or relationship and what challenges you will face. This two-card layout can be used daily to take your emotional pulse and stay attuned to various aspects of yourself. It's also perfect for getting an update on a situation, issue, or problem examined in an earlier Cross of Awareness reading.

(3) The *Triad* layout (see Figure 6, Chapter 14) uses three cards to help you (a) get a quick look at where you are in your life, (b) clarify the influence of your inner triad (mind, body, spirit) on your situation, and (c) answer yes/no questions.

(4) The *Daily Opportunity* layout (See Figure 7, Chapter 14) uses four cards to help you consider what your inner work for the day might be. It is also a good, quick layout to use when you travel.

(5) The *Fountain of Creation* layout (See Figure 8, Chapter 14) gives you an idea of what energies or psychological factors are active in your life.

(6) The six-card *Star Guides* layout (See Figure 9, Chapter 14) helps you evaluate, from six different perspectives, an action or project you are considering and place it in the larger context of your personal growth and inner development.

To Reverse or Not?

A question that comes up in every Tarot book is whether or not to place special value on reversed cards. For readers who use the cards as divinatory devices, they are "hot" cards, warning of something dangerous or negative in your path.

Those of us who use the cards for personal growth work[10] do not gasp audibly whenever a reversed card appears. We think each card contains a full spectrum of possibilities to consider. Occasionally a reversed card will seem to serve as a personal pointer signaling you to pay extra attention to its message. It may also point out energy that is blocked off[11] or just working its way into your conscious awareness,[12] as some Tarot writers suggest. To others an upside-down card brings to mind that card's shadow and is thought to express an aspect of yourself that you may not consciously recognize or willingly show to others.[13]

If you are going to acknowledge reversals, then the way you turn over cards will affect whether or not they are reversed; and you will need to use the same method in all your readings. You can either keep the bottom edges of the cards toward you (that is, always at the bottom) as you turn them (see Figure 2), or you can flip the cards so that the bottom edge becomes the top when you lay them down (see Figure 3). There is no right or wrong way, so adopt the one that seems the most natural for you—and for the sake of consistency in reading reversals, stick to it.

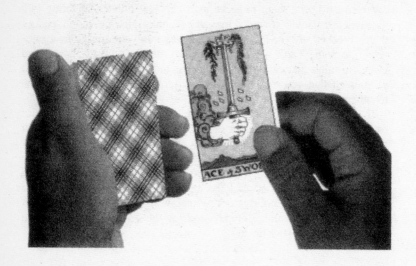

Figure 2
Keeping the bottom edge of the card
toward you as you turn over your cards

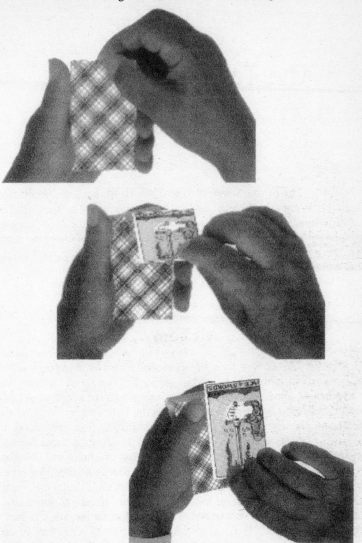

Figure 3
Turning the top edge of the card
towards you as you turn over the cards

4 ✹ The Tarot and . . .

Before we give you some of our ideas about how the individual Tarot cards express personal and spiritual growth issues, we'd like to explore some of the ways the Tarot in general connects to various metaphysical, mystical, and psychological schools of thought. Each has the potential to help you remember and relate to the symbols in, and meanings of, the cards that turn up in your readings.

Alchemy

Alchemy, an ancient form of chemistry aimed at changing *prima materia* (rock) into lapis or gold, originated as the art of the Egyptian craftsman or jeweler. Its ultimate goal, the search for a "philosopher's stone," came later. Somewhere between the third century B.C. and the thirteenth century A.D., alchemy made a transition from metallurgy to mysticism. Metals and the processes that transformed them became the basis for a complex allegory about human psychological development. On its surface the task remained the same: to engage in a series of operations to transform one element into another of "higher" value. Only the goal was to release the world soul, *anima mundi*, imprisoned in *prima materia* (the human body) and transform it into the "higher" or enlightened self. It is quite possible that early designers of the Tarot were cognizant of the alchemical allegories and their emblems, and included the same stages of the psychological journey in their cards, using some of the same symbols. We'll point out a number of them in our descriptions of the cards.

Astrology

Many Tarot writers have assigned astrological signs or planets to the Major Arcana cards. While working on *The Lovers' Tarot*, we discovered that astrologically oriented authors often assign different signs to the same card. For instance, Aries, Mercury, and the Sun have all been linked to The Magician. And various authors have suggested that the signs of Gemini and Libra and the planets Jupiter, Venus, and Mercury are the appropriate astrological connections for The Empress. Since the viewpoints of these authors differ so considerably, we suggest that those of you who want to delve further into the connections between astrology and the Tarot pick one system and use it consistently. Authors to choose from include: Eileen Connolly, Steven Culbert, Irene Gad, Craig Junjulus, Sandor Konraad, Emily Peach, A. E. Thierens, and Robert Wang. See the full reference to their publications in the bibliography.

Cabala

The Cabala, also spelled Kabbalah or Qabalah, is the embodiment of the esoteric and mystical wisdom of Judaism. The word, which first appeared in the eleventh century, comes from the Hebrew root word KBL (to receive), which suggests that originally its wisdom was transmitted orally.

From the fourteenth century on, Cabalistic teachings appear as a diagram, known as the Tree of Life, which consists of 10 spheres or Sephiroth representing eternally emanated divine qualities of God, plus an 11th invisible Sephira. They are connected by 22 paths. Tarot writers differ considerably as to which Hebrew letters should be assigned to the Major Arcana cards and which Tarot cards should be assigned to the paths between the Sephiroth.

The Cabala teaches that all manifestation is based on duality or polarity, thus the Sephiroth are arranged in three columns or pillars: the pillar of judgment or severity (left), the pillar of mildness or equilibrium (middle), and the pillar of mercy (right).

Because of its ability to relate to and encompass varying mythologies and religious beliefs, Gareth Knight calls the Tree of Life the foundation stone of the Western mystery tradition.

Some Tarot authors believe that each of the 22 Major Arcana cards is linked to a path between the Sephiroth and to a specific letter of

the Hebrew alphabet. The nineteenth-century French occultist Eliphas
Lévi was the first to maintain this.

Waite, who was hostile toward Lévi's work, did not include Hebrew
letters in his deck; however, the black-and-white deck developed for
the Builders of the Adytum (BOTA)—and based on Waite's deck—
does display them.

Manly P. Hall, founder of the Philosophical Research Society in
Los Angeles and dedicated researcher of all mystical traditions,
doubted that the connection was anything "more substantial than the
coincidence that both consist of 22 parts."[1] Yet when Hall created his
own deck, he did attribute Hebrew letters to each of the Major Arcana.

Understanding them is a must for anyone combining spiritual Tarot
work with studies of the Cabala. To learn more, consult the works of
Corinne Heline, Irene Gad, or Robert Wang.

Chakras

The term *chakra*, which means "wheel" in Sanskrit, refers to a
whirling vortex of invisible energy. There are seven of these centers
aligned along the spine from its base to the top of the head and
slightly above the head (crown chakra). Each chakra has its own
vibration, resulting in a distinct pattern and color.

Beginning at the base of the spine, the seven chakras are:

(1) the root, base, or sacral chakra (Sanskrit, *muladhara*), associated
with self-preservation, the expression of basic instincts, sexuality,
vitality, life energy, the planet Saturn, and the alchemical metal
lead.

(2) spleen (*svadhisthana*) chakra, associated with strong, deep feelings, unconscious influence, decision making from deep, almost
intuitive knowledge, the planet Mars, and the alchemical metal
iron.

(3) solar plexus (*manipura*), associated with action based on sensory
and emotional reactions, the use and expression of your vital energies, the planet Jupiter, and the alchemical metal tin.

(4) heart (*anahata*), associated with emotional reactions, especially
compassion and understanding, our sense of values, the sun, and
the alchemical metal gold.

(5) throat (*vishudda*), associated with creative originality, individual-

ity, self-expression, and communication, the planet Venus, and the alchemical metal copper.

(6) brow or third eye (*ajna*), associated with the rational mind, as well as psychic abilities, the moon, and the alchemical metal silver.

(7) crown (*sahasrara*), associated with abstract learning and the capacity to recognize and react to opportunity, the seat of high aspirations, our connection with the Source, the planet Mercury, and the alchemical metal quicksilver (mercury).

In using the term *alchemical metal*, we refer to a transformative process rather than to an actual metal. Jewels or decorations over specific locations in Tarot figures refer, and call our attention, to the energy of that chakra.

Whenever seven of anything appears in a Tarot card, at least one of its meanings likely refers to the chakras (the seven "interior stars"), which in symbolism are connected to the seven planets known at the time the cards were developed, the seven archangels associated with those planets, the seven colors of the rainbow, and other systems of seven. In metaphysical work, regardless of the system they fall into, all sevens by their action and color are related to one another and the meaning of their respective positions extends the meanings of each position in all the systems of seven.

Color Symbology

What images come to mind when you see a particular color? How do you react to red . . . yellow . . . orange . . . or blue? Your answers will determine that color's symbolic significance for you, and that level of connection may suffice in the beginning of your Tarot work. As you grow, however, you may want to know more. Grasping the symbolic meaning of various colors can enhance your understanding of the cards in which those colors appear.

For almost as long as people have been creating art, they have used color to convey certain ideas or evoke any number of feelings. The most traditional and easiest interpretations come from a color's appearance in nature. For instance, green, which is associated with growing things, can symbolize our basic nature, life, growth, or the spring cycle.

As you continue your studies, you will discover that colors have both negative and positive qualities. Take red, for example. Being the color of blood, it symbolizes life, passion, a vital force pumping us up for action. Of course, it also can conjure up images of death, and has even been used to suggest coexistence of the opposites "life and death."

Alchemy used colors to refer to various stages of the inner work of transforming the human spirit. Black, for instance, represented the first stage, and green the second stage, of the transformational process.

Jung thought that lighter colors referred to the more conscious aspects of the mind, while darker, more vivid colors referred to the unconscious and, ironically, more subtle aspects of what the artist was trying to convey. However, other scholars believe that just as lighter colors are diluted versions of a darker color, the message conveyed by the lighter colors is less intense. A third viewpoint proposes that lighter colors have more white in them and, therefore, more illumination, so they likely symbolize closeness to divinity.

As we write about each of the cards, we will try to give you some idea of what we think various colors stand for in that card. If you want to learn more about the *extensive* symbology associated with colors, the symbol dictionaries by Hans Biedermann, J. E. Cirlot, J. C. Cooper, James Hall, and Boris Matthews are good places to start.

Mystery Schools

These secret groups or cults flourished largely from the sixth century B.C. to the fifth century A.D., but have been revived in this century. Through a series of initiatory steps or ceremonies, they claimed to raise the consciousness of their members to include the esoteric knowledge of the true and ancient wisdom of the universe. A basic premise of mystery schools or systems is that the material and earthly world of man is a "microcosm," or duplication, of the divine or cosmic universe, the macrocosm.

It is likely that their knowledge was revealed and passed along through modified pagan rituals incorporating archetypal principles and elevated to the level of allegory and symbolism—some of it incorporated into Tarot cards. A particularly influential group in this regard was the Hermetic Order of the Golden Dawn, a relatively recent secret occult order founded somewhere between 1886 and 1888 (authorities differ) and active until 1903. Although the Tarot was only one of a number of techniques its members were schooled in, the Golden Dawn deck has directly or indirectly affected almost every major twentieth-century Tarot writer or designer. Among the order's members were Aleister Crowley, designer of the Thoth deck, Arthur Edward Waite, designer of the Rider-Waite deck, and the poet William Butler Yeats.

Personality and Year Cards

A number of years ago we attended a Tarot conference in San Francisco that included a workshop taught by Angeles Arrien, author of *The Tarot Handbook*, a companion for the Thoth deck. In that seminar we learned how to identify the Major Arcana card that portrays what you have come into this lifetime to learn. Arrien calls this the *personality card*. Here's how to determine yours.

Add together your month, day, and year of birth, as follows:

$$\begin{array}{r} \text{September 17, 1935} = 09 \\ 17 \\ \underline{1935} \\ 1961 \end{array}$$

$$(1 + 9 + 6 + 1) = 17 = \text{The Star}$$

If the numbers total more than 22, reduce the number down to 22 or less by breaking it down into single digits and then adding them. For example,

$$\begin{array}{r} \text{July 31, 1940} = \quad 07 \\ 31 \\ \underline{1940} \\ 1978 \end{array}$$

$$(1 + 9 + 7 + 8 = 25 = 2 + 5 = 7) = \text{The Chariot}$$

We also learned how to find our annual "year card," which indicates the tests or lessons important for us during the current year. To determine the Major Arcana that is your *year card*, which changes each year, of course, add the month and day of your birthday to the current year. For instance,

$$\begin{array}{r} \text{July 31, 1995} = \quad 07 \\ 31 \\ \underline{1995} \\ 2033 \end{array}$$

$$(2 + 0 + 3 + 3 = 8) = \text{Strength}$$

When your personality card or your year card appears in a reading, it signals an especially important reading for you.

PART TWO

LEARNING THE CARDS: THE MAJOR ARCANA

5 ☀ Archetypal Mysteries

Every author will give you his or her idea about the archetypal energies or issues each card expresses. We're no exception. We offer our interpretations in this chapter and the next seven.

You'll want to read our definitions. Later you may want to read definitions written by others as well. Their perspectives may call attention to details you hadn't seen previously.

Before you start reading a card's "definition," however, form initial impressions of your own. Here are some questions to consider or answer in your Tarot journal for each card:

1. What does the card convey to you?
2. Of what life experience does it remind you?
3. Have you had this experience or only heard about it?
4. How close to or removed from the depicted character(s) do you feel?
5. Overall, do you like this card?
6. Are there some parts of it you are more drawn to than others?
7. Are there parts of it you don't like or that make you uncomfortable?
8. If the characters on the card could speak, what would they say? Speak as them; write it down.
9. What does a figure's depicted position on the card suggest to you about his/her goals or state of mind? If you were the character(s) in the card, how might you change your placement in the scene, or your posture?
10. What might this character do next?

Then examine each card as you read about it. Notice what we (or other authors) emphasize that you did not. Does it make sense to you? Does it add to your understanding of the scene? What did *you* miss? What did *we* miss?

Please note that in describing and elaborating on the meaning of each card, we have used the gender of the major figure on the card in our explanation of that card. Consequently we refer to The Hanged Man as "he," because the figure is a male. As an archetype, however, the qualities that The Hanged Man embodies are in us all, male or female, and so it is with all the cards in the deck.

The Fool
(Major Arcana 0 or XXII)

"I exist to help you sample all aspects of life. I step out without fear to experience and investigate. 'This way. Follow me. Take action,' I say, and urge you on when you hesitate, perhaps from past disappointments.

"In fairy tales I am the young lover, often a prince in disguise, who wins the hand of a lady through his pure-hearted acts and bravery in a crisis or a contest against an older, manipulative suitor. In other stories I am the 'dummling,' a worthless, unlucky, seemingly stupid character who turns out to be a hero or finds unexpected success.

"I encourage you to take risks and to look at things in your own unique way. 'Nothing ventured, nothing gained,' I always say. Yes, I could pay more attention to details and preparation, but if I stopped to think out everything, I'd never get ahead.

"Mine is the innocent wisdom of the impetuous. I am the impulse

to leap forward into the unknown, and I'll serve you again and again
as you encounter the challenges, conflicts, and the joys—especially
the joys—of the symbolic life. I represent your ability to be fully
yourself and to be true to your own nature. I hope that you never
cast me aside, for I am a crucial part of your humanness.

"*A key phrase to remember me by is* the limitless energy of spirit."

The Rider-Waite Fool depicts a young person standing on a cliff.
His yellow boots convey that he intellectually understands the need
to be grounded in physical experience. He wears a black mantle of
ignorance, lavishly decorated with spoked wheels. They are mandalas
(pronounced **mun**-deh-lehs). In Jungian psychology they represent the
Self. In occult tradition, the wheel with eight spokes symbolizes the
whirling motion of the creative universe.

Seven green leaves surround each mandala. They correspond to the
body's seven chakras or energy centers, as well as all the symbolic
meanings of the number seven. The lower wheel near the back of The
Fool's mantle contains the Hebrew letter Shin, symbol of the spiritual
energy that brings things into existence.

Under his mantle he wears a white shirt, signifying purity of spirit
with the Tetragrammaton embroidered at the throat (or creative)
chakra.

According to Waite, The Fool is poised "at the brink of a precipice
among the great heights of the world."[1] And a precipice or abyss is
a place of spiritual transformation. It is the spot from which we can
leap into the unknown, or delve into the unconscious. It is "where
we all must go, stripped of our preconceived ideas, ego expectations,
possessions, and whatever else holds us back from making the necessary radical turn needed for personal and social transformation."[2]

Over his right shoulder, The Fool carries his personal identity and
psychological potential in the form of a wand, with a "curiously
embroidered" wallet[3] attached to one end. The eagle embroidered on
the wallet links The Fool to the Greek all-father god, Zeus. As a bird
of the day or light, the eagle itself represents self-renewal and messages made clear.

The Fool wears a green hat with a red feather, traditionally said to
be an eagle feather. At his feet a white dog, guardian of conscious
awareness, barks and jumps.

The white light (pure spirit) of the sun, which has not yet reached
its zenith, shines upon him from a yellow sky of divine intelligence.
Snow-covered mountains in the distance stand for the principles of
"The Path" on which we and The Fool are about to embark. With

each step toward greater understanding, the snowcaps melt a little and flow into the valley of our inner life.

The Morgan-Greer Fool is essentially the same except that he carries a staff and wears a laurel wreath (evidence of past accomplishments and promise of future success) around his golden hair.

The Aquarian Fool, bundled up against the weather and the vicissitudes of life, is without companions or encumbrances other than the white rose of purified desire and a budding wand of intuition. The bubbly design in his lapel, which will be repeated and embellished in many later cards, represents access to the divine feminine aspect of Spirit. Note that it is turned outward and follows the alignment of the spine but does not quite overlay the spinal chakras. This reminds us that we have not yet begun our inner journey. Our energies are not yet activated.

Around his throat chakra, the energy center for communication, and at his temple, the Aquarian Fool wears the divine triangle. Wherever the triad or the symbol for it—a triangle—appears in the Tarot cards, it can be read as representing any and all of the following ideas, depending on the reader's own orientation: the Christian Trinity of the Father, Son, and Holy Spirit; the inner human triad of body, mind, and spirit; the psychological inner mother, father, and child aspects of ourselves; the three elements (salt, mercury, sulfur) necessary to start the alchemical process of transformation; and the several triads formed by the pathways that connect the Sephiroth on the Cabala's Tree of Life.

The Aquarian Fool is aware of the threefold nature of the universe and has spiritual aspirations as indicated by both the upward-pointing triangle and the reverse-V design in the background.

The Aquarian card, especially, hints that when The Fool appears, our activities need to include a synthesis of the physical and the spiritual. It's time to consider what it takes to achieve union and harmony with inner, outer, or any other seemingly opposite forces in our situations or ourselves.

The Fool takes life as an adventure to be enjoyed. He inspires us to be open with others and within ourselves. He is the trickster/clown archetype who is allowed to see and say what others, because of societal or peer pressure, will not. The Fool represents the psychological state we are in when we begin any new endeavor. He is the originating and animating principle, the suggestion of possibilities yet to come. His journey will take him from a state of innocence to one of personal spirituality and creative power, and so will ours as we confront and integrate the experiences and challenges of the other Major Arcana cards.

In all three decks The Fool faces toward the left, toward the unconscious. In the positive sense, he will have to delve into previously inaccessible or consciously unavailable psychological material in order to grow. In the negative sense, he may just be acting out his impulses with little conscious thought. This idea is reinforced by his position at the brink of a precipice.

The Fool embodies our capacity to move toward change without having to know what lies ahead. He is "the spirit in search of experience."[4] To some the left side of the card also represents North, the direction of initiation in the mystery school tradition, and another clue that The Fool is looking for enlightenment.

Tarot authorities differ as to whether The Fool should be numbered zero or 22. We think it is appropriate that he be numbered zero, since zero is symbolic of the infinite, the unknowable, or as one Tarot symbolist put it, the state "prior to coming into being as an extended being" and, therefore, still full of potential.[5]

Paul Foster Case, founder of BOTA, writes that it is appropriate that the Tarot begins with The Fool because many of its scenes *are nonsense* "in that they run counter to the testimony of superficial sense experience" and will, therefore, be regarded by the worldly as "utterly foolish."[6]

Spiritually The Fool is open, unbounded, and unquestioning love of the Universe. Depending on your own understanding of cosmic forces, The Fool can be called the God-Self, Christ consciousness, the God within, the Tao—or whatever words you use to describe the mysteries and unknowable processes observed on earth.

Each of us on our respective quests is part Fool. Guided and touched by the unknowable, experiencing and expressing that energy within, he travels light, unencumbered by the worldly luggage of society's values. He is the "power of the soul to make life interesting."[7] He directs us to add some levity to our lives. The Fool reminds us that we may be taking our situations far too seriously, and not seeing the possibilities for growth and insight of a more happy-go-lucky nature.

Our talents for seeing the truth in a situation and our desire to seek the highest good in all situations is The Fool's handiwork. We act under his influence when we explore fantasies and realities, act spontaneously, and behave naturally without malice. Both his position on the precipice and the barking dog at his heels remind us to pay attention to that first step, so we can enjoy the rest of the trip.

The shadow aspects of The Fool include: an inability to commit to tasks or relationships; remaining psychologically stuck and refusing to try the new; being reluctant to see or admit our own foolishness; having no energy; being overwhelmingly solemn with no sense of playfulness; and having difficulty being spontaneous or appreciating the spontaneity of others.

Depending on its position in a layout, if The Fool appears:

- Take more risks.

- Take a deep breath, tell yourself to be brave, and be open to the next adventure that comes your way.

- Realize that there is both cosmic knowledge and hidden depths (light and shadow) to be gleaned from your situation. Look to both for direction.

- Rigorously examine your attitudes for insight into the obstacles you are encountering. Stop being so naive.

- Seek the highest qualities in yourself and others. If you find them in others, they have to be within you also.

- Open your eyes, mind, and heart. A time of unfolding has arrived or is at hand.

As we and The Fool prepare for our encounters with the other Major Arcana cards, we want to remind you of what the Chinese philosopher Lao Tsu had to say on the subject:

> *When the wise man learns the Way,*
>   *He tries to live by it.*
> *When the average man learns the Way,*
>   *He lives by only part of it.*
> *When the fool learns the Way,*
>   *He laughs at it.*
> *Yet if the fool did not laugh at it,*
>   *It would not be the Way.*
> *Indeed, if you are seeking the Way,*
>   *Listen for the laughter of fools.*[8]

6 ☀ Ten Archetypal Strengths and Resources

The first 10 Major Arcana cards depict the crucial strengths we need to acquire on our journey toward wholeness. The first five cards (Major Arcana I–V) serve as the foundation for the developmental tasks and experiences that help us build the next five strengths (Major Arcana VI–X). The 10 together supply the inner resources we'll require when we face the trials of Major Arcana XI–XX in Chapter 7.

If your progress has been shaky or nonexistent lately, these building blocks may need repairs or rearranging. By taking on the challenges described in this chapter, you can rebuild what you need for success.

The Magician
(MAJOR ARCANA 1)

"I confidently take care of any situation that arises. And you can, too, with the tools lying on my table: the Wand, the Sword, the Cup, and the Pentacle. I bring higher wisdom down to a practical level, and demonstrate the discipline you need to translate ideas into action. I am your focused inner guide. It is my energy that helps you establish priorities and act on them.

"I can sort through the physical, mental, and emotional elements of a relationship to determine which need attention, and then channel higher energy in that direction.

"I want you to seek the higher purpose in all you do. Honoring the spirit within gives dignity and importance to your activities and relationships. I am both your potential and your experience. I remind you of your past accomplishments and give you the confidence to take the next steps for advancement.

"A key phrase to remember me by is <u>creative focused attention</u>."

The Rider-Waite Magician stands against the yellow background of divine intellect, wearing the white gown of true purpose underneath a red cloak of power and authority. Around his waist is a purple belt in the shape of a snake devouring itself—an ancient symbol of transformation known as the uroboros. The Magician is framed by the climbing red roses of cultivated desire above and a bed of red roses and white lilies of spiritual truth at his feet. A lemniscate sign symbolizing eternity hovers above his head.

In the Morgan-Greer card, The Magician's red cape is also clasped together by the lemniscate. His uroboros belt is green, indicating that his inner processes are active and creative. Both magicians wear a white band around their heads, activating their ajna centers and tying back the black hair of ignorance.

In both the Rider-Waite and Morgan-Greer cards, the positioning of The Magician's arm suggests that he connects the divine to the worldly. He both receives and dispenses gifts of the spirit and channels them into productivity. Holding the "magic" wand of authority, mastery, action, and command, he can create heaven on earth and activate all the upcoming cards.

The Aquarian Magician wears a red cap over his crown chakra. Its blue edge of conscious understanding fits over and activates his ajna center.

Although he does not adopt the position of the Rider-Waite and Morgan-Greer figures, the triangles, circles, and the V-shaped lines behind him all suggest his connection to the Divine.[1]

In addition, he has access to the masculine aspect of Spirit, as symbolized by the dominant geometric pattern on his table, and to the feminine, represented by the design on the shield in the lower right corner.

The Magician sets forth the theme of our quest. His actions demonstrate that we have embarked on an *inner* journey and reveal some of the skills we'll need for each of the challenges we will encounter.

The Magician brings out our "can do"/"will do" attitudes and the ability to concentrate on our goals. He is the part of us that changes ideas into actions. His curiosity allows us to experiment and try new things. Failure does not daunt us. It merely adds to the store of experience from which we draw.

This card calls attention to the discipline we need in order to see through illusion to divine reality and effectively deal with problems. The Magician, with his "tools" of action on display in front of him, points up the many problem-solving approaches available to us.

The know-how of The Magician is magnetic. In addition to promoting keen perceptions of the actual and potential problems in a relationship, it also draws higher-self energies to our relationships.

When The Magician is drawn, creativity and initiative are at work. His appearance can be a suggestion to pursue studies leading to various kinds of growth, a reminder to remain open to new ideas and opportunities, or a signal that there are new patterns for us to consider. He urges us to focus our will and define our goals.

Another of The Magician's functions is to bring spiritual strength into our lives. The lemniscate (figure eight) above his head points out a need to connect the physical (or seen) with the spiritual (or unseen) realms and to recognize how divine force expresses itself through our personal actions.

In Jungian terms, The Magician is the shaman promising knowledge of the unknown. He embodies our archetypal belief in the power of magic and our wish for miracles. Mythologically he is related to Hermes/Mercury, the guide to travelers who brought sudden changes in fortune. He was also the patron of education and architecture (note the Ionic capital at the top of the Rider-Waite table leg), and is associated with the number eight (on its side as the lemniscate).

The shadow traits of The Magician include: engaging in trickery and deceit; using black magic for personal or destructive intent; abusing power for selfish or hostile gain; dominating those who are easily dominated; and lacking respect for universal law. At its worst, the shadow of The Magician becomes the con man.

When The Magician appears in your layout:

- Examine your skills to make sure you are not overestimating them or using them inefficiently.
- Make a choice and take an appropriate action rather than simply wishing for success or fulfillment.
- Only concentrate on the business or project at hand.
- Presume that there's more here than meets the eye, and look for spiritual elements in your everyday life.
- Attend to the wisdom of your higher self.

The High Priestess
(MAJOR ARCANA II)

"I am the eternal keeper of ancient wisdom. Mine is the quest for knowledge. I show the balance of dark and light in this world, as

well as the harmony between the spiritual and the mundane. I am not
merely an observer; I radiate the energy of experience.

"As the 'divine feminine,' I stir deeper feelings of personal and
universal love than you have ever known. As a result, you are free to
be receptive and active in your relationships.

"My scroll contains the laws of the universe, the core truths that
lie at the heart of all spiritual and moral teachings. If you lose contact
with me, you also lose family and racial ties.

"I am your memory, the storehouse of all your successes, failures,
dreams, and fantasies. I am your dream guide. I inspire through meditation. Use me to translate your experiences into personal wisdom.

"My presence encourages you to become discriminating in your
choices and to become conscious of the difference between the image
you have of yourself and who you really are.

"There's more here than is obvious at first. My key phrase is
<u>ancient and unrevealed knowledge.</u>"

In the Rider-Waite and Morgan-Greer cards, The High Priestess sits
between two black and white pillars, marked in the Rider-Waite card
as "B" and "J." This alludes to Boaz and Jachin, pillars from the
Temple of Solomon, and to all pairs of opposites in our lives. A
miniature version of them stands beside the Aquarian priestess. The
lotus atop each pillar, which gives them an Egyptian look, represents
(in Egyptian symbology) the watery origin of the world and of life.

Both the Rider-Waite and the Morgan-Greer High Priestesses have
the moon at their feet and on their headdresses, showing the influence
of unconscious memories on our conscious behavior. The moon also
calls our attention to the cycles in our lives and their effect on us.

The gown of the Rider-Waite priestess, which looks as if it is
dissolving into water, suggests that hidden knowledge is about to
emerge into consciousness. Water also alludes to the flow of life
energy and growth potential. Metaphysically, it symbolizes secret doctrines or esoteric teachings. Tradition has it that all the waters on
subsequent cards in the Major Arcana originate here.

The High Priestess inspires us to examine our motivations as we
confront life's experiences. She represents the combined qualities of
analytical thinking *and* intuition. "Look around," she warns. "There
is much to consider before drawing conclusions." Take time to reflect,
she tells us, and to search for deeper meanings.

The conscious decisions we make while under the influence of
strong emotion become our automatic reactions and unconscious habits. The High Priestess gives us the opportunity to rethink and modify
those choices.

The Rider-Waite and Morgan-Greer priestesses sit on thrones (seats of transformation) before veils, hinting that there are divine secrets and sacred mysteries to be learned. In the Aquarian deck, the veil is drawn. Mountains, signifying the inner journey, and the barest hint of a castle, a symbol of the Self, are seen in the distance. However, the path leading to them is seen only in the reflection. In other words, the way is through inner reflection. In addition, the reflection of the mountains in the water illustrates the quality of mirroring that the High Priestess embodies.

The pomegranates embroidered on the background veiling in the Rider-Waite and Aquarian decks symbolize one source of creation manifesting in many. The combination of the palm tree and the pomegranate on the Rider-Waite veiling represents the union of masculine and feminine elements.

Mythologically, the pomegranate connects The High Priestess to the maiden Persephone, who was tricked into eating a pomegranate seed after her abduction by Hades, lord of the underworld, and then condemned to spend six months of the year with him. Like Persephone, The High Priestess is privy to the workings of both the upper and lower worlds.

The Rider-Waite priestess wears the horn and moon crown of Hathor, Egyptian goddess of love and fertility, and of Isis, the Egyptian all-mother. She is also the mythological equivalent of the moon goddess, the archetype of deep feminine understanding. She has access to knowledge through sleep and dreams. Spiritually she is Sophia, the holy spirit, the mother goddess of wisdom.[2] Her feminine sexuality and inner wisdom make a powerful combination. Waite calls her the "highest and holiest" of the Major Arcana cards.[3]

The shadow traits of The High Priestess include: an inability to trust our intuition; literal-mindedness; superficiality; an attitude of fatalism; and duplicitous behavior.

When The High Priestess appears:

- Either you have been relying on your intuition too much, or you need to rely on it more.

- It is now possible to balance the masculine/feminine (or known/unknown) aspects of your personality.

- You may soon become aware of earlier memories or conflicts that apply to your present situation. Be patient and receptive to their appearance.

- Hidden influences or unidentified motivations are at work in your situation.

- Attend to basic lessons in spiritual growth.

The Empress
(MAJOR ARCANA III)

"I wait here to help you fulfill your heart's desires. I spring from the soil of your imagination. Bring your seeds of desire to my garden, plant them, water them with intelligent activity, and they will flourish. I am the mind's power to make new connections. I supply in abundance to those who till my soil in love and who respect their own nature, and the laws of Mother Nature as well.

"I am the archetype of fertility, nurturance, and renewal. I am the energy that works to produce the abundant life. Without me nothing comes to fruition. My movement is upward and outward. I am the doorway of life entering the physical, emotional, and mental activities of earthly existence. I ground you in the pleasure of the senses.

"In relationships, I provide passion and creative ways to bestow your feelings. In business and other projects, I guide you to seek creative possibilities.

"My key phrase is <u>creative abundance</u>."

In the Rider-Waite deck, The Empress sits outdoors against a yellow sky symbolizing intelligence, lush trees, and a flowing waterfall. Grain, representing fertility and renewal, grows all around her and connects her with several mythological harvest goddesses, including Demeter, the Greek grain mother, the Mediterranean mother goddess

Cybele, and Ceres, the Italian goddess of grains and harvests.[4] The "grain-near-a-waterfall" motif was a Gnostic symbol of fertility, later adopted by the Freemasons[5] to symbolize earth-and-sea fertility.

The Empress holds a scepter of life, topped by a globe, giving us our first hint that we create our own world. She wears the white robe of purity, embellished with flowerlike Venus symbols of fertility. The "mirror of Venus" shield at the base of her chair, which is duplicated in the design of the pillow at the back of her throne, provides a "backing" of love-wisdom. Her golden hair, emanating divine energy, is held back by a wreath of myrtle leaves, symbol of immortality. The 12 six-pointed stars in her crown, which represent the signs of the zodiac, give her universal authority.[6] They connect her, mythologically, to the Egyptian goddess Isis and the Roman goddess Juno. Traditionally she is considered to be pregnant.

The Morgan-Greer Empress holds the eagle shield of spiritual power (emblem of Zeus, king of the gods) in her right hand to protect all that she creates and nurtures. In her left hand she holds a bouquet of grain and a lotus blossom, symbolizing the Self. She demonstrates the cycles of blossoming and seeding.

The flowing stream to her left indicates access to the unconscious, as does the crescent moon on which she rests her foot. It also implies respect for nature's cycles. The pomegranate in front of the moon is another symbol of fertility. The cross and heart at her bosom, or heart chakra, represent the union of spirit and matter in divine love. They also call our attention to the idea of creating from the heart.

The Aquarian Empress holds a brown rod of earthly authority. The high rock formations behind her suggest earthly strength, as well, while the cutting action of the green waterfall over the cliffs illustrates unconscious energy and activity. The bright red and aqua design on the front of her gown tells us that the heart and throat chakras are activated and that she has the ability to convey her love and compassion. The pattern on her headband clearly points to the masculine aspect of spiritual activity. And the 12 stars on her crown, which extends upward beyond the card's frame, emphasize her connection with divine forces.

As the sum of 1 + 2 and the product of 1 × 2, The Empress unites the concepts found in The Magician and The High Priestess cards. She has the abilities necessary for taking action. In addition to symbolizing birth, motherhood, and sexuality, her generative forces help to bring ideas to fruition. Waite describes her as "the outer sense of the Word."[7]

The Empress reminds us to patiently nurture the things we believe in. "Use your imagination to create the environment you want to live in," she advises, and promises pleasure and passion in return.

This card can be a signal to look for old longings and unfinished business that may have gotten buried beneath the duties of daily life. Consider how you can germinate those seeds with new awareness.

The shadow of The Empress includes: feeling emotionally barren; regarding our need for love as a bottomless pit; dwelling on the pains of the past rather than moving forward; feeling that life is chaotic; planting the seeds of mistrust and deceit; destroying instead of creating; and engaging in "love" that smothers individuality.

When you draw this card:

- Take care to cherish and protect the people and projects in your life today.
- Exercise more self-discipline and creative courage.
- Give yourself credit for your accomplishments and others credit for theirs. Fully experience and enjoy that success.
- Review the cycles of your life; identify your present cycle, and redefine your priorities accordingly.
- Look at the destructive situations and negative feelings you hold onto. What can you learn from them and use? Let the rest go.

The Emperor
(Major Arcana IV)

"I have developed the strength and vigilance to accomplish the tasks necessary for civilization to advance. The decrees I send out establish standards for justice and determine how they will be interpreted.

"I am the producer and planter of seeds, as well as the one who determines which seeds are worthy of being sown, grown, and nurtured by The Empress. I take information from The High Priestess and translate it for use in the outer world. I pass on the secrets of worldly success, and teach you how to survive.

"My position requires the clear thinking of a scholar and the discipline of an athlete. Though I consult advisors, the final decision is mine. Once I make it, I go forward with supreme confidence.

"I inspire you to lead those who look to you for guidance. Follow me and you'll have the energy and the determination to exercise your authority.

"I am at the heart of order, rationality, and the methodical approach. I organize the ideas generated by my partner, The Empress. I give you the ability to penetrate to the core of an issue and make appropriate, responsible decisions. When you announce your principles, and assume responsibility for your actions, I am at work within.

"My key phrase is <u>reasoned authority</u>.*"*

The Rider-Waite Emperor sits on his gray stone throne, the seat of wisdom. Its four ram's-head ornaments, along with the card's orange background, symbolize vitality and sexual power. Female sacred principles are represented by the earthly orb in his left hand, and male sacred principles by the scepter of life in his right.[8]

The Morgan-Greer Emperor sits in profile, suggesting that we can discern only part of his personality. His throne is decorated with the eagle of Zeus, which also appears on his crown.

The Aquarian Emperor wears a red crown of active power over his crown chakra and a red jewel over his ajna chakra. His throat chakra, a source of creativity, is closed, as indicated by the black adornment covering it.

Mythologically The Emperor is related to Zeus and is the archetype of the all-father, who makes the rules, issues the edicts, and passes on the traditions of society. Metaphysically The Emperor has been linked to the God-Self or "Supreme Authority" enthroned within the personality.[9] We think he represents only the masculine aspect of the God-Self.

The Emperor's strong male energy teaches us to use reason in handling our problems, to set limits, to respect and live within society's regulations, and to pursue our ambitions with confidence and courage. His discipline leads to self-sufficiency; however, his position *is* geared to resist any change other than his own. Be aware of this tendency when you draw The Emperor.

His presence in a layout can be a suggestion to delegate responsibility. Perhaps you could let would-be emperors make mistakes and learn from them while you remain available to advise and teach. Also consider exposing *your* inner "student emperor" to a variety of teachers.

The Emperor asks us to examine our own authoritative behavior or lack of it. Look for your control issues, he advises. Question your passivity.

The shadow aspects of The Emperor include: getting angry or vindictive when our authority is challenged; exercising oppressive self-control or hardly any; depending on others to control our behavior; difficulty making definitive decisions and carrying them out; and confusing authority with aggressiveness or domination.

When you draw The Emperor:

- Check your recent behavior for signs of stubbornness or lack of responsibility.
- Recognize and appreciate how you utilize your strengths and self-discipline.
- Use more logical reasoning when evaluating your immediate problem.
- Consider accepting more responsibility for a project or for your actions in a relationship.
- Review your ideas or behavior regarding a current authority in your life.

The Hierophant
(Major Arcana V)

"I set forth and teach ideas and traditions that have proven their worth. My keys have unlocked doors for others before you, and al-

*lowed them to explore the teachings that inspired some of our civiliza-
tion's greatest thinkers and achievements.*

*"I urge you to reevaluate mundane standards in terms of higher
principles and to consider that the true source of inner strength comes
from awareness of your divine origin. I pass on to you the truths of
the Universal Mind. Personal power and integrity grow as you draw
on this knowledge.*

*"I urge you to develop a philosophy to live by. I encourage you
to set high standards for your interactions with others, and to respect
people of all backgrounds and cultures.*

*"I am a teacher, guiding your inner growth through contemplation
and inspiration, and your outer development through philosophical
inquiry.*

"My key phrase is <u>inner teacher</u>."

In all decks, The Hierophant raises his right hand in blessing, two
fingers down. He understands what is and what is not yet ready to be
known. The three extended fingers stand for the divine Trinity.[10] The
gold and silver crossed keys of heaven and earth rest at The Hierophant's feet. They also represent the inner and outer divine, sun/
consciousness (golden key), and moon/unconscious (silver key), the
ego and the Self, indeed, all of the dualities that we need to resolve.

In the Rider-Waite card, two priests kneel before The Hierophant.
One has red roses of earthly passion on his robe, the other white lilies
of divine love and purified mental aspiration.

Both the Rider-Waite and Morgan-Greer Hierophants sit between
the pillars last seen in The High Priestess card. He has changed their
outer duality to inner balance, evidenced by their gray color.[11] By
living amid the interplay of opposites without anxiety and without
being destroyed, he inspires us to balance the spiritual and the material
in *our* lives.

At the time Waite designed it, he meant this card to represent the
ruling power of religion in its "utmost rigidity of expression."[12] Now
seen in a kinder light, The Hierophant encourages self-control and
mastery of the inner self.

The Aquarian Hierophant wears the oranges and purples of God
consciousness. The mountainlike design on his crown symbolizes the
spiritual path, while the upward-pointing triangles suggest the worldly
appearance of God in human nature.

If religious associations present a problem for you, think of The
Hierophant as a wise and successful elder who is the preserver and
carrier of spiritual tradition. He is our inner spiritual teacher, the facet
of ourselves that seeks to understand our relationship to the greater

Universe. The Hierophant is associated with Osiris, the resurrection god of Egypt, and as such represents the rising up of the creative process.

The name *hierophant*, which belonged to the high priest of ancient Greek mysteries, means "revealer of sacred things." He is a mediator, providing a link between the spiritual and the worldly, a bridge between outer life experience and inner illumination. Psychologically he can be either the benevolent or the intolerant father figure within and with whom our intellect (lilies) and instincts (roses) often try to find their rightful place.

Through The Hierophant we are able to understand and participate in rituals and celebrations; adopt an inner code of moral values; and behave ethically in our interactions with others.

The shadow aspects of The Hierophant include: adopting principles without thinking them through or considering whether we can live by them; exhibiting hostility or intolerance toward the established order or toward persons whose religious ideas differ from ours; placing too much importance on outer appearances or affiliations; and allowing beliefs to become personal dogma that rules rather than guides.

When you draw this card:

- Give credit to mentors who have traveled this road before you. Consider how their experience and wisdom applies to your situation.

- Look at the effect of both material and spiritual values on your issue or situation.

- Review the principles of established religions, or your own culture's traditions, for insight into your issue.

- Ask your own inner teacher for guidance.

- Consider whether you are being too dogmatic or unprincipled about your issue.

The Lovers
(MAJOR ARCANA VI)

"We want you to know that forming a loving union with another can increase your understanding of life. Love and commitment offer significant potential for growth.

"We're also here to remind you that, first and foremost, you must have a relationship with yourself. As you integrate the masculine and feminine aspects we represent, you'll feel complete, confident, and capable of relating to others with openness and sincerity.

"While we can be understood literally as physical and sensual lovers, we also represent instinctual energy transformed to a higher level through the direction of both conscious and intuitive 'reasoning.' Ultimately we represent your personal union with the Divine and the recognition of the divine within you.

"Our key phrase is the healing union."

In the Rider-Waite card, the archangel Raphael, robed in fiery red and regal purple, floats in the radiance of the sun's life force. Raphael is the angel for guiding the way and for arranging propitious marriages.[13] He blesses and protects two nude figures, who embody the innocence of love before it is contaminated by material desire.[14]

The female looks upward at the angel, creating a direct link to the spiritual source of inspiration. The reasoning male looks to the passionate female side of himself for wisdom and to confirm his insights.[15]

Psychologically this suggests that our consciousness (the male) gets its direction from our unconscious (the female). With the angel's divine influence, our unconscious also can be the reservoir in which we develop inner holiness. If we do not deny our basic nature (nudity), then the inner aspects of ourselves will become lovers rather than enemies.

Behind the woman, a female serpent[16] of kundalini energy wraps itself around the Tree of the Knowledge of Good and Evil. Behind the male, the Tree of Life bears the twelve flaming "leaves" of zodiac energy.

The Morgan-Greer card simply presents two nude figures embracing under a golden halo in a lush setting that suggests natural creation blessed by the spirit.

The Aquarian Lovers are portrayed in lavish headgear, which activates their ajna centers. The male wears elaborate, peacocklike robes, pointing to the development of the Self that can occur in relationships.

The female's headdress, with its upward-pointing triangles, shows that she aspires toward the higher spiritual and creative process represented by the circle enclosing a dot. The downward-pointing triangle over her ajna center tells us that she brings the Divine into their physical union.

Psychologically The Lovers card directs us to look beyond surface appearances and to examine our own conflicting desires and beliefs. It encourages us to let go of ego judgments and become vulnerable, trusting, and forgiving.

This card depicts the "tension of opposites" with which we must all wrestle, and the unity that can occur when we recognize that opposites can survive in paradox. It also represents the union of the feminine emotional or intuitive aspect of our psyches with masculine, conscious understanding. The Lovers card reminds us to acknowledge and draw upon the inner sexual aspect that is the opposite of our outer sex.

The shadow aspect of The Lovers includes: an inability to get close in relationships; infidelity; difficulty trusting others; and trouble recognizing conflicting aspects of ourselves.

When you draw this card:

- Do not dismiss the importance of either your conscious intellect or your intuition, especially when you have to make relationship decisions. You need them both for personal wholeness.

- Look at all aspects of the situation—the hidden, the obvious, and the possible—to understand the implications of any choice you are considering.

- Seek to identify any opposites that need to be balanced in your situation.

- Become aware of the loving nature of your higher self, in contrast to the ego of your personality.

- Work toward personal integration.

The Chariot
(MAJOR ARCANA VII)

"I am an inner director, a spiritual driver. Think of your life as a flower-bedecked parade float. I am underneath the display controlling the vehicle's progress.

"My two sphinxes, or horses, which usually veer in slightly different directions, help you consider opposing viewpoints of a situation. They make you aware of the range of emotions and experiences available to you and the choices you can make. I bring you the strength to proceed with focused determination. Instead of denying your aggressive instincts, you'll be able to use them to direct your activities.

"From me you draw the power to accomplish what you want. I embody the warrior energies of courage and singleness of purpose, which assist you in achieving goals. Even when you're involved in seemingly mundane tasks, you are functioning in a greater Universe. I remind you of this, and in so doing, help you move toward a deeper understanding of the meaning of your life.

"My key phrase is <u>the determined search for greater understanding.</u>"

In the Rider-Waite card, the charioteer, representing the psyche, controls the chariot of the personality, keeping it in perfect balance as he triumphantly leaves a conquered city (mastery over human problems) to pursue new adventures and conquests. The charioteer moves from the past into the future, from the known into the unknown. He represents the archetypal victorious warrior/hero and "conquest on all planes."[17]

His may be a tainted victory, however, as the charioteer appears to be *embedded* in his stone chariot and not yet able to fully deal with his instinctual nature. Or, as Waite puts it, the "planes" of his conquest are not yet within himself.[18]

The blue canopy with its bright stars, the eight-pointed star on the charioteer's crown, and the crescent moons on his shoulders indicate the influence of celestial cycles. He holds a wand of authority, showing his ability to use consciousness and purposeful concentration to control the sphinxes.

The white sphinx represents the pillar of mercy on the Cabalistic Tree of Life, described in Chapter 4. The black sphinx stands for the pillar of severity and justice. The red Hindu lingam/yoni design at the center of the chariot symbolizes the uniting of opposites and the balance between male and female energies. The winged solar disk above it links him with Egyptian heaven gods and Divine Spirit. This is the vehicle of the Spirit, and the charioteer is the "Lord of Light."

In the Rider-Waite and Aquarian cards, the charioteer needs no reins. His control is mental. The chariot's yellow wheels have just emerged from the water of unconscious energy, suggesting that illusion has been conquered through conscious awareness and action.

The Morgan-Greer charioteer wears a golden crown of five-pointed stars—representing his higher nature—atop his free-flowing golden hair. Holding the reins of his horses, which capture the principle of opposites and the conflicting urges of our basic instincts, he controls and guides their expression. The Hindu symbol from the Rider-Waite card is replaced with the Buddhist yin/yang symbol on his belt. Or, depending on your orientation, it can be identified as the zodiacal glyph for Cancer.

The Morgan-Greer charioteer rides forth with purpose. On his chariot, a strong gold framework of divine law and action supports a blue canopy of honor and protection. The indigo interior suggests the primal matter to which he has creative access. The solar medallion on his breastplate indicates his connection with universal forces and masculine energy.

The Aquarian charioteer looms large. A five-pointed star on his helmet, over his ajna chakra, shows his access to and use of spiritual energy.

Because only the wheels on either side of the card give the impression of a chariot, the Aquarian chariot is less obvious than those in the Rider-Waite and Morgan-Greer cards, yet its color and strange shape make it an unusual feature of the card. Its front is formed by V-shaped lines of force that shape our ego ideas. The chariot's headpiece is formed from a pure white sphere decorated with the creative feminine aspect of the Divine.

In the Rider-Waite and Aquarian decks, the moons on the charioteer's shoulders are sometimes said to have the "faces" of Urim and Thummim, a poetic interpretation at best since *urim* and *thummim* are Hebrew words for certain divinatory objects used by Old Testament high priests to seek the divine will of God.[19] Pollock says they represent the "supposed shoulder plates of the High Priest in Jerusalem.[20]

In metaphysical terms, chariots are often the equivalent of a throne, and the charioteer can be seen as a younger version of The Emperor. He takes the action that creates the experiences and memories the older Emperor can draw upon. He carries The Magician's magic wand, at least in the Rider-Waite card, and thus The Magician's energy supports his action.

The Chariot is a card of strength, determination, and encouragement. It embodies great potential for movement, accomplishment, leadership, responsibility, and authority. Often signaling a time of changes based on high principles, The Chariot reminds us not to dissipate our energies, but to stay focused on our goals.

This card speaks of our life journey, both inner and outer. It encourages us to get in touch with our inner self and receive guidance through meditation, study, and service. In a sense, *we* are The Chariot, the vehicle through which spirituality takes form, grows, and expresses itself in the material universe.

The Chariot steers us toward stability, the ability to balance our need for change with our desire for security, and the capacity to switch directions when necessary.

The shadow aspects of this card include: a lack of self-control; being too controlling of others; being overbearing; acting irresponsibly; and not having a sense of direction in our lives. In its extreme, it could express itself as someone who wants to control the world.

When The Chariot appears:

- Identify past experiences that have helped you develop the fortitude and control to solve your present problem. You have the skills you need.

- Determine if you are trying to force issues that really need to be negotiated. Reflect before making demands.

- There are past issues you need to discover, consider, and possibly resolve before charging ahead.

- Enhance your understanding of the situation and its possible solution by considering it from another angle. There may be more than one avenue open to you.

- Realize that you cannot disown your aggressive drives without damage to your psyche. Accept them and learn to direct them into appropriate action.

Strength
(Major Arcana VIII)

"I want to share my secret with you. I have learned to tame the beast within, and I do it without strain. I use my spiritual powers. I know that they are the true basis for my outward actions.

"Instead of trying to shut down forces that appear to be dangerous, I transform them into energy that can be used constructively. I neither condemn nor ignore my animal nature, but respect and direct it for my purposes.

"With my guidance, you can develop the inner vision to use human energies more gently and productively. I foster the expansion of awareness, giving you greater control over your personality.

"When I love, I recognize and encourage the best in my partner. In my relationships, I recognize and acknowledge the strengths of others. I demonstrate my principles rather than preach them. I teach you the power of the spirit to create the person and to be in charge of its soul development.

"My key phrase is <u>spiritual strength</u>."

The Rider-Waite card pictures intuitive insight as a young woman dressed in a long white gown of purity. Her crown of flowers and the garland of flowers encircling her waist symbolize creative imagination and organic processes. She is the maiden aspect of The Empress and the feminine equivalent of the preceding card's charioteer.

The woman ministers to an orange lion, symbol of basic instincts and masculine willpower. (In some alchemical texts lions also represent different stages of personality development.) Although experts differ on whether she is gently closing,[21] opening, or immobilizing the lion's mouth, his extended tongue suggests that he is licking her to show he approves of and accepts her caress.

The lemniscate above the maiden indicates that we are witnessing a transitional moment of mastery in the eternal now. Devouring energies are transformed into personal strength. Bestial and spiritual powers are integrated.

In the Morgan-Greer card, the woman and lion sit amid the lush plants and palm trees of the lion's domain. The high mountains in the background suggest elevated consciousness. Palm leaves, a traditional sign of victory and eternal life, replace the missing lemniscate. (Growing palm trees also symbolize the soul, according to Jung.)

The Aquarian card shows a man of great determination, elaborately clothed. The sword to his right represents our conscious, logical nature. A dog seated in front of him and to his left, the side of our unconscious, animal nature, guards against untamed human impulses. The divine triangular decorations on the dog's headdress support the cultivated expression of man's animal energy.

The man's triangular headdress, topped with feathers that extend up out of the frame, shows his connection to higher levels of consciousness. The background pattern of the V-shaped lines, which take the place of the lemniscate found in the Rider-Waite card, symbolize divine influence pouring down onto the scene.

All three Strength cards encourage us to get in touch with our desires and create a harmonious union between the conscious, rational and the unconscious, intuitive sides of ourselves.

The Strength card declares that its forces and those of the cosmos can be controlled by human consciousness, if we are "attentive, watchful, vigilant."[22] We have the ability to face life with hope and eagerness and to live passionately while maintaining an inner peace.

The Strength card also announces that the situation now challenging us has a deep spiritual component. It assures us that problems can be solved if we change our frame of reference and see them in a new, more loving context.

In Egyptian mythology, the two aspects of the Strength card are represented by Sekhmet, the lion-headed goddess of destruction *and* healing, and Bast/Bastet, the cat-headed goddess who personified life and fruitfulness. There is also a mythological connection to Heracles, who battled the Nemean Lion and, victorious, wore its skin ever after, making him invincible.

The shadow traits of this card include: lack of courage or integrity; insecurity; lack of self-control, possibly expressed in abusiveness, destructive aggression, or sexual abuse; rage; scattered energy; and loss of focus.

When Strength appears in a spread:

- Listen to other people's ideas and figure out how to blend them with yours.
- Honor both your masculine willpower and your feminine intuition.
- Courageously use compassion to bring harmony to a situation or relationship.
- Recognize the energy bound up in strong feelings, so you can be in charge and direct it.
- Appreciate your strength and determination. If you have not already done so, put it into action.

The Hermit
(Major Arcana IX)

"I bring higher knowledge from the past, which can shed new light on your present situation. Think of me as a teacher, counselor, thera-

*pist, or spirit guide, whichever role appeals to you when you seek
advice. I will not give you the answers, but I will help you to find
them for yourself. Using my principles of patience, contemplation, and
examination before action, you can step back from troubling situations
and see them from a broader perspective.*

*"I hope you are willing to explore your unconscious. That's the
key to inner growth. 'What are your goals in this area?' I ask.*

*"If you let me, I can add spiritual love to your earthly relationships,
and show you how they can contribute to your search for a meaningful
life. I remind you to consider the real purpose of your daily activities
and to set high standards for business operations. Does your work
contribute to the general welfare? Does it add meaning to your life?
Will the part you play provide a model for others to follow?*

"My key phrase is <u>light of the higher ways.</u>"

Standing on a snowy mountaintop of spiritual attainment, the Rider-
Waite Hermit lights the way to higher levels of wisdom. He has
traveled this road himself at least once, as his beard of experience
indicates. His light is intended to pierce spiritual darkness. He represents both the one identity of which we are all a part, and the idea
that in our quest for personal understanding of the Divine, we are all
ultimately alone. His gray robe reflects the resolution of all opposites.
His hooded cloak of contemplation envelops the knowledge of the
ages. The blue background indicates that this same wisdom is all
around us.

Held in his right hand to signify conscious awareness, The Hermit's
lantern is both a divine focal point and the spark of divinity in us all.
The six-pointed star, or Solomon's Seal, that lights the lantern is
formed by interlaced upward-pointing (physical) and downward-
pointing (spiritual) triangles, representing insight and wholeness. As
we consciously aspire "upward," divine knowledge flows down to
us, and the delusion of opposites is resolved. This star is also an
ancient symbol of the divine sexual union that maintained life in
the universe.[23]

With his left hand, The Hermit holds the yellow staff of intellect
and higher knowledge. If you use your imagination to outline the
lantern and figure in the Rider-Waite and Morgan-Greer cards, they
take the shape of the Arabic number nine.

The Hermit in the Morgan-Greer card wears the earthy brown,
hooded robe of humility and service. Surrounded by the bluish purple
background of divine wisdom, he is born of this world and above it.
And like the Rider-Waite Hermit, he stands on snow. It symbolizes

solidified ideas and values that will periodically melt and become part of the waters of the collective unconscious.

The Aquarian Hermit wears the pink hood of Divine Force[24] and a purple robe with elongated triangles radiating from the neckline and sleeve. Some believe they are a stylized version of the mountains present in the other two hermit cards. The geometric background pattern on the upper left side of the card suggests that The Hermit has incorporated the masculine aspect of God into his anima or feminine side. He can draw equally on consciousness and intuition.

While the other two hermits face the left or north, leading us into the direction of initiation, the Aquarian Hermit moves toward the right, indicating that he has passed one initiation and is heading for the next one. He also has his back to us, suggesting that "the work" will never be complete. We will never discern it all.

As a result of his aspirations, service, and discipline, The Hermit has attained an elevated level of understanding that allows him to be a light in the dark night of the soul. In Jungian terms, he is the archetype of the Wise Old Man or the Wise Old Woman, carrier of a tribe or culture's spiritual knowledge and traditions.

Although The Hermit appears to be alone, he may merely be ahead of the spiritual seekers to whom he is showing his "tried and true" path.

The shadow aspect of this card includes: feelings of isolation and boredom; the emptiness found in "traditional forms of exclusively rational doctrines";[25] engaging in meaningless activities or trying to make the meaningless more important than it is; overdependence on a guru or spiritual leader; inflated egotism or pride derived from advancement in our religious experiences; and the idea that isolating ourselves will automatically produce a spiritual experience.

When The Hermit appears, it is time to:

- Ask yourself: "How did I get here and where do I want to go?"

- Reevaluate your priorities and goals for their real substance, perhaps by retreating from everyday routines.

- Consult reliable, experienced sources, including classes and mentors, and learn from their experiences.

- Let your light (ideas, talents) shine.

- Determine what specific understanding your current issue could teach you that would promote spiritual or psychological growth.

Wheel of Fortune

(Major Arcana X)

"I am the creative, formative aspects of your life. I am the circle that has no beginning or end. I am also the rotation of events within the fixed elements of the universe, pictured at the corners of my card. I advance and improve your life.

"Where I go, confrontation and change may follow. I'll help you to adapt to new circumstances and remind you that nothing is permanent. Everything goes through change cycles. I give you the strength to let go of whatever is no longer profitable or appropriate for you.

"I teach you to expect the unexpected, and to understand it when it happens. Look to earlier events or cycles for clues. Look for patterns in your relationships to others. Be tolerant of your own and other people's ups and downs.

"Consider the important occurrences in your personal life. What events taught you the most about living? Let me inspire you to take what life gives you and use it more creatively.

"My key phrase is <u>universal cycles</u>."

The Rider-Waite Wheel of Fortune is comprised of three concentric circles representing will, love, and creation. In the outer circle, the letters TARO are interspersed with the Hebrew letters Yod, Heh, Vau, Heh of the Tetragrammaton. Together they make up the original formula for the universal creative process. The eight-spoked wheel stands for Spirit.

On the left side of the wheel, Typhon, one of the Greek angels of death, descends. On the right, the jackal-headed Anubis, Egyptian guardian of tombs, rises (just as consciousness evolves from lower to higher levels.[26]

The blue sphinx atop the wheel is a symbol of the contradictions and paradoxes with which we must learn to live. It also represents our eternal Self and the completion of our earthly cycle. The sphinx head shows conscious control, the masculine sword, discrimination, and its placement over feminine breasts, compassion. At the same time, it is also a symbol of contradictions or paradoxes with which we must learn to live.

Symbols in the middle circle stand for the four basic alchemical elements: mercury (air) points toward the sphinx; sulfur (fire) toward Anubis; salt (earth) to Typhon; and solution (water) downward.

In clouds at the four corners of the card, animals are connected to both the four elements and four fixed signs of the zodiac: bull (Taurus), lion (Leo), eagle (Scorpio), and man (Aquarius). They represent the unchanging reality in which the rotation of events takes place.[27]

In some cards, including the Rider-Waite, the four corners are also winged archangels, acting as cornerstones for experiences sent from above. They are: Auriel or Uriel (Taurus), Michael (Leo), Gabriel (Scorpio), and Raphael (Aquarius).

In the Morgan-Greer card, a young king and queen cavort at the top of a large wooden wheel. They are at the highest phase of existence. The king holds a golden goblet of abundance. The queen holds her gown steady against the pull of someone who has already fallen off the wheel, suggesting she is aware of the precariousness of their position. While he looks toward the left and remembers the past that got them there, she looks to the right and considers the possibilities of the future.

The wheel, set beside a large plateau, is turned with a handle held by a hand reminiscent of the ones on the Rider-Waite aces. It is the influence of higher forces, the impact of a divine plan, or more mundanely, the hand of fate.

The Aquarian card shows the wheel in front of a man's chest. He wears a sphinxlike headdress and is backed by radiating lines representing spiritual aspiration. The man incorporates the symbol for mercury that appears on the other cards. He is the personification of the Mercury/Hermes psychopomp, our guide to the "underworld" represented by the next ten cards.

In the Wheel of Fortune card, the mandalas on the costume of The Fool have taken full shape. The *mercurius* personality of The Fool has developed into the full-blown personality of Mercury/Hermes. And we have not only acquired the attributes needed to face the challenges of the next ten Major Arcana, but incorporated those attributes into our physical and mental bodies, as well.

The two serpents slithering up the sides of the Aquarian wheel symbolize action and reaction. They also represent the kundalini Ida and Pingula energies[28] rising up from the base chakra to the throat chakra, where they can be creatively expressed. Inside the wheel is the bubbly design that expresses the feminine aspect of the Absolute. The ribbonlike design at the bottom expresses the masculine aspect.

Mythologically the Wheel of Fortune is associated with the goddess Fortuna, whose symbol was the wheel of time. It signifies far more than good or bad luck. It is a symbol of advancement, of cycles of manifestation, of energy that can be harnessed without stopping the rhythm of natural unfolding and periodic repetition. It is the archetype of our quest for the Holy Grail, for self-enlightenment.

The Wheel of Fortune can teach us endurance and fortitude, how to analyze situations and make decisions accordingly, and how to keep our psychic balance in the midst of fluctuation.

Shadow traits of this card include: experiencing ourselves as victims of fate; procrastination; feeling stuck; fighting change; and lacking the persistence necessary to carry out tasks.

When The Wheel turns up:

- Be prepared to roll with the "punches" of life.

- Determine how past events could be affecting your present attitudes and behavior.

- Be alert to unexpected opportunities. Recognize the opportunities in seemingly negative situations.

- Become attuned to your own, other people's, and your environment's natural cycles. You may not be acting in harmony with them.

- Concentrate on finishing what you have started and left undone, especially highly emotional situations and relationships left hanging.

Armed with the knowledge and respect The Magician has for natural law and the ways of the universe, we gain access to the personal and collective wisdom of The High Priestess. The Empress and The Emperor archetypes, which represent both external parental figures and our inner parents, force us to develop the inner control and a code of values represented by The Hierophant.

Given these basic understandings, we further develop our personality by incorporating opposites as The Lovers did, persevering in our search for understanding as The Chariot did, and resolving the conflict between instincts and intellect as Strength did.

Finally, through The Hermit's wisdom, we come to recognize the God-Self that resides within and become more skilled at living within the Wheel of Fortune's divine cycles.

With these lessons forming our personal and spiritual foundation, we enter a new phase of growth guided by the next 10 Major Arcana cards.

Table 1 summarizes the strengths and skills portrayed by the first 10 Major Arcana cards.

TABLE 1

Summary of Ten Archetypal Strengths/Inner Resources

Major Arcana Card	Key Phrase	Strengths
I-The Magician	Creative focused attention	Discipline to translate ideas into action; knowledge of natural processes
II–The High Priestess	Ancient and unrevealed knowledge	Seeker of deeper meanings; tuning into hunches
III–The Empress	Creative abundance	Motherhood; feminine sexuality; generative forces that bring ideas to fruition
IV–The Emperor	Reasoned authority	Fatherhood; masculine sexuality; confidence; courage
V–The Hierophant	Inner teacher	Mastery of the spiritual self
VI–The Lovers	The healing union	Recognition of opposite aspects of personality

MAJOR ARCANA CARD	KEY PHRASE	STRENGTHS
VII–The Chariot	The determined search for greater understanding	Ability to achieve and persevere
VIII–Strength	Spiritual strength	Ability to resolve conflicts between the conscious and unconscious
IX–The Hermit	Light of the higher ways	Recognition of The Divine within
X–Wheel of Fortune	Universal cycles	Adaptation to change; recognition and understanding of cycles

7 ☀ Ten Archetypal Tests and Dilemmas

Major Arcana I–X depict our inner potential and establish strengths we can draw on for our life journey. Major Arcana XI–XX give us a look at the challenges we must face to "come of age." They are like the American Indian concept of the Vision Quest and the Australian aboriginal concept of the walkabout. They are our shamanic trial.

The first five cards in this new sequence represent some of the toughest tests we will ever experience. Surviving their challenges unlocks the door to the last five tests. On the surface, several of these later cards, such as The Star, The Moon, and The Sun, don't look much like tests. They do present dilemmas, however, and we can only truly resolve them after much inner work and preparation. Success here raises us to an inner realm hitherto undreamed-of, opening the Universe (Major Arcana XXI) to us.

Justice

(MAJOR ARCANA XI)

"I sit poised between my two pillars to encourage you to discover the truth in your own life. I want you to become a self-directed, balanced personality, and I am one of your gateways to accomplishing that. I inspire you to take responsibility for your own life and for the outcomes and consequences of your actions.

"Do not mistake me for judgment. My job is evaluation. My sword of discrimination cuts away illusion. I appear to remind you not to be misled by the lure of easy or greedy solutions, for 'as a man soweth so shall he also reap.' You have the opportunity to be an agent of justice in the way you live. Even in what appear to be small matters, strive to maintain your own moral strength and integrity. Act from your ethical principles. Be concerned with the observations, opinions, and rights of others. Listen to all the facts and information before taking action.

"My key phrase is <u>the search for equilibrium.</u>"

In all three decks, Justice sits in a balanced position between two pillars, which emphasize the card's number, eleven. These pillars—severity on the left, mercy on the right—with their hidden center pillar of equilibrium call to mind the Cabalistic Tree of Life. The pillars extend off the card into the sphere of cosmic justice.

Justice wears a crown with three turrets representing knowledge, argument, and decision, and a square stone in the center, forming a combination of the circular (eternity and divine awareness) and the square (integrity and earthly awareness). The square stone indicates that decisions must be made with and reflect third-eye or ajna insight. In the Rider-Waite and Morgan-Greer cards, this symbol is repeated in the pin that clasps Justice's cape at the heart chakra, suggesting that compassion in decision making begins in the heart. In Jungian symbolism, the squaring of the circle is a symbol of totality, wholeness, the Self.

In the Rider-Waite and Morgan-Greer cards, Justice, wearing the slipper of conscious understanding, extends her right foot. She is ready to rise and act. Her right hand (consciousness) raises the double-edged sword of decisiveness that cuts through illusion. It can also be seen as the sword of consciousness defending against unconscious or shadow elements.[1]

In her left hand, with fingers pointing earthward toward the unconscious, the Rider-Waite figure holds golden scales of solar light balanced to measure our actions. The unbalanced scales held by the Morgan-Greer figure imply that equilibrium must be achieved through transformation and the balancing of conscious knowledge and unconscious intuition. The Rider-Waite Justice sits on the basic, unalterable stone throne of wisdom, symbolized by its gray color. The stone thrones can also represent the Self.

Both figures wear robes of scarlet, the color of courage and passion. Their capes are green for creativity, growth, or fertility. The complementary colors signify both opposites and balance. The blue cowl at the throat chakra of the Morgan-Greer Justice clothes her words in divine energy.

Representing confidence and inner wisdom, the temple veil behind Justice is royal purple, the healing color attributed to authority. Its color lets us know we've come to the highest court of justice. Yellow behind the veil signifies intensified or higher consciousness, the source of all true knowledge.

The Aquarian Justice sits between bundles of blooming rods, for pillars. The patterns at the base of her scarf—which itself represents the spine and kundalini energy—show that the feminine and masculine attributes of the Absolute are integral within us as we begin this time of challenge.

The lack of a veil between the pillars signifies that the "light" of understanding from above is available to shine through and illuminate our development of inner justice. The elongated handle of the Aquarian scales has a red jewel at the top to symbolize the placing of passion above and away from the balancing process.

By situating the scales in light and shadow, this card calls on us to balance the opposing forces within us—the conscious/unconscious, masculine/feminine, divine/earthly—so we may utilize all, and not deny any.

The Aquarian Justice wears a black glove on her left hand, the symbol of feminine attributes. Its placement suggests her capacity to dissolve old values and adopt new ones, while her right hand holds the sword of action that can cut away outdated values. She wears the gray glove of balance on her right hand, which symbolizes masculine attributes, while holding the balanced scales in her left hand—a double balance.

This card represents cosmic equilibrium and what Jungian analyst Marion Woodman refers to as "holding the tension of the opposites," letting each have its own voice without trying to do away with either.[2]

Justice challenges us to live in paradox and not regard it as chaos. It invites us to look deep inside ourselves and identify the contradictions within. It asks us to balance our inner promptings with our conscious mind's ability to analyze and assimilate. It moves us into a position of power, with great potential for growth. In Egyptian mythology justice is associated with Ma'at, frequently defined as the goddess of truth. More accurately, however, she represents "the right order."[3]

Shadow characteristics of this card include: failure to take responsibility for our actions; inability to accept the consequences of our decisions and actions; blaming others for what happens to us; leaping to a decision without taking into consideration all available information and resources; overconcern with whether or not something that has happened to us is "fair"; and denying our inner opposites.

When Justice appears:

- Make an appropriate assessment of the problem and your part in it. Are you being judgmental? Are you acting with integrity?

- Look for a previously unidentified inner contradiction with which you are struggling.

- Consider how resolving or releasing feelings from the past and living more in the present might help you achieve inner balance.

- Gather all the accessible information regarding your current situation. Is there a "solution" that includes more than one viewpoint?

- Consider where your life is out of balance and how you could modify your activities to restore harmony.

The Hanged Man

(Major Arcana XII)

"Here I am, suspended comfortably between heaven and earth, pausing to reflect before making important decisions. I know the value of surrendering to higher wisdom. I am patient and will suspend my usual actions, waiting for the insight I seek from above.

"When I appear, expect a turnaround. My function is to push you into looking at your situation from a perspective that is 180 degrees from your original one.

"I encourage you to see things from other people's points of view. I remind you to turn your attention from the obvious and consider new approaches. I warn you, however, that although you may uncover information that enables you to go confidently in another direction, your actions may be disruptive for others. Your motives may be misunderstood.

"As you let go of worldly pride and alter your views on how the world should work, a new set of truths will be revealed. The challenges I present to you ultimately permit the relocation of your center from the ego to the higher self.

"My key phrase is <u>reversing false images</u>."

The Rider-Waite Hanged Man, suspended upside down from a *Tau* or T-shaped cross, has a radiating gold halo around his golden hair. He has already received divine inspiration. With his feet in the air, his position suggests that his "under-standing" comes from above. The center of his consciousness has shifted to the Self, which is expanding and becoming the Cosmic Self.

The Hanged Man's jacket is blue, the color of infinity and spiritual values. His hose and belt are the red of passionate endurance. His shoes are golden, symbolizing high ideals and spiritual goals, as is the rope that suspends him from the cross, which is the symbol of divine selection.

Wearing the same colors, the Morgan-Greer figure hangs suspended between two leafless tree trunks that act as a "doorway" to a new way of being. The deep purple rolling clouds reveal access to divine creativity.

The pattern on the shoulders of the Aquarian Hanged Man's gray-violet shirt shows support from the feminine aspect of the Absolute. The jagged patterns at his wrists and over his abdomen hint at an upcoming union between the actions of his arms and his "gut" instinctual forces. A bolt of energy for inspirational change extends from his throat chakra (creativity) to his base chakra (vitality), reminding us that a direct connection between these two chakras gives us the most access to creative energy.

The Aquarian Hanged Man is suspended on a living cross, which represents the living Divine and the Divine in living. To further emphasize this principle, the top of the cross extends beyond the card.

In all three pictures, The Hanged Man has one leg crossed behind the other, forming the divine triangle. In the Aquarian and Morgan-Greer cards, it is his right leg, with the straight *left* leg suggesting the act of waiting to receive and the patience we need when our world is turned upside down. In the Rider-Waite, the left leg is bent, and the straight right leg tied to the top beam. This reflects a more active desire, a reaching for spiritual understanding.

The legs of the Aquarian and Morgan-Greer figures form the number four,[4] the number of stability between the material and the psychical. It is also a sign of synthesis and psychological growth. When three, the numerological breakdown of the card's number (12 = 1 + 2 = 3) and four appear together, striving toward wholeness is indicated. Inasmuch as three is a masculine number and four is a feminine one, the card suggests that The Hanged Man, perfectly centered and balanced, has accepted both his inner masculine and inner feminine aspects.

The hands of The Hanged Man, behind his back with elbows out, form a spiritual triangle, as do all the spaces between both legs and arms. His hands are not seen, suggesting surrender to a higher purpose and the end of extending outward (for either giving or grasping) from ego concerns.

In Jungian terms, The Hanged Man loses his sense of self and experiences the "collective unconscious," a timeless source of knowledge and inspiration shared by all. He connects with universal or transpersonal consciousness. In esoteric or spiritual terms, he gives up personal self and aligns with God—the Universal Mind, a higher will or higher purpose. His tale is the archetypal myth of the willing sacrifice that leads to greater understanding and wiser action. Many writers have likened The Hanged Man to Odin, the Norse god of wind and spirits, who suspended himself from the world tree Yggdrasil for nine nights in order to attain the secrets of the runes. This card also embodies the Zen concept of searching for the Buddha in the world only to find—usually when we have given up the search—that we were the Buddha all along.

The Hanged Man offers us two major challenges. The first involves what psychologists call "reframing." This is the ability to set aside our typical viewpoint and perceive a situation in another way. We can find positive value or opportunities in what originally seemed oppressive or totally negative, for example, and, by redefining our situation in those terms, enhance our soul's development. The Hanged Man also challenges us to step out of our limited personality perspective and to see ourselves in a greater context.

Finally, the card urges us to wait for the right moment to receive knowledge or initiate action. "I'll know it when I see it" is a favorite phrase of The Hanged Man.

Shadow aspects of The Hanged Man include: an inability to consider change; rigid values or holding onto old values rigidly; unwillingness to make the necessary sacrifices or do the work necessary for success; sacrificing too much of ourselves for others; or regarding ourselves as victims rather than learning from our experiences.

When The Hanged Man appears:

- Be willing to reverse your attitude or approach, even if only temporarily. Look for the true meaning or essence of the situation.

- Consider doing something that, for you, is "out of character," but that you may have been longing to do.

- Consider whether a short-term sacrifice could bring long-term gains or satisfaction.

- Evaluate how or in what situation you are "hung up" or your "hands are tied." Have you been sacrificing too much, having difficulty giving up a rigid perspective, or uselessly struggling against a situation over which you actually have little control?

- Identify your inner or higher principles and align yourself with them in your actions and attitudes. Honor your vision.

Death
(Major Arcana XIII)

"I ride forward to announce natural changes that bring about transformation and renewal. Although I am the archetype of physical death, in the Tarot I express feelings that accompany the death of old ways of being.

"I end the 'status quo.' I release limited thinking so new forms can be built. I help you end old patterns of interacting, so that new ideas and understanding can evolve. With me around to inspire the development of new attitudes, you can make room in your life for new opportunity, face changing circumstances, and put aside old beliefs that no longer ring true.

"I promise rebirth and renewal following the disintegration or abandonment of those things that are no longer useful to you. I bring a new dawning with all the potential it implies, and with all the fear and excitement it engenders.

"My key phrase is <u>new opportunities and transformation.</u>"

In the Rider-Waite card, Death is portrayed as a golden skeleton (the spiritual foundation of our growth), holding a black banner, representing matter before it takes form, and decorated with the five-petaled rose of the senses. Its white color symbolizes matter that *has* taken shape. Death rides from the unconscious left toward consciousness on the right, with a river flowing behind him—possibly the River Styx, which the Greeks believed was the transport to the land of the dead. The river carries a ship toward the future. Above it, a great lake of the unconscious falls over high cliffs into the river. In the East, the golden sun rises between the two stone pillars that we first saw in The Moon card, representing the dawning of a new day or time of life. Four figures, or aspects of ourselves, face Death: a deceased or wounded king representing our *persona* or personality, a child (our innocence), a maiden (our immaturity or purity), and a priest (our spiritual beliefs).

The Morgan-Greer card shows a skeleton facing forward to look transition in the face. His hooded cape is clasped at the throat with a square yellow brooch representing the material world. He holds a wooden scythe (ending cycles). Its crescent blade (related to the crescent moon, therefore to cycles) encloses a large single white rose, growing from the right side of the card where the future and developed consciousness await. The rising sun casts a red color over the sky and the background river, hinting at our mortality, yet flying birds hold spiritual promise.

In the Aquarian card, the mental aspect of transition is emphasized by depicting only the head of a figure, whose breastplate bears the pattern of the masculine aspect of the Absolute. The cowl beneath his helmet resembles flowing blood.

While red often does represent blood, it also symbolizes passion and represents the fourth stage of alchemical transformation (*rubedo*), wherein the "illuminated/aware life process is now ruled by the enlightened, 'spiritually objective' self. It preceded/foretold of the completion of inner work."[5]

The emphasis on brown, an earthly, creative color, in the Aquarian card suggests not only our earthbound state but the fertility that abounds with the change of attitude this card represents.

On a symbolic level, the Death card represents the cycles that constantly occur in nature as well as in our own inner development. It expresses both our feelings regarding physical death and the feelings that accompany the death of old ways of being. In Jungian terms, Death is the archetypal "night sea journey" or descent into the "underworld" of unconscious material. A successful return to reality by overcoming the malignant or devouring aspects of the unconscious dramatically changes our conscious awareness. This mystical or symbolic death is also part of primitive or shamanistic initiation rites and the old mystery school tradition.

Recognizing personality masks (the *persona* in Jungian terms) is a necessary part of developing from lower to higher consciousness. Spiritually this card tells of the death of personality or ego desires, which prepares us for a new life with a new perspective. It is a continuation of the work begun in The Hanged Man, but on a more intimate and less intellectual level. The two cards work in tandem, one beginning the reorganization, the other deepening it.

The shadow aspects of this card include: resistance to change; physical or mental stagnation; either inertia or wildness; and needing more and more worldly power or possessions.

When you draw the Death card:

- Recognize that it's time to let go of patterns, action, habits, or attitudes once useful, but now outdated.

- Consider whether or not you have some unfinished mourning to do, or whether you are extending your mourning too long as a way of avoiding moving forward.

- Identify any unresolved feelings of abandonment, rejection, or isolation.

- Identify the cycle you think is about to be finished and consider how you feel about that ending and a new beginning.

- Identify the many masks you wear to see which ones are still appropriate, and which, if any, complicate your situation or issue.

Temperance
(Major Arcana XIV)

"My principle is that of blending and combining to create something new or distinctly different. My guidance and energy inspire you to create tangible products or to work on yourself psychologically, and become more unified.

"My name derives from the Latin temperare *("to mix"), and the*

Latin tempor, *a seasonal time period. Taken together they mean the ability to combine or mingle properly at the appropriate time.*[6]

"*I encourage you to combine spontaneity with knowledge and memories of the past. I help you rebalance inner and outer matters that at first may not seem to fit. Under my guidance, you are able to adapt your behavior to changing circumstances.*

"*The water I pour does not spill. It flows in both directions, bringing internal integration. When you allow my influence into your life, your conscious and unconscious natures are not at conflict.*

"*I am the eternal now and akin to the Zen concept of living the fully conscious life.*

"*My key phrase is* the higher self in action.*"*

The Rider-Waite card shows the archangel Michael wearing the sign of solar and divine energy on his brow. He is the purifying fire of the soul. At the neckline of his white robe, as on the shirt of The Fool, are the Hebrew letters that form the Tetragrammaton. An orange triangle in a white square over his chest represents matter in its purist form.[7] Israel Regardie, who wrote on the ceremonies of the Golden Dawn, calls this image the solar emblem of Tiphereth—the sixth Sephira on the central pillar of the Cabalistic Tree of Life—and describes it as the place of the heart, a central point of balance, and the synthesis of form and energy.[8]

In the Rider-Waite and Morgan-Greer cards, the angel stands with one foot on the ground of the sensual, material world, and the other in the water of the emotional, spiritual world. Providing a glimpse of our place in the Universe, he pours water from his higher left hand of divine consciousness. By pouring the water without spills, he demonstrates the discipline and self-control that come with maturity and arise from what we believe to be proper action.

The path beside the angel's feet leads to the mountains of wisdom and enlightenment, where a golden light of divinely inspired knowledge hovers.

The yellow irises to the angel's right symbolize illumination and messages from another realm. The irises' location on the right side of the card foretell the blossoming influence of the Divine in our future work.

The Aquarian card shows a seemingly feminine, ornately garbed angel. Like all angels, she guards the threshold between the Divine and the mundane, between the unconscious and the conscious, between historical time and sacred time.[9] As a winged creature, she suggests transition and gifts from the Divine, so perhaps her ornateness is intended to remind us of the full force and beauty of bringing the Divine into earthly life.

The Aquarian angel's headdress bears the sun disks of power and healing. Triangles of divine communication decorate her throat chakra. The feminine aspect of the Absolute is incorporated in her feathery front.

Temperance reminds us not to discard the past, but to preserve the best aspects of it and find new and creative uses for them in the present. Its appearance tells us to pay attention to experiences related to our current situation or issue. By pouring them back and forth in our minds like the water in the angel's cups, we can gain new understanding of their place in our lives.

Temperance urges us to recognize unconscious material and mix it with conscious awareness so that it "flows" into one. It symbolizes the ongoing work of dissolving and integrating the tension of the opposites, so we become better able to recognize, accept, and live with paradox. Gareth Knight, who relates the Tarot to Cabalistic symbolism, calls this the "tempering of the soul" to make it a suitable tool for the "Great Works of God."[10]

As a five card (14 = 1 + 4 = 5), Temperance is related to The Hierophant, and takes that card's principles of mediation and balancing to a more spiritual level.

The shadow aspects of this card include: being extremely self-centered; being out of harmony with ourselves—possibly reflected in mood swings and unstable actions; overindulgence or addiction; impatience; lack of self-control; and action without thought to previous experiences or potential consequences.

When this card appears in your spread:

- Use moderation and self-restraint.

- Reflect on past mistakes to determine what you have learned about your needs and motives. How could that apply in your current situation?

- Evaluate rigid ways of thinking that may lock you into a one-sided, disharmonious way of relating. Consider how you could be more flexible in your attitude.

- Consider how selfish motives might be impeding your inner or outer progress.

- Consider what is out of balance in your life and work to reestablish harmony.

The Devil

(MAJOR ARCANA XV)

"Urrrrrgh, am I scaring you? That's not really my purpose. They put me in this book of life experiences to help you recognize your shadow side, and it's a heavy burden.

"I am the undeveloped, unlived aspects of your personality that keep higher wisdom from coming through. When you understand yourself, and what gives you true worth, my power melts.

"Are you overly concerned with clothes, social or professional positions, appearances? Are you envious of others? Do you have secret sexual fantasies?

"They all come from me, because I am that part of you that must be put aside to live in civilized society. As long as you fear or deny those kinds of feelings and attitudes, you live in bondage. I'm here to remind you that someday you must recognize them, slip your chains, and reclaim them as your own.

"Whoa, now! Wait a minute. Don't think I'm giving you permission to run rampant. I didn't say you needed to act on your feelings. Claiming them as your own will be enough to free you. Frankly, I'm tired of being your scapegoat.

"When you see through the illusion I present, you are on the way to true freedom. You will cease to blame others and find your way past me into your inner center.

"My key phrase is <u>acknowledging your hidden recesses</u>."

The ram-horned, donkey-eared, shaggy-legged devil in the Rider-Waite card perches with clawed feet on a one-dimensional cube or pedestal, which represents limited knowledge and the illusionary base from which we make judgments. He has a navel, so we know he is not the fallen angel Lucifer. Instead, he is comprised of our own projections—the negative, disowned fears and attributes we fail to recognize in ourselves and instead attribute to others.

The burning torch he holds in his left hand lights the tail of the male, suggesting both overpowering, destructive sexual needs and dormant kundalini energy that could lift sex to the sacred. Which will he choose?

Unlike the blessing of The Hierophant, The Devil's upraised right palm has all fingers extended.[11] It bears the astrological glyph for Saturn, the planet of "bondage to circumstances that devour emerging creativity."[12] The open hand hints that nothing is hidden—that's the great challenge of this card. We must not be deceived by superficial appearances.

On The Devil's forehead is the outline of an inverted pentagram. When its point is turned upward, the pentagram symbolizes man aspiring to higher ways. The reverse, as shown in The Devil card, represents disregard for all laws, especially moral and spiritual ones. It also symbolizes valuing sensual gratification and material gain above all else.

The two nude, horned, cloven-footed figures suggest delusion or false knowledge bestializing human consciousness to the point of apparent bondage. Of course, the chains are loose enough for the people to slip out of them any time they choose. Self-absorbed, the figures, who represent duality and immaturity, don't see this.

A blue fly inside the large inverted yellow pentagram on the Morgan-Greer card represents the negative noise in our heads that distracts us from creative endeavors.

Like the Rider-Waite figure, the Aquarian Devil has huge bat wings, making him a creature of the night (a symbol of the unconscious). He looms over the nude figures of a man and woman whose featureless faces depict their primitive nature. These figures suggest that turning away from awareness leads to loss of identity and lack of self-knowledge.

The positions of the figures in The Devil card make it almost a caricature of Major Arcana VI, The Lovers, to which it is numerologically related ($15 = 1 + 5 = 6$). We must recognize our bondage to limited knowledge and our need to more fully understand ourselves, this card suggests. The darkness of ignorance is dispelled by allowing light to enter into our daily lives. One way to do that is to accept, and even laugh at, our human foibles. This is the devilish gift comedians offer us.

Mythologically The Devil is reminiscent of all the horned gods of antiquity. With the torso of a human and the lower body of an animal, he symbolizes one whose consciousness has not yet reconciled with his animal instincts. So why does The Devil appear *after* the reconciliation challenge shown in the preceding Temperance card? To free us for the tasks the next five cards ask us to tackle. The horns he wears *are* an ancient symbol of new life and spiritual regeneration.[13]

This card embodies the Jungian idea that demands for growth often come from the shadow aspects of ourselves, and that acknowledging our shadows releases creative energy.

According to Jungian author Robert Johnson, the shadow is our "dumping ground," the unlived side of our human potential.[14] It is where bigotry, violence, rebellion, revenge, repressed sexuality—and any of the many other ways we humiliate, override, or dehumanize another—reside. It is also where we hide our "untamed" or uncivilized instincts, especially sexual ones. We tend to see these things first in other people, and the challenge of this card is to identify what angers or scares us about others and accept them once again as aspects of ourselves.

When this card turns up:

- Pick at least one thing about the situation or issue at hand that angers you. Consider that the reason it angers you is that some part of *it* is also in some way part of *you*. Can you identify the connection?

- Make a list of attitudes you think contemptible in others. Can you recognize them as part of yourself?

- Identify your strong beliefs and consider how they prevent you from being open to new ideas or action.

- Examine any areas of your life in which you feel "imprisoned."

- If you feel someone or something is holding you back, look to see how you are chaining yourself to that situation.

The Tower
(MAJOR ARCANA XVI)

"I am the ego structure you have built, and I have a burning desire to get your attention. I am the outer facade you have constructed so people cannot see your inner shadow. Sometimes I am also regarded as a house of lies, false values, and ignorance. I am the pride that goeth before the fall.

"One of my functions is to shatter existing modes of thinking. When rigidity and delusion are overthrown, a flash of clear vision may follow. Sometimes entrenched situations only need a little jolt, but I'm prepared to deliver more if necessary. Don't tempt me.

"I carry the spiritual force that releases the imprisoned inner self to go on to higher fulfillment. Suddenly being thrust into an alternate awareness can be a liberating experience, even if you do not understand it as such until later.

"My key phrase is <u>reorganizing the personality.</u>"

In the Rider-Waite card, a tower of false wisdom set on a jagged pinnacle suggests both a mountain fortress built for defensive purposes and a pedestal on which we hold ourselves aloof or separate. Suspended in the sky nearby is the golden crown of personal will and materialistic thinking. It bears no jewels of understanding.

The three flaming windows depict false security and false pride being burned away as the Divine Triad of Father, Son, and Spirit is established within. Two figures, one male, representing rigid ego attitudes, one female (rigid emotional attitudes), plummet earthward. Both wear red and blue clothing, reflecting a mixture of conscious and unconscious attitudes. They fall headfirst, symbolizing a clean break from the past. Against a black sky of ignorance, a bolt of lightning flashes (divine intervention) over 22 yellow Yods (signs of spiritual wisdom and grace). They represent the 22 paths of the Cabalistic Tree of Life and all the powers of the Major Arcana.

The brown Tower in the Morgan-Greer card resembles a rook, or castle piece in a chess set, suggesting the limitation of an ego that can "move" in only two directions (i.e., think only in dualities). Lightning flashes of insight strike from beyond the card's frame, forcing the acknowledgment of the stunted or shadow aspects of our personality, represented by the tiny, falling, black figures. Meanwhile, the blue waves of emotion beat at the rigidity of the personality.

The Aquarian Tower also looks like a rook. It is caught in a storm of personal turmoil, and waves of turbulent unconscious material threaten its foundation. There are blowing clouds created by powerful winds of change and flying birds, representing the presence of Spirit. The full moon holds the promise of a new cycle.

In its most positive sense, The Tower reflects the ability to go our own way, follow our own direction, possibly even defy social conventions or other organized traditions, and make it work for us. Tower "people" have strong character, and they often need it for the ups and downs in their lives.

More traditionally, The Tower represents an abrupt awakening, usually from unforeseen happenings. Delusions are overthrown, old notions upset, and false conceptions destroyed as we learn the contents of our shadow. The more rigid the personality, the more severe the disruption. The good news is that as a seven ($16 = 1 + 6 = 7$), The Tower is a card of initiation.

It is linked to Major Arcana VII, The Chariot, and therefore to victory and a new direction for the future. Further, 16 is one of those "magic" numbers. If we total all the numbers in the sequence preceding it ($1 + 2 + 3 + 4 + 5$, etc.), we arrive at 136 or 10 ($1 + 3 + 6 = 10$) and 1 ($1 + 0 = 1$), both of which depict the beginning of a new cycle.

The Tower is of our own making. In relationships it may point to a false sense of security or self-importance. If we are functioning in a limited world, or if our successes in meeting the challenges of the previous five cards have given us an inflated sense of our capabilities, it may be time for another lesson in self-realization. This card warns us to let in the light of greater awareness before lightning strikes and topples our inflated egos.

The upheaval shown in The Tower can break up spiritual arrogance as well. It shatters barriers of creed and dogma, plunging us into the pursuit of new personal and spiritual truths. Knight writes that the roof lifts up to allow the "Fire of Heaven" to enter and "unify the opposite poles of the self to the very highest level."[15]

The archetypal dark night of the soul depicted on this card calls for awareness and recognition. Its shadow aspects include: lack of insight; avoidance of change; and holding onto rigid ideas or attitudes.

When this card appears:

- Be ready to see things in a new way. Are you holding onto beliefs that may complicate your situation?

- Look to what needs balancing in your life. Where have you been overly intellectual or overly emotional?

- Make room for the unexpected, especially a flash of insight.

- Ask where and how you have been presenting a false image to yourself or another.

- Be ready for some heavy soul-searching, possibly stimulated by activities beyond your control.

The Star
(MAJOR ARCANA XVII)

"I bring you the bright light of understanding. I stimulate your imagination through intuitive awareness. I am fully engaged here, and there are no paths to lead you away from discovering what is really going on now. I stimulate your imagination through intuitive awareness.

"I will guide you as you search for meaning and direction. I can

*help you find and fulfill your destiny. I offer you access to the collec-
tive and personal unconscious so you can develop your conscious
awareness. From me you can obtain a sense of security and confidence
in your own inner truth.*

*"I encourage you to still your mind and connect with the Spirit.
Let the water from my vases remind you that the Universe provides
a continuous supply of guidance. You can tap into it and receive what
you need by listening to my voice within yourself. The divine gift I
bring you is freedom of the soul.*

"My key phrase is <u>universal guidance</u>."

In the Rider-Waite card, a woman with golden hair, signifying
spiritual wisdom and blessing, rests on one knee at a pool that represents the collective unconscious. Her left foot is on land and her right
foot on water, but not in it, suggesting that spirit supports matter, and
that conscious knowledge is propped up by unconscious intuition.

The female figure, whose nudity shows she has nothing to hide,
pours the water of life from a pitcher in each hand. The stream from
the vase in her right hand falls directly into the pool to show that she
is making a conscious choice to expand the Self. The flow from the
vase in her left hand (unconscious/intuition) falls on the land, where
it divides into five rivulets, representing the five human senses. The
ripples in the pool form an expanding circle or mandala, suggesting
expansion of the Self or the inner soul.

Above the female figure is a large eight-pointed yellow star—a
symbol of spiritual sustenance and the psychological equivalent of the
eight-spoked wheel. It is surrounded by seven smaller, eight-pointed
white stars that bring to mind the main chakras, or energy centers, of
the body.[16]

In Jungian terms, stars symbolize the archetypes that influence us,
the Spirit of the Universe, and the Spirit of humans. Their presence
on this card suggests our access to divine guidance.

The stars total eight, which is also the number of this card (17 =
1 + 7 = 8), and a number of balance. Jung considered it a number of
wholeness and, therefore, a symbol of the Self. It also represents
regeneration and the ceaseless breath of the cosmos, containing both
the outbreath and inbreath of the Divine.[17]

An Ibis, sacred to both Hermes, protector of heroes, and Thoth,
Egyptian god of wisdom, perches on a nearby tree, which traditional
interpretations of this card associate with the brain and nervous system. The tree and the bird represent the ability to focus or concentrate
in order to receive higher wisdom.

The Morgan-Greer Star also depicts a nude woman kneeling. Unlike the Rider-Waite card, however, her right foot is *in* the pool while the left rests on greenery. As she concentrates, she is grounded and balanced in both her physical and emotional natures. Lush greenery, representing natural fertility and creativity, fills the foreground. Trees grow on the hills behind her.[18]

An elaborately designed star shines forth on the Aquarian card. The star's orange and black colors, plus indigo, are duplicated in the brilliant plumage of a bird that rests on a berry-filled bush (ripeness). The bird is often identified as a peacock, symbol of the Self. Through the peacock, which Japikse defines as humanity, "the light of the star shines forth and illuminates the shadows of earth."[19] The modified V-shape of the white background shows that the divine wisdom has descended and is available to us.

If The Tower is the jolt that disrupts our so-called security, then The Star offers the inspiration and guidance to rebuild with a greater perspective. She is the stabilization and peace that occurs after the revelations of The Tower.

Mythologically this card is related to the *anima mundi*, or soul of the world, who was depicted as naked, with a halo of stars, and with one foot on land and the other in water[20] to show her dominion over earth and sea. It is also linked with the Sumerian mother goddess Inanna, queen of heaven, often addressed as the light of the world and the morning and evening star. Inanna's shield bears an eight-pointed starlike design. She is the Great Mother, the source of the earth's "lifeblood,"[21] who brings the substance of the Divine and of the elements to the living world in the measure that we can receive them.

The Star is the card that inspires us to develop inner calm and peace. As our mind stills, the lightness of being and of the Being finds room to enter and influence every area of our lives. Concentration and focus facilitate the release of our imagination. Creativity flourishes. Waite calls this the card of the "Gifts of Spirit."[22]

The Star represents wholeness, healing, and universal truth unveiled. It challenges us to discover basic tenets of our being and apply them to daily activities. It calls our attention to a new inner focus and heralds a time of renewal. Embodying the Jungian principle of individuation, the guiding star asks us to develop a unique, personal vision and understanding of our destiny in a divine Universe.

The card's shadow aspects include: denying (or failing to recognize) our talents and abilities; loss of self-esteem; loss of hope; avoiding or failing to be open to both inner and outer truths; holding onto a narrow attitude; and getting lost in too many idealistic causes.

When this card shines in your spread, it suggests that you need to:

- Look for new insights into a situation.

- Make a careful comparison between your ideals and what is actually available to you in relation to your situation/issue. Does part of the problem lie in a discrepancy between the two?

- Evaluate how you are attuning yourself to, or failing to align with, higher consciousness.

- Rely on your self-confidence and inner focus to help you fulfill current goals or plan new, more meaningful ones.

- Prepare yourself to receive and participate in a time of healing and renewed direction.

The Moon
(Major Arcana XVIII)

"I am another stage of your unconscious unfolding. I am the intelligence of all the cells of your body, and your deep sense of connection with nature, which intellect can never fully understand nor words adequately explain.

"You first encountered me in my cousin The Hermit. You were still looking outside yourself for wisdom then. As a result of your subsequent experiences, however, you now know that what you are seeking is, and always has been, an integral part of you.

"I am the wisdom of the heart. In my present phase I signal a time for increased creativity. In other phases I can be moodiness, inner

darkness, changeability. Some call me a scavenger because I derive my energy from digging deeply into memory. In me you see the reflection of your thoughts and actions.

"Welcome the sleep and dreams I bring. They are a source of new knowledge and psychological repair. I inspire you to become aware of cyclic patterns of instinct or emotion so you can decide whether or not to continue them.

"My key phrase is <u>cycles of inner development</u>."

The Rider-Waite card portrays a yellow moon with a human profile, suggesting all the cycles we must go through to attain spiritual wisdom. Fifteen yellow Yods of divine energy, or "dew" as Waite calls them,[23] fall from it. They symbolize renewing and fertilizing inspiration.

A violet lobster or crayfish representing instinctive energy or the beginning of conscious growth[24] emerges from a blue pool of cosmic chaos at the base of the card. On the dry land of physical manifestation, a wolf, our natural animal instincts, and a dog (domesticated instincts) bay at the moon, implying that we must acknowledge and integrate both states of being. The animals are mythologically related to the Greek watchdogs of the underworld (shadow) and to Hecate, goddess of the moon, for whom the dog was sacred. To continue our journey toward wholeness, we must get past them successfully without killing them.

A path symbolizing our spiritual direction winds through the land of experience to unknown heights. It passes between two towers of human achievement and through the gateway to spiritual enlightenment. The path undulates, suggesting the different planes of consciousness open to us during sleep, trance, or meditation. This undulation, the cyclic activity of the moon, and the possibility, as Jungian analyst Irene Gad suggests, that the crayfish can go backward and forward,[25] convey the idea that the route to wholeness is never easy or straightforward. The "twin motif" of the two animals and the two towers "duplicates" the message of new material working to emerge from the unconscious.

The Morgan-Greer scene is similar except the path meanders between two stone towers that are each constructed differently, suggesting differences in creative expression.

You certainly can't miss the moon on the Aquarian card. It almost seems mounted like an icon. The designs on each side of the base of the Aquarian card hint at the pillars in the Rider-Waite and Morgan Greer cards, while the horizontal lines between them likely replace the path rather than the pool (since they are red, not blue). The sharp and rounded angles in the Aquarian Moon card suggest the masculine and feminine elements of our unconscious as well as the complexity or difficulties of following the path of The Moon. Its promise looms large, however, and is difficult to ignore.

The Moon represents the active imagination, which has access to our shadow aspects. It is a doorway to the unknown. Intuitive material can be brought forth through it and organized for use in everyday life.

Associated with inner feminine energy, this card stirs up deep feelings. They can motivate us to accomplish our goals, although they may need to be examined first. "Moon spirit" can erupt as intense, fiery revelation or dreamy, meditative productions.[26] Either way, it asks us to open ourselves to the creativity it stimulates, and incorporate it into our overall viewpoint.

The challenge of The Moon card is to wait for hunches to "ripen." Moon ideas become material realities in the light of day and with the energy drawn from the next card, The Sun.

Shadow aspects of The Moon include: failure to acknowledge our sensitivity and imagination; resistance to recognizing and accepting our shadow; mood swings/depression/"lunacy"; and difficulty recognizing the illusory nature of some experiences or feelings.

When this card appears:

- Consider whether you have feelings about your situation that you have been unaware of or have avoided dealing with.
- Become aware of the impact your own cycles and feelings have on your situation/issue.
- Be open to information from dreams and memories.
- Determine whether you could be completing an important phase in your life, or beginning a new one.
- Be careful not to let other people talk you into doing something you intuitively feel is not right for you.

The Sun
(Major Arcana XIX)

"I serve as an unfailing energy source for all earthly creatures, sending out rays of creativity and spiritual renewal for you to use. I fuel the mini regeneration you go through each day and the cosmic regeneration you experience as you approach the successful completion of inner work.

"I encourage you to celebrate being with others in my warmth. I represent union in earthly and spiritual matters and urge you to see worldly unions as possibilities for personal and spiritual growth.

"In all your pursuits, I provide the vital energy you need to achieve your goals. I teach you to be more receptive to new ideas and to have confidence in your own abilities.

"I sponsor the merger of unconscious parts of yourself with the conscious so that rebirth will take place. I bring conscious self-revelation that leads to inner growth.

"My key phrase is <u>triumphant renewal</u>."

The Rider-Waite Sun features a child sitting astride a white horse, telling us that the shadow aspect of our animal nature has been mastered. The child, who is naked (i.e., innocent, authentic), needs no saddle or reins. He has perfect balance and control.

His head is wreathed with flowers and a red feather similar to the one The Fool wears. Having gone through the experiences of the preceding cards, The Fool is reborn and ready for the next spiral through his archetypal journey.

Turning his back on limitation and restriction, the child sits in front of sunflowers (solar energy in physical form), which grow behind a gray stone wall.[27] The alternating straight and wavy beams of light radiating from the sun symbolize our masculine and feminine natures.[28]

In the Morgan-Greer card, a golden-haired woman and man gaze into each other's eyes. They represent the union of opposites, the incorporation of the masculine and feminine aspects of ourselves.

The Aquarian Sun card contains no human figure. Bands of energy radiate out from a personified sun to the four corners of the card, which represent the four corners of the earth. Their patterns suggest abundance.

As our solar star, The Sun collects and distributes the power of the Universe to us and to the universal Spirit within us. The vital energy of our inner and outer suns is what makes us feel alive.

Our "Sun Spirit" challenges us to learn to balance unconscious and conscious material by recognizing and respecting the importance of each. By blending the two, conscious action flows from intuitive knowledge. Intellect is accompanied by its partner, affect.

The sunflowers on the Rider-Waite and Morgan-Greer cards suggest the "marriage" of Mother Earth and Father Sun,[29] and a spiritual rebirth as a result of that union. The newborn aspect of our personality and our life is what Waite calls "consciousness in the spirit."[30]

The Sun card fosters transformation. Its shadow aspects include: failing to acknowledge or listen to our inner child; being afraid to trust anyone; rejecting knowledge of our oneness with the Universe; and feeling "burned out" or as if we are merely surviving rather than thriving.

When this card appears:

- Prepare to engage in a more integrated, confident way of relating or behaving.

- Get ready to develop a new image of yourself, which may feel awkward for a time but which will ultimately enliven your life.

- Celebrate and share your emotional abundance with others.

- Evaluate how authentically you've been living and how your societal masks serve or inhibit you.

- Face the ways you promote closeness, or avoid it, in your relationships.

Judgement

(Major Arcana XX)

"Harken! I sound this call to awaken you to a new awareness of spirit and an expansion of personal consciousness. I am the creative word that liberates you from learned limitations. Wake up and arise from constrictions of self-doubt, guilt, and the false judgments of others. I will show you the way to revitalize your life and move into a new phase of higher awareness and purpose.

"With my prodding you can be free from illusion and blend with universal consciousness. As you perceive events and situations from my higher perspective, you will experience a new lease on life. Daily activities will take on different meanings, and you will no longer be held back by the 'tyranny of the trivial.'

"I may sometimes bring a time of soul testing as you use your changed awareness to adjust to new circumstances. Through it all, your body and personality can remain vehicles for divine energy.

"My key phrase is the <u>summons that is 'heard and answered from within.'</u> "[31]

The people on the Rider-Waite Judgement card are naked and gray, suggesting assimilated wisdom and the integration of opposites. They rise from opened coffins that represent mental restrictions opening to liberation and that float on cosmic natal waters. As they come up from the depths of the unconscious to full awareness, everyone looks up at an archangel, who is traditionally identified as Gabriel. Gabriel blows his golden horn, which emits the sound of our inner voice or spirit. A golden-haired woman opens her arms to accept its seven vibrational rays, which represent awakening chakra energy, as well as the powers of the seven archangels, each of whom represents one aspect of God.[32] As in The Lovers card, the unconscious feminine domain is more responsive to the divine than masculine consciousness.

The background figures in the card suggest that with our "new" attitude, we will experience more of a sense of Self within a greater community, although not necessarily a personal or earthly one.

The background figures may also point to a new inner life or relationship in which we have access to our inner child, inner parents, inner masculine or feminine aspects of ourselves, and other disowned or undeveloped attitudes. The smallness of the background bodies and their indistinct features hint that there is more work to be done in our next growth cycle.

Gabriel's banner bears the equal-armed Greek cross that served as the Christian cross into the ninth century. Much earlier it was the emblem of Hecate, goddess of crossroads. As such, it represented transition and the union of male and female symbols, both meanings that are appropriate for this card.[33] The snowcapped mountains in the distance symbolize eternal truth and higher attainment.

In the Morgan-Greer card, the figures of a man, woman, and child face *us*, the man and child extending their arms upward and outward. Dark blue, these figures exemplify the release that arises when we respond to the call (trumpet) to face our shadow aspects, using the inspiration or purifying flames of divine energy. The flames emanate from spiral-like clouds, suggesting that our awareness will be cyclic. Our feminine, or inner mother, aspect will protect us in our work, signified by the female with her hands protectively over her breasts.

In the Aquarian card, the angel, rooted in the earth, blows his orange trumpet up and out to the world as the sun radiates from behind fluffy white clouds. The dark shadows covering the land (our psyche) recede. Flowers bloom. The arched pattern on the angel's robe represents the power of aspiration and decision. The V-shaped lines at the base of the card and extending below it indicate that we are in the presence of, and grounded in, divine energy.

The Judgement card brings a higher level of awareness than any previous card. It challenges us to release the personal ego in the service of a new "awakening," and encourages us to view this as a lesser loss for a greater gain.

This card has been associated with the "Last Judgment," the archetypal theme of cycles, descent into the underworld, and resurrection. Waite thought it represented the higher self calling upon the personality to rise up from self-imprisonment. It is the shedding of our final worldly or ego illusions so we may have a more spiritual life on earth and understand that we live in the eternal now.

Judgement represents human consciousness blending with the Divine Spirit in order to glimpse immortality and begin to trust that there is a higher purpose of our existence. If often leads to dramatically different choices, certainly to new directions and goals. As we fully realize our connectedness to the human race, some decisions may seem more difficult to make than they had been previously.

Our enlightened state attracts both people who are in the same place and those who need help in reaching it. It can take a good deal of soul-searching and discrimination to know when not to link our lives with people whose behavior or demands deplete our energy.

The shadow aspects of the Judgement card include: being mired in a personal point of view that we refuse to give up; projecting our shortcomings onto others and judging them negatively; being critical of others; and feeling isolated from others or from divine influence in whatever way we define it, (i.e., God, our soul, our inner God, our higher self, the universal or cosmic process).

When this card appears:

- Depending on its position, it is either the dawning of a new perspective or an indication that work needs to be done to give up old, dead ways of thinking and to bring about a fresh viewpoint.

- Let go of any value judgments that could keep you from fulfilling aspirations that are trying to surface now.

- Allow for a renewal of love, and ground your personality in higher purpose.

- Get in touch with the judgmental aspect of yourself and consider whether you have been too hard on yourself or another. How has your judgment been incorrect, or blinded you to a more expansive awareness?

- Ask yourself what "rite of passage" or new phase of your life you could be facing.

Table 2 summarizes the tests and dilemmas represented by the Major Arcana cards of this chapter.

TABLE 2

Summary of Ten Archetypal Tests/Challenges

MAJOR ARCANA CARD	KEY PHRASE	CHALLENGE
XI–Justice	The search for equilibrium	To balance instinctual and analytical abilities; to identify opposing qualities
XII–The Hanged Man	Reversing false images	To redefine situations; expand perspective
XIII–Death	New opportunities and transformation	To abandon outmoded or false attachments
XIV–Temperance	The higher self in action	To resolve tension of opposites
XV–The Devil	Acknowledging your hidden recesses	To identify projections and shadow content
XVI–The Tower	Reorganizing the personality	To destroy false conceptions
XVII–The Star	Universal guidance	To develop meaning and direction in life
XVIII–The Moon	Cycles of inner development	To develop ability to wait for ''hunches'' to ripen
XIX–The Sun	Triumphant renewal	To learn to balance unconscious and conscious material
XX–Judgement	Summons that is heard and answered within	To develop a sense of self within a greater community; explore inner aspects of self

Most of the challenges expressed by the 10 cards covered in this chapter (Major Arcana XI-XX) have to do with the need to change or enlarge our perspectives in order to achieve maturity and a "new vision." That expanded awareness then leads us to consider our place in the Universe and ultimately to acknowledge our oneness with it, as we see in the next chapter.

8 ✺ Achieving Unity

The World
(MAJOR ARCANA XXI)

"Come, join me in this dance of completion and awareness of all life. I want you to enjoy freedom from fears and falsehood, to clearly see the world within yourself as well as the outer one, and to know they are the same.

"I will teach you to love one and all, without conflict, to use your abilities to the fullest in all endeavors, and to work for success at tasks both large and small. By fulfilling your potential, you add to the Universe in a way no one else can.

"Pursuing the path of inner growth brings a sense of participating in the cosmic plan for humanity. Having accomplished the tasks of all the cards that precede me, you now live in an entirely different world, a world you have created by perceiving things differently.

"I bring you back to that childlike wonder of seeing the world through new eyes. You now dance life, not just walk through it.

"My key phrase is the <u>essence of one spirit</u>."

In the Rider-Waite card, a nude figure, draped with the flowing purple scarf of divinity, dances freely. She symbolizes the merging of the conscious and unconscious states. She also represents the idea that the Universe is a living organism.[1]

It is sometimes said that the scarf conceals the fact that the figure is actually an androgyne, the all-in-one. In Jungian terms, this represents the goal of successfully blending both male and female aspects into full humanness. The tension of the opposites is resolved. There is no conflict.

The figure is poised within the world womb, a mandorla or almond-shaped wreath of thick green leaves. Bound at the top and bottom by red bindings, which form the lemniscate (eternity) also seen in The Magician and Strength cards, it suggests the creativity and protection that comes from our connection to the cosmic process. The figure also wears a red wreath or ribbon of victory and accomplishment in her hair.

The smaller wreath symbolizes the smaller, worldly victories achieved through the trials of the preceding Major Arcana cards. She resides in the world of form (the greater wreath), but is no longer bound by its restricted perceptions.

The four animals in the corners of the card represent the four fixed signs of the zodiac. They are the bull (Taurus), lion (Leo), eagle (Scorpio), and man (Aquarius), seen earlier in the Wheel of Fortune card. There they had wings of divine potential. Now they are fully realized. They also represent the Tetragrammaton as it operates in the four elements of the world, and parallel The Magician's tools: wand (fire/lion), cup (water/eagle), sword (air/human), and pentacle (earth/bull).

Psychologically the central figure and the corner figures demonstrate the "squaring of the circle," an alchemical and Jungian symbol for the process of becoming fully realized and transformed humans.[2] In The World card, the inner work is symbolically complete. In reality it never truly ends.

In the Morgan-Greer World card, we see a person dancing within an *ellipse* of thick green leaves (a symbol of continuous and natural wholeness). This is sacred space. It protects and at the same time hints of more to come.[3] The sky inside the wreath is star studded to signify restored perfection. Outside the wreath are dark dots of energy yet to manifest as matter.

A woman holding a flowering rod of spiritual knowledge and wearing an "earthy" olive-brown dress stands in the world circle of the Aquarian card. She wears a circular red jewel over her ajna chakra and a triangular orange jewel at her throat chakra. A russet turban covers her crown chakra, and even appears to extend it outward. Her spirit is awakened and she is able to communicate her wisdom. She is a contemporary version of the Divine Female, the conscious soul.

The World card is akin to the myths and fairy tales in which a hero or heroine returns from an arduous journey victorious and wiser. It signifies attainment of cosmic consciousness, of feeling rapturously connected with the Universe in a very real, personal way.

In the Golden Dawn deck, this card is called The Universe. The figure is related to Shiva, lord of the dance and God in the form of a cosmic dancer. Shiva dispels fear, assists us to dwell in the bliss of the Self, and is considered a god of transformation.[4]

Like the Hindus, the Egyptians also conceived of the "active principle or heartbeat of the cosmos as a dance," but their cosmic choreographer was female: the mother goddess, Isis.[5] Walker says the figure is the World Mother, the primordial Mother Center-of-the-Earth.[6] We have been transformed from the unknowing or innocent Fool to the carrier of the "world soul."

The World card indicates that we now know how to act within the appropriate structure. We have creative freedom to develop and express our ideas and in this way give birth to ourselves. We are the eternal dancer in a world of opposites, which we now have the skills and maturity to accept.

The card represents integration and wholeness on all levels: physical, emotional, mental, and spiritual. The personality with its ego ideas has lived through and been refined by the preceding 10 trials. Psychologically the Self has now emerged as the reigning center within the Universal Center. We have reached our true maturity.

We can recognize the worldly in the Spirit and the Spirit in the worldly. It is what metaphysicians call "unity consciousness." We are "capable of perceiving that the absolute and the relative are both the same and different."[7]

The shadow aspects of this card include: those personality traits that keep us isolated and egocentric; emotional stagnation; the inability to recognize and acknowledge all the aspects of ourselves; and fear of restriction.

When this card appears:

- It heralds the completion of one cycle and the potential beginning of a new one.

- Find ways to use your energies and enjoy the freedom of your personal dance, even as it necessarily takes place within the restrictions of your daily life.

- Become more self-regulating, take charge of yourself, and trust your inner authority.

- You are too caught up in your own tiny world and need to see the larger picture. This does not have to be cosmic, although it may. It can also mean allowing the perspective of another to widen your understanding.

- A temporary attitude of detachment from your situation may give you a more liberated perspective.

- Recognize the inner spirit that supports you.

Throughout our lives as we do our inner work, the archetypal insights of the Major Arcana will occur again and again. Often their appearance or effect will only be recognized after we have experienced some of the more mundane ''lessons'' represented by the Minor Arcana. So let's see what now awaits us in the outer world and how it interacts with and shapes our inner world.

PART THREE

LEARNING THE CARDS:
THE MINOR ARCANA

9 ☀ Minor Arcana: Ten Growth Opportunities and Four Levels of Maturity

The 56 Minor Arcana of the Tarot are usually thought to represent everyday experiences that have happened, or may happen to us. We regard them as stepping stones toward higher consciousness and as stimulation for our spiritual or personal development. They reveal our present level of awareness.

The aces to tens in each of the four suits depict growth experiences, opportunities, and lessons to be learned. Whether they have come and gone, are occurring now, or are due to occur in the future depends on where in the layout the card falls.

With regard to each suit, we consider the ace as the gift of or power behind the suit. It is the launching platform that gets us started on the experiences of that suit. Cards two through nine represent the kinds of experiences we must go through to prepare ourselves for the suit's higher wisdom. The tenth card is a transitional one. It is the "insight" or turning-point card of the suit, and represents our realization that there is something beyond the two through nine experiences. It propels us into the initiate stage embodied by the Page of each suit and begins the process—illustrated by the court cards—of achieving full awareness and insight in the area governed by the suit.

Looking at the Minor Arcana cards of each suit in sequence can help us understand the general lessons that suit has to teach us. Of course, in everyday life, we will not have these experiences or insights in sequence. They occur when the circumstances of our lives are ripe for them.

Ten Growth Opportunities

In addition to their quantitative function, numbers have qualitative aspects to which the unconscious mind responds. These qualities can be both personal and cultural. Thus, to understand the growth task portrayed by a Minor Arcana card, you need to understand, among other things, the card's numerological attributes. Cirlot calls them "idea forces."[1] Jung identified them as primary archetypal symbols.

ACES

The aces in each deck introduce the basic message of the suit. Presented by an omnipotent hand emerging from a cloud in the Rider-Waite and Morgan-Greer decks, they express the essence of each suit and indicate that its creative energies are now accessible to us. We are in the presence of a motivating force that will move us through the suit's experiences. However, the cloud serves as a veil to protect us from the full truth, which might overpower and destroy us at this point in our journey.

"The unknown awaits," aces tell us. They invite us to step across the threshold and explore. All is new; the potential is there. Ones and aces remind us it will soon be time to make a decision, time to begin the hunt. In Jungian terminology, ones show we're ready to begin the growth process toward wholeness. Where will it lead us? What principle needs to be expressed in our life? In fairy tales the bountifulness of ones is often represented by the finding of a treasure.

TWOS

Twos of any suit point to a choice and the need to consider two positions or alternatives. Twos bring the potential for integration and the opportunity to unite complementary or opposing energies.

The "test of the twos" is to figure out how to handle the dualities in our lives rather than remaining locked in one position or another.

According to Jungian analysts, when a symbol appears twice or as twins in a dream, a new aspect of the psyche is at work and moving into conscious awareness.

THREES

Three completes activities or events, paving the way for new situations. It also reflects the conflict between higher ideals and more worldly concerns, and tests our ability to "handle the mundane, and the disappointments" of our idealizations.[2] To Jung three was a restless number, symbolizing urgency and striving.[3]

Threes cause us to consider what our duty is in any situation. Will we embrace it with joy or resistance? Threes announce the arrival of a transformative moment.[4] Will we recognize and act upon it? Will we grow from it, or will we fight all the way?

FOURS

Fours represent natural order, personal logic and reasoning, inner organization. They are the sweet smell of earthly success arising out of the creativity of threes, the transforming of the idealistic into the practical.[5] They often represent personal and societal boundaries that attempt to put an end to chaos. Greer thinks fours represent the *conflict* between our desire for order and security, and our desire for change.[6]

Fours depict the natural plateau we reach after periods of intense creative activity. They represent renewal and a time for new ideas to germinate. Fours advise us to learn new concepts, develop new strengths, test new abilities. They offer the opportunity to release the past and to stabilize recent changes.

FIVES

Five is the symbol of humans and of our sensory life. It often represents the opportunity to change direction. As a midpoint, it can denote mediation and adaptation. Fives can also signal a time of testing, and the presence of an inner struggle that will soon require a decision.

They can encourage us to direct our sensory input and feelings into actual creative projects, or suggest that we regard our lives or activities from a more positive, satisfying perspective. Will we take advantage of the opportunity or continue to define our reality in the same way as before?

SIXES

Six, which is represented geometrically by the six-pointed Star of David (also known as Solomon's Seal), symbolizes the union of masculine and feminine energies and facets of our personality, and the need to look both earthward and heavenward for guidance. Sixes remind us to draw upon both consciousness (outer knowledge) and intuition (inner knowledge) in order to understand and sustain conditions and relationships.

Sixes can bring balance, equilibrium, and coordination. As a sign of wholeness and the completion of efforts, they speak of willingness and the self-discipline necessary to accomplish whatever we set out to do. When we can resolve the sixes, we will be ready to move forward once again.

SEVENS

A sign of initiation, seven deals with ordeals or obstacles, tests or temptations, and how to overcome them. Also a traditional sign of victory or achievement, seven stimulates an increase in energy, ideas, and insights.

Seven speaks of movement, development, and the creation of consciousness leading to transformation. As the combination of three (The Divine) and four (matter), sevens can also represent unification.

EIGHTS

Although eights can be a number of balance, rhythm, and renewed energy, they also may call for a choice. From them we get another opportunity to evaluate and possibly reorganize our priorities. Are we spending too much time on one project or activity to the detriment of our inner life? Have we excluded spiritual energy from our worldly projects? Are we harboring attitudes that prevent us from enjoying the fullness of life?

Dr. Fritz Perls, the founder of Gestalt therapy, used to ask his clients if they collected gold coins (positive feelings) or brown stamps (negative feelings). Eights press us to consider what kind of collectors we are.

NINES

While they *can* suggest material success, from a spiritual point of view, Tarot nines ask us to reflect on whether or not we have learned enough from numbers one through eight to have a new sense of inner fulfillment. They offer another chance for completion.

To obtain the wisdom of the runes, Odin, the Norse all-father god, hung on the world tree for nine nights. As the highest single-digit number, and the pinnacle of achievement before a new phase begins, nines also present us with another choice. Once again we are initiates considering the next phase of our journey toward self-realization. Nines offer us one last opportunity to gain insight before moving into the next cycle.

From a Jungian perspective, nines ask whether or not we have come to realize that life's meaning won't be found in wealth or personal advancement, but rather in the shifting of our focus inward to the development of the Self, or inner God. Do we now regard our activities differently and give them a different emphasis?

TENS

Tens represent culmination. Numerologically they are related to ones (10 = 1 + 0 = 1), and share some of their same symbolism, only on a higher experiential level.

In the Tarot, tens tell of transitions and higher wisdom to be gained. Tens are the beginning and the end. They are a temporary respite that allows us to acknowledge the success of our previous efforts and prepare for our next spiral of growth.

As the sum of the first four numbers (1 + 2 + 3 + 4), tens represent the totality of the union and creativity that those numbers symbolize. While the aces portray the abstract ideal of a suit, the tens illustrate the culmination of "ordinary" experiences of the suit and offer a glimpse at something more and quite different to be discovered.

The Four Levels of Mature Knowledge

Traditionally, when court cards appeared in a reading, they were presumed to represent people with the physical characteristics pictured, who would exert influence on us.

We think the court cards illustrate aspects of ourselves at various stages of maturity. In metaphysical terms, they represent levels of initiation, our progression on the path to a specific form of mastery and power represented by their suit. The knowledge, attitudes, and skills we will acquire before moving from one level to another are determined by the different tasks and experiences the suit calls upon us to undertake.

From a Jungian perspective, the court cards represent different energy systems active within us. Each of them shows the characteristics of a particular energy, and our goal is to direct and empower the energies that have been undervalued and to rein in or redirect the tyrannical ones that run roughshod over us.[7] Although Jungian Rose Gwain equates Jung's four energy functions as Swords = thinking function, Wands = feeling, Cups = intuitive, and Pentacles = sensing function, Jungian writer Irene Gad reverses the functions of Wands and Cups,[8] corresponding with our own approach:

$$\begin{array}{rcl} \text{Swords} & = & \text{thinking} \\ \text{Wands} & = & \text{intuition} \\ \text{Cups} & = & \text{feeling} \\ \text{Pentacles}^9 & = & \text{sensing}^9 \end{array}$$

PAGES

Pages represent a state similar to adolescence. They already have been through the sensual experiences of the suit at least once. They have not yet had enough experience to comprehend their journey's full meaning or integrate what they *have* learned into the totality of their life.

They represent us at the beginning of higher awareness. We understand that we don't know it all. We realize we cannot complete certain tasks totally on our own, and are willing to seek out additional experiences or training.

As elevens, Pages move us into a new cycle of understanding and independent activity. They are the "young, delicate beginnings of the qualities of the particular suit,"[10] the initiates whose skills and responsibilities gradually increase. According to Greer, Pages are "the least developed [of the court cards] but the most open and willing to take risks."[11] They often act as messengers to ourselves and can represent our inner child.[12]

Numerologically Pages are related to twos (11 = 1 + 1 = 2), but have a more sophisticated sense of duality and need for recognition. They call for resolution, and send us searching for inner harmony and balance. We're at a pivotal point in our emotional development. Will we enter this new stage with excitement and confidence, or kicking and scratching in protest?

KNIGHTS

Knights represent a state similar to early adulthood. Having learned our "pagely" lessons, and acquired many new skills, we now polish and put our personal stamp on the ones that seem most valuable to us, as well as discarding what we think we don't need.

Knights are wanderers and, therefore, encounter numerous opportunities for new insights. They are energetic and adventurous, but often headstrong and volatile, too. They can rush forward without planning or thinking of anyone but themselves. We love Mary Greer's description of them. Knights have "reached the stage of thinking they know something,"[13] she says.

Whether we're male or female, our knightly task is to figure out where our place is, to evaluate our experiences and decide what new attitudes and approaches best suit us. That journey and the adventures, victories, and obstacles we encounter along the way, prepare us to assume our roles as Queens and Kings. If we stay too long on the path, however, we run the risk of becoming perpetual adolescents—always seeking, roaming, resisting authority, and remaining out of touch with our higher selves. This fate parallels the one that befell the knight Parsifal in the King Arthur legends. While seeking the Holy Grail (symbol of the God within), Parsifal enters the castle of the Fisher King for the first time, but lacking the maturity to consciously understand his travels, condemns himself to continued wandering.

In the Rider-Waite deck, all of the Knights wear armor to protect the physical body while the psyche and soul develop. They are seated astride horses, indicating that they are now seriously into the work of balancing conscious awareness with unconscious needs or instincts, as represented by the horse. They are also challenged to control their need for power, which is one of the mythological meanings of horse.

Numerologically the Knight's 12 is related to three $(12 = 1 + 2 = 3)$, which warns of premature, incomplete solutions and restlessness, which is likely to persist until we Knights finally get it right and fit the insights obtained from our worldly experiences into their rightful place in our inner wisdom.

QUEENS

Queens are fecund, feminine archetypes. They understand the way of the land and what must be nurtured for both the inner and outer worlds to remain fertile and creative, for the "soul life" to be nourished. They are finished with the superficialities of their knightly journey.

Queens embody female maturity. They are stable, receptive, and have a deeper appreciation of the qualities of their suit.[14] Their energies are "held within . . . concentrated and focused, so that greater power might emerge."[15]

With skills and accomplishments equal to a King's, their talents lie in the personal and interpersonal realms.[16] Psychologically they represent one aspect of the *anima* in a man, or the sense of self for a woman.[17]

Numerologically related to fours (13 = 1 + 3 = 4), Queens know their way around. They understand what must be done to bring ideas into reality. They represent tribal or cultural wisdom, emanate teaching energy, and make the deals necessary for tasks to be accomplished without violating values or ideals.

KINGS

Kings are the archetypal masculine principle and represent characteristics of male maturity, such as social responsibility and outward accomplishments.[18] Operating from a position of extended experience, they take charge, establish procedures, organize and build empires. They capture the "dynamic, ongoing, directive" qualities of the suit."[19] There is a saying in psychology that mothers (Queens) tell you what to do and fathers (Kings) show you how to do it. Mother has the ideas and understanding. Father puts it into action.

Having completed their journeys and acquired the wisdom they sought, Kings make appropriate and necessary decisions—reflecting their numerological relationship to fives (14 = 1 + 4 = 5)—and help others progress in their own journey. They act from their worldly knowledge, life experience, and regard for what they believe to be others' ultimate good rather than from dominating, oppressive attitudes; however, they can be inflexible at times.[20] The King can represent one aspect of the *animus* in a woman, or sense of self for a man.[21]

10 ☀ Pentacles:
Grounding the Psyche

Members of the Pentacles family are earthy people. They value the traits of hard work and productivity. They represent the "grounding" in material matters that allows us to feel comfortable and secure enough to proceed with our spiritual growth. That is why we think "pentacle experiences" come first in the order of experiences we need to propel us through various stages of personal and spiritual development, and unlike many other Tarot authors, who save them for last, we have chosen to start our discussion of the Minor Arcana with the Pentacles.

In addition, each Minor Arcana suit represents one of the four letters that make up the Tetragrammaton (or name of God). According to the Golden Dawn tradition, God's descent into matter occurs in the order of Yod (Wands), Heh (Cups), Vau (Swords), Heh (Pentacles), while our spiritual ascendance progresses in the opposite direction: Heh (Pentacles), Vau (Swords), Heh (Cups), Yod (Wands). This is our other rationale for ordering the chapters of the Minor Arcana as we have. (Of course, in reality we don't have Pentacles, Swords, Cups, and Wands experiences in any orderly sequence.)

Psychologically, Pentacle experiences relate to ego development and to the sensory experiences that help us learn who we are and how we function in the world. If you think of money as energy, the suit's esoteric message deals with how to use one's energy for expression and development of the Self.

Along with the letter Heh, Pentacles represent the active world of matter, the spiritual element of earth,[1] and Jung's sensing function.

Stars, which have long been associated with the heavenly realm and the five human senses, appear within the circle of the pentacle, and symbolize the growth required for humans to achieve wholeness. Ultimately the suit of Pentacles refers to the development of work as service and a spiritual exercise. To borrow from Thomas Moore, the suit of Pentacles deals with the "economics of the soul."

On the down side, the materialistic Pentacles are sometimes so work oriented and goal directed that a flock of birds could fly overhead and they wouldn't look up. They might not even hear them, unless they were hunting. They do love the fruitfulness of the world around them but have little appreciation for its beauty or mystery.

Still all the Pentacles in the Aquarian deck are drawn against a light blue sky filled with puffy clouds, suggesting that no matter how mundane the work, heavenly influences oversee it, and opportunities to raise our work to the celestial level are ever present.

Numbered Cards

ACE OF PENTACLES

"*I offer you a new opportunity, a path leading to new expression and fulfillment. I want you to gain greater control over the material resources of the earth and prosper to your fullest potential.*

"*I am the theme card of the Pentacles. I provide stimulation and inspiration to develop your skills and talents for the pleasure of activity. I encourage you to learn to enjoy the fruits of your efforts.*

"*I bring the energy you need to take initiative. I give you the courage to explore new projects and to put your ideas to the test.*

"*I caution you to use the gifts of the earth wisely to increase the general prosperity both of yourself and of humankind. I urge you to look for higher meaning in your worldly efforts and to seek ways to express your values and ideals in your creations.*

"*My key phrase is <u>the power of earthly endeavors</u>.*"

In the Rider-Waite card, a white hand, radiating cosmic energy, emerges from the clouds, holding a large pentacle. White lilies of purity and truth bloom in a sheltered garden beneath the gray sky of divine wisdom. The yellow path of applied intelligence leads through an arched gateway (transition) of roses (passion/energy)[2] to blue mountain peaks that indicate greater knowledge to come.

The Morgan-Greer card includes essentially the same symbology except the hand is flesh toned.

The Aquarian Ace of Pentacles is centered between orange flowers and berries, which bloom on curving gray stalks that cross near a bud of new opportunity.

The Ace of Pentacles represents new beginnings in material activity. It brings a surge of personal power that can be focused on practical developments. The card represents favorable conditions for manifesting ideas and using talents that have not yet been tapped. The Ace's thrust of energy is ideal for starting new business enterprises, professional projects, artistic creations, or purely pleasurable endeavors.

The card also represents the unity of matter and Spirit leading to both inner and outer riches. It affirms the potential for self-worth and Self-worth in our endeavors.

The shadow aspects of the Ace of Pentacles include: a false or premature sense of security; extreme competition where financial gain is concerned; blinding ambition; and reluctance to "leave the garden" and make our own way.

When this card appears:

- Conditions are favorable for taking the initiative, or the next step, in any projects you are involved in or considering.
- You are on the first step of a more fulfilling attitude toward your work or other activities.
- Refocus your goals, especially if you have been floundering.
- Consider how your work or endeavors do, or can, contribute to your feelings of security.

TWO OF PENTACLES

"I carefully juggle these pentacles, first to demonstrate the importance of flexibility in perspective, and also to show you that it is possible to recognize, even enjoy, the dualities of life.

"I urge you to consider alternatives and achieve a balance in situations. I know that will seem difficult initially. You may want to dance around the issues. Even that can be fun. Just don't decide that you must take one and only one position. Like the divine loop that connects and contains my pentacles, dualities exist and interact within a higher principle.

"As the churning water behind me indicates, although you think of yourself as a creature of logic, much of what you do is influenced by your unconscious. This is one of the dualities you will need to acknowledge.

"My key phrase is <u>physical dualities</u>."

In the Rider-Waite Two of Pentacles, a young man in the green shoes of creative understanding and individual development dances on smooth gray pavement that represents a need for balance. He holds two pentacles within a green (growth) band twisted to form the horizontal figure eight or lemniscate, (potential for transformation). As indicated by his red clothing, this is a vital, passionate person who needs to integrate his conflicting energies.

In the Morgan-Greer card, the two pentacles partly out of the picture suggest that the figure wavers in integrating his dualities. In the past (background), he has merely sailed over the ocean of his unconscious material rather than delving into it. But he is, after all, only a two.

Black areas at the heart, throat, and crown chakras of the figure in the Aquarian card tell us that these energy centers are not activated.

His emotions (rolling water) are, however, and he has trouble making a passionate decision (pink hat rather than red).

The Two of Pentacles is sometimes referred to as the juggler because he represents keeping two or more projects going, or working toward two goals, at the same time. He also embodies cleverness and the ability to keep a careful eye on more than one situation.

The rolling sea suggests emotional ups and downs as we wait for more input (ships). This makes it difficult to keep ourselves grounded, as the one uplifted foot in the Rider-Waite card implies. Well, progress *is* made step by step, this card reminds us. If we are patient, our ships will arrive in due time.

The Two also represents the linkage between the spiritual and material aspects of our life activities. Our task here is to recognize both and let neither "drop" from our awareness.

The shadow aspect of the Two of Pentacles includes: failing to consider alternatives in any situation; clinging stubbornly to one extreme position; and false gaiety when we're really worried or struggling to attain inner balance.

When the Two of Pentacles is turned up:

- Look to see what aspect of your life you may have been neglecting. Reevaluate your priorities for more balance.

- Changes are taking place in your psyche or your self-concept. Be patient, and you will be able to recognize and sort them out.

- Consider that all new awareness doesn't have to come from serious contemplation. Having fun offers insight, too.

- Realize that there is a broader perspective or meaning to the situation than you have been experiencing.

THREE OF PENTACLES

"I am here to show you the nobility of work. Perform your tasks as though commissioned by God or your own highest principles, and you'll establish a reputation for quality as well as avoid being bored with your efforts.

"I emphasize the concept of work as a spiritual exercise. Through concentrated focus and the 'cultivation of ordinary things,'[3] you can begin to hear how your soul expresses itself in physical activity.

"Take the time to ground your creative visions in physical effort. Pay attention to the progress you're making according to your own goals or plans. Whether routine or creative, the value you put on your efforts adds to your feelings of self-worth and nourishes your soul.

"My key phrase is <u>the spiritual force of work</u>."

The Rider-Waite card displays three workers in a church or monastery made of gray stone. The sculptor represents technical skill. The monk symbolizes the spiritual understanding of work, and the architect stands for energy and desire.[4] He also holds out the blueprint, suggesting the need for an overall working plan, and also that he is the architect of our soul, possessor of the divine plan. His polka-dotted clothes and the long tail on his hood imply that he brings elements of humanism and humor to serious work.

The sculptor wears a yellow apron, indicating that intelligence takes precedence over instinct in his work. His elevation symbolizes the dignity of labor.

The three pentacles form an upward triangle, which represents aspiration toward the spiritual. They are surrounded by a decorative band with a fleur-de-lis (illumination) at each tip. Directly below, a flower in its own downward-pointing triangle suggests that within the work situation, we can find personal flowering and spiritual growth. Likewise, the three figures can also represent our inner triad: body (sculptor), mind (architect), and Spirit (monk).

The sculptor in the Morgan-Greer card wears dark gray and brown earthy colors as he stands overshadowed by the lighted window of pentacles. The tip of the downward-pointing triangle is juxtaposed near his head. He is about to be awakened but does not yet realize it and is still very much in the realm of the senses, as symbolized by the five he is chiseling on the left column. The five also hints that his realization will be a struggle for him.

The Aquarian sculptor works alone beneath a vaulted ceiling, which arches off the card into the infinite. The usual variegated background pattern of the suit mingles with the pillars in this card to give the impression of a temple-of-the-Spirit realm. It suggests that physical work is only part of what is needed to build the temple.

In its mundane sense, the Three of Pentacles represents the mastery of skills and their use in the marketplace. It stresses the personal and spiritual benefits of producing goods of lasting quality. It encourages us to set our own standards of integrity, and to commit ourselves to focus physically, mentally, and spiritually for the best outcome. The card also signals the need to build our own inner "temple," or cathedral, the sanctuary of our Self.

The shadow aspect of this card includes: failure to establish goals and priorities; neglecting to carry out our responsibilities or being indifferent to the way we do carry them out; and thinking that we can or have to do everything ourselves.

When the Three of Pentacles appears:

- Consider the gains that may be made by working with others, or seeking their input regarding your situation.

- Develop an overall plan for your situation or project.

- New tasks or projects may offer you the opportunity to recognize the spiritual aspects of your work.

- Expand your satisfaction or pleasure with your work. You may have to change your style of working, your attitude, or redefine your role so you can express glory through your efforts.

FOUR OF PENTACLES

"I take care of the things I have worked to get. Sometimes I get a little paranoid or greedy and think that I have to protect my money and my position from others who might try to take what is mine. Other times I can look at myself more gently and feel proud of how skilled I am at collecting and utilizing the resources I need.

"I do think it's a lot easier to accumulate material comforts before taking up self-improvement projects. 'God helps those who help themselves,' I always say. Still, being miserly isn't exactly an impetus for personal development. Just look at that Ebenezer Scrooge fellow Charles Dickens made famous.

"On the other hand, my key phrase—feeling truly wealthy—does refer to a subjective attitude and an inner evaluation."

The Rider-Waite card shows a royal person with a yellow pentacle balanced atop his plain gold crown. He holds another pentacle to his bosom, while his orange, booted feet rest on the two remaining pentacles.

The Morgan-Greer Four of Pentacles depicts a royal woman wearing a brown robe for earthly grounding. On her forehead a mandala activates her ajna center. A wall of psychological defenses separates her from divine knowledge symbolized by the yellow sky.

The Aquarian Four of Pentacles carefully balances an elaborate crown decorated with a large pentacle. Another pentacle covers his chest or heart center. The two lowest pentacles are partly out of the frame.

The Four of Pentacles assumes responsibility . . . for himself. This obviously has both positive and negative consequences. Having gained a measure of success, he feels the best course is to hang on. So he hangs onto position, power, people, attitudes, and, above all, to money.

He surrounds—some say closes off or insulates—himself with his economic dependence. In the Rider-Waite card he has blocked his crown and heart chakras with pentacles and closed off his connection to the earth (reality). Sometimes he is seen as having grounded himself in money. He tends to be defensive with others, feeling he has no need for their input into his life. He cloaks himself in a black shawl of ignorance.

When understood in this way, the card suggests that difficulties in sharing play a significant part in the issue we are hoping that the Tarot will clarify. Spontaneity and generosity are noticeably absent, and we may be excluding some innovative ideas by not listening to outside input. Perhaps we also need to examine and share our own reactions.

The Four of Pentacles can be a confusing card, however, because although the figure appears rigid, its opposite can be the inability to structure and organize our life. Are we giving too much of ourselves away without considering our own needs or priorities?

The placement of the pentacles, especially in the Rider-Waite card, offers the possibility that instead of being closed off, the figure has succeeded in laying a foundation of material security (pentacles at hands and feet) that will facilitate spiritual development via the pentacles at the heart and crown chakras. From this viewpoint, the houses in the background represent the material and worldly success the figure has already achieved, and the gray in the foreground says his future task is to balance and organize the material with the Divine.

In occult writings, "poverty" refers to the delusion that we are separate from the other things in our environment. Therefore, its corollary, wealth, marks the end of illusion and the recognition of our God-Self and oneness with all.

The Four of Pentacles can be considered as a shadow card when it is defined as representing greed. Other shadow aspects include: mistaking material possessions for our sense of identity; using material or financial gains to insulate ourselves; having limited interests in anything but wealth; and keeping our feelings from being readily accessible or understandable.

When the Four of Pentacles appears:

- Consider what you have been holding onto and whether it might really be holding onto you.

- You may need to reorganize your situation or project, including getting more input from others.

- You may be too inflexible in your demands or your view of your issue/situation.

- Determine whether you now have the security and confidence to permit you to be more generous in situations or relationships, or, conversely, whether you give too much of yourself away and need now to protect yourself.

FIVE OF PENTACLES

"I'm focused on my woes these days. I don't want to do anything about the causes of my problems, and I certainly don't want you to tell me that I may have been responsible for my situation. I want you to tell me that I don't deserve what has happened to me.

"I don't want your help, only your pity. I prefer companions who share my belief that the world is a cold and hostile place.

"I am too busy just hanging on from day to day to think about spiritual things, although I certainly feel lost and unfulfilled. I worry about the things I've done in the past, and I worry about what's going to happen to me in the future.

"Some have told me to regard my crisis as an opportunity and think of my anguished feelings as a signpost for looking within to see what I need to do. When I follow that advice, I feel a little more hopeful.

"My key phrase is the need for soul work."

In the Rider-Waite card, two tattered and wounded wayfarers tread along in a snowstorm of darkness. They pass a stained-glass window but fail to see its five lighted pentacles offering opportunities for growth. Although their clothes are ragged, they are still colorful, suggesting that they still have some hope for uncovering their potential to change. They also have retained the ability to color their view of life.

In the Morgan-Greer card, a woman consoles a man who wears blood-soaked bandages around his head (wounded awareness) and his left wrist (inflexibility in receiving).

In the Aquarian card, two pilgrims pass under an arched window that floats on a layer of snow. Their downcast eyes indicate that they seek gratification from daily life, rather than looking inward.[5]

The Five of Pentacles does at first seem to paint a picture of deprivation. It depicts feelings of isolation and the inability to secure the essentials for a balanced and rewarding life. Inspiration and help are as near as the church, but the two figures don't see this. Even so, in the Rider-Waite and Morgan-Greer cards, they *are* moving, and therefore making *some* progress.

Occurring as it does midway in the first ten Pentacles, the Five of Pentacles is a transition card. It depicts the wounding and spiritual isolation that can occur from overreliance on material Pentacles energy. Look around and come in out of the snow, this card signals loudly. It's time to change our attitudes, take personal responsibility, and start working toward recovery. There *is* potential for growth in every crisis.

Psychologically the two figures also represent our masculine and feminine aspects, while the window represents our higher self. If we plod along ignoring our spiritual needs and our inner yearning for renewal, we will feel wounded and impoverished. Our Spirit cannot soar and we cannot see its rhythm and harmony until we look inward.

In the Rider-Waite and Morgan-Greer cards, the male is more obviously wounded than the female. This suggests that the masculine (your inner masculine energy, or animus if you are female) sustains more injuries by engaging in the physical action associated with Pentacles. In the Morgan-Greer card, our feminine aspect (your inner feminine energy, or anima if you are male) is still able to nurse those wounds and offer consolation. All the cards imply, however, that we haven't paid much attention to either of these facets of ourselves. We've been looking outward for solace instead of turning inward.

Although this appears to be a shadow card, it is actually a transitional one. It is the ''dark night of the soul'' before the anguished personality turns toward higher spiritual values. We feel abandoned and are unaware that it is our own pride, stubborn independence, or failure to acknowledge our vulnerabilities that leave us out in the cold.

This card hints at the healing that must occur—the uniting of our male/female aspects and the renewal of faith in ourselves or our spiritual values—before we can experience The Hierophant's energy, to which this card is numerically related.

When you get this card:

- Determine what you are doing to limit yourself. Are you just trudging through life without enjoying it?

- Your present concern is surely testing your basic ideals or self-confidence.

- Consider whether hardship, or feeling like a victim, has become a way of life for you. How can you change your viewpoint?

- Ask yourself if you have rejected a religious or other established doctrine without replacing it with some kind of guiding ideals or principles.

SIX OF PENTACLES

"I'm careful, I am. It's not evident at first glance because I appear to be generous and to relate well to other people. But I know precisely how much I can give without tipping my scales. I'm pretty stable and fairly predictable.

"The Buddha said we should strive to realize that fortune goes with misfortune. To be enlightened, we need to transcend both. I kind of understand that, but mostly I'm still geared toward acquiring a fortune or other outward proof that I'm a success.

"I grasp the idea that those of us who have achieved a certain level of success need to 'give back' to our communities, and in our

professions, act as mentors. It is far easier for me to do that than to be benevolent to myself.

"My key phrase is <u>balancing the inner scales</u>."

In the Rider-Waite card, a man dressed as a merchant weighs out gold coins (energy) and drops them into the outstretched hands of two kneeling, needy supplicants with blankets draped over their shoulders.

Which person are you today? In your present situation, do you regard yourself as successful or needy? Do you measure your success in what you give or share, or in what you get? Are you taking care of yourself? The Six of Pentacles offers us another opportunity to achieve balance, this time between our intellectual (yellow blanket) and emotional (blue blanket) processes.

In the Morgan-Greer card, the hands of two unseen people (our needy aspects) reach out to receive a coin. Six pentacles are set behind a red column extending off the top of the card. The red of the column is duplicated in the red button over the philanthropist's heart chakra, showing this suit's intimate connection to personal and divine love.

In the Aquarian deck, black and pink patterns of energy-available-to-draw-upon decorate the sleeves of a guild member's jacket. Pentacles appear in the sky and also on the table to indicate that "spiritual values are applied to material life."[6] The person sits in front of a central, deep pink pillar. It symbolizes divine love and, like the Morgan-Greer pillar, extends up out of the card. Its color is duplicated in the hat's scarf and vest. Both touches tell of the intermingling of earthly and divine energies. The six brings us to a second level of completion, spelling out the spiritual integration only hinted at in the Three of Pentacles.

Superficially, the Six of Pentacles represents someone who has made it and enjoys the attention of being in a dominant position. The Six thinks of sharing primarily in material terms. He connects with and perhaps attempts to control others by taking care of their physical needs.

At a deeper level, this card tries to teach us that "true" giving results from discerning what another person truly needs or is able to accept, regardless of his request, and giving that. Because few of us have sufficient understanding of the human psyche to be able to do this, we tend to project our needs or fears onto another instead, and then give accordingly.[7]

The clue to still another meaning of the card is that the coins the merchants give in the Rider-Waite and Morgan-Greer cards can be considered "change." While obtaining these coins may represent a success of sorts, all the figures on the card have more to learn.

In Jungian terms, the supplicants may represent the "bum" or needy side of us that we ignore and force to beg for comfort, while the merchant could be our lofty ego state. At this point in our journey through the Pentacles suit, we have yet to realize that we are *all* of these figures.

The shadow aspect of this card includes: poor money management; greediness; being so generous we deplete ourselves, possibly for appearance' sake; poor self-discipline; and holding back emotionally in relationships.

When you draw the Six of Pentacles:

- Examine your attitudes toward giving and receiving money. Work to achieve a balance between them.

- Consider how your attitudes toward giving and receiving also apply in other areas and relationships of your life. What do you gain by being too generous? How does it serve you to withhold things or aspects of yourself from others?

- Consider the ways you fail to nurture yourself.

- Evaluate the role that issues of control and gratitude play in your life. Do you have trouble with either?

SEVEN OF PENTACLES

The Seven of Pentacles speaks in a contemplative tone:

"I'm satisfied with what I've done so far even though there's still more to do. I've worked hard to build a good foundation, and I'm considering my next step. My task is to model for you the value of

hard work, evaluation, and planning. When you see the potential in a project and get busy, you put my energy into action.

"Few people realize that hoeing the weeds out of a project can be as fulfilling as gazing in satisfaction at the finished product. The reward is in the work itself as well as the outcome. I call it enjoying the intangible fruits of the harvest.

"I counsel you to be patient while seeking integration and wholeness. There is always a next step, so don't forget to stop and give yourself credit for what you have already accomplished. The patience and determination you develop under my inspiration build self-confidence for future endeavors.

"My key phrase is <u>soul regeneration</u>."

In the Rider-Waite card, a young man leans on a hoe—his tool of creation—while surveying seven pentacles (his cultivated projects) on a nearby vine. He wears one brown boot of earthly understanding and one orange one of divine knowledge.

The Morgan-Greer figure stands in thick greenery, holding his hoe prominently as the symbol of his dedication to accomplishment. Behind him, green slopes signifying growth rise to a blue mountain peak of aspiration.

The chin strap of the Aquarian figure is decorated with pink and black spiritual designs. The orange and hot pink colors of his hat show that he has opened his crown center to the soul satisfaction and passion that can come from work. His left hand rests on a cane carved with the head of a duck to signify destiny and cosmic plans.

The card depicts someone who has done well so far and pauses to evaluate and consider additional ways to transform ideas into the successful achievements that the pentacles represent.

On another level, the Seven of Pentacles represents progress toward regeneration. Clarissa Pinkola Estés writes that the gardener is the cultivator of the soul. He harvests new energy in order to replace what is worn out. "He keeps track of the need for change and replenishing."[8]

Waite describes the pentacles as the young man's treasure, and says that this is where his heart is.[9] For Greer the challenge of this card is to *cultivate* patience and to "move through self-doubts that raise [our] fear of failure and apprehension that [our] work will be for nothing."[10]

The shadow side of this card includes: work or money becoming more important than relationships; experiencing a conflict between ambition or competition and other values; feeling discouraged about or doubting the value of our efforts; and failing to evaluate our progress at regular intervals.

When the Seven of Pentacles appears in a layout:

- Take stock of what you have done and plan for what you might like or need to do next.

- Consider that one aspect of your wealth is your ability to help nourish the earth, as well as to enjoy and partake of its bounty. Do you emphasize one over the other?

- Evaluate your role in a relationship to determine if you place more emphasis on the financial aspects of it than the other person might like.

- Reorganize your priorities and decide where you need to cultivate new attitudes.

EIGHT OF PENTACLES

"I'm pretty busy here. Just observe all I've done so far. I get better with each one I make, and the more I do, the better I feel. So pick your thing and do it as I have. Any activity you choose has its own challenges and rewards.

"Whatever task is before you, if you focus on doing your best, you will experience an increased sense of satisfaction and inner worth. I'm here to remind you that every project contains the potential for personal and spiritual growth—if you pay attention to the details of your activity, that is. If you don't, it may seem as if you're doing the same thing over and over.

"Metaphysically I am sometimes understood as a student or initiate in a school of higher learning. My willing commitment requires concentration and endurance, as I persevere and progress step by step.

"My key phrase is <u>dedication to service</u>."

The Rider-Waite and Morgan-Greer apprentices sit at their workbenches industriously fashioning pentacles. Their completed products are mounted for display while they work on another one. In the Rider-Waite card, the yellow-green ground indicates an underlying mental foundation for purposeful activity and growth. A yellow path leads to the city in the background, showing the worker's connection with and contribution to the general welfare of his community.

The Aquarian deck shows an artisan in an upper room. He wears a brown studded hat, revealing that his crown chakra is activated to receive higher energy. The three nails in the pocket of his apron represent comprehension of the three aspects of the One Reality: matter, force, and mind. (One of the meanings of the Hebrew letter Vau is "nail," which represents the revelation of truth through intuition.)

The Eight of Pentacles represents the effort involved in mastering skills or harnessing energy and then using them to their best advantage. It takes discipline and often tedious, repetitious practice to hone our abilities and talents, this card reminds us. The artisan symbolizes the intrinsic value of working hard and persistently to form a better society for all to enjoy. Contributing to our community promotes inner growth and assures us of our connection with the whole of life.

This card also reminds us to work with the awareness of how a current project fits into our personal life plan. It suggests that we order and organize our daily experiences within the larger context of spiritual service. By working on our inner attitudes as well as our observable products, we can make our daily life sacred.

Shadow aspects of the Eight of Pentacles include: impatience or unwillingness to take the time necessary to master skills for a profession; "workaholic" ambition with subsequent "burnout" because the work is not fulfilling; a strong need to get ahead fueled by greed or envy; and shoddy workmanship.

When this card appears:

- Evaluate your work from a different perspective. Consider how you might alter your attitude or methods to achieve more satisfaction. Perhaps you need to do other work or look to the satisfactions of a hobby or avocation for balance.

- Coming up with an organized plan and/or attending to the little details may be necessary to resolve your issue or situation.

- Get some advanced or different training.

- You need to realize or remind yourself that your daily activities and your spirituality are not separate. Each enhances the other.

NINE OF PENTACLES

"I am content to be here alone on my property. I deserve this good life. I have become used to it, so I don't really need any other people around for fulfillment.

"To achieve this level of success and satisfaction, I have functioned from a position of dedication, clarity of purpose, and single-mindedness. I must admit, though, that the cost of that much self-discipline has sometimes been the loss of the spontaneity and freedom I treasured when I was younger.

"Still, I have no regrets. I did my work, paid my dues, and had the patience and perseverance to see my efforts through to their successful conclusion. I am now self-reliant. I have become all that I could be at this time, which is why my key phrase is <u>sensual fullness and fulfillment</u>."

The Rider-Waite "lady nine" wears a luxurious gown decorated with the astrological signs of Venus (feminine creative power). Her beaded hat is red. A red-hooded falcon (control of the soaring spirit) perches on the glove of her upraised left hand. Standing before fruit-laden grape vines symbolizing the sweetness of life successes, she rests her ungloved right hand on one of nine yellow pentacles positioned against the vines. For the moment at least, growth (two trees) and spiritual aspiration (purple mountains) are behind her, or at least not foremost in her mind. Nevertheless, the tiny snail of cyclic development at her feet slowly progresses toward the future. It is only a small part of her awareness at the moment.

The Morgan-Greer card shows a turbaned woman "dressed to the nines" in exotic clothes. In a setting where purples (higher energy) dominate, she stands near a pine tree of immortality laden with cones signifying fertility. Her feathered turban displays a blue jewel over her ajna center. She wears the pentacles like a necklace on her green suede vest. They are much more a part of her personality than the Rider-Waite figure's, as if connecting the "diverse constituents of success."[11] A colorful bird perches on her left hand.

The Aquarian card holds more spiritual promise than the other two nines. In it a woman holds an exotic white bird (her higher self) near her shoulder. Three pentacles decorate its long tail, representing the triad of her inner spirit. She has completed as much of her personality development as she can, signified by the remaining six pentacles set on the unusual mauve cloak that falls from under her brown hat. The hat's earthy color suggests that her thinking is still dominated by material concerns. The black garment underneath her cloak, with its mauve decoration beginning at her throat chakra and extending down the spinal alignment, tells us, however, that she has already entered the first stage of the transformation process, whether or not she realizes it.

The Nine represents achievement and self-interest, self-reliance, and sensual pleasure. It is the completion of the Pentacles cycle, and as such, a time of safety and comfortable circumstances. There's very little to do except enjoy.

A secure financial base now exists along with a foundation of inner satisfaction and confidence. Our accumulated experiences allow us to recognize our self-worth without needing outside validation.

The hooded bird in the Rider-Waite card and the controlled birds in the other cards can be understood in several ways, depending on the other cards in the layout. They may imply that self-discipline is the secret to the lady's abundance. She has her aggressive or "hunting" instincts under control, but has lost her spontaneity and freedom as well.

The birds might also signify that the lady is so settled and secure that it will take aggressive action to move her out of this time of luxury and toward further spiritual development. Yet another interpretation could be that once unleashed, spiritual development is far from passive. The Aquarian figure, with her elegant bird wearing a trinity of pentacles on its tail, seems closest to hearing this call for spiritual growth.

All of us *will* be called upon to move from this position to a higher stage of development, however. The snail is evidence of that, and the

Nine's overseeing Major Arcana cards, The Hermit (IX) and The Moon (XVIII), virtually guarantee it.

Shadow elements of this card include: failure or disappointment linked to lack of discipline or dedication; restlessness; a feeling of not knowing what we want; imbalance between what we want and what we are willing to do to achieve it; and reticence to make decisions about moving forward.

When this card appears:

- Take time to fully appreciate what you have.

- Find new ways to enjoy your life. Are your interests too solitary?

- Use your solitude to sort your priorities. Whatever your measure of financial security, you still may have a sense that something is missing. Be ready to seek higher meaning in your activities.

- Prepare to move into your next cycle by examining the experiences that led to your present situation. You may need to place more value on, or conversely, to release and stop clinging to, past attitudes, behaviors, and relationships.

TEN OF PENTACLES

"I have lived a rich and full life and want to share my experience with all who are interested. I pass on a rich legacy of insight and wisdom to those who seek my company and my guidance.

"I have carefully attended to all the lessons of my suit. I'd like to leave my understanding of them with others who follow. Subsequent

generations can gain security and success of both an inner and outer nature by examining the way I have lived my life.

"Of course, I hope they will be more concerned with their inner natures, since I believe that will bring the most magic and joy into their hearts. As I sit here remembering, it seems to me that tending to relationships and maintaining childlike curiosity are ultimately more enriching than all the wealth one can acquire.

"My key phrase is insight through experience."

The Rider-Waite card is one of the most symbol filled in the Pentacles suit. Some authorities describe it as showing a patriarch sitting at ease in the foreground, surveying his family and comfortable estate through an archway (an opening to a new future). His hand is on the nose of one of two gray dogs, while the child's hand is on the tail of the other. Although the elder's hair is white, his beard is the gold of valued wisdom, and his coat of many colors is decorated with grapes (growth) and magic symbols that represent power over nature. The female or mother figure wears a red gown emanating the power of love. The male or father figure wears an outer cloak of blue over a brown undergarment to show that his earthy aspects are not yet fully cloaked in divine realization. He holds a "magic" wand tipped by a Yod.

The stone archway bears the family coat of arms, their ideals. It is also decorated with the scales of justice, suggesting a balanced sense of order and values in the family's life.

A tapestry with a checkerboard border symbolizing the forces of "dark" and "light," or the tension of opposites, hangs at the far left edge of the pillar. The pentacles are arranged in the pattern of the Cabalistic Tree of Life, revealing that the card deals not only with material wealth, but also with emotional and spiritual prosperity.

Other authorities regard the old man as an outsider and link him to the god who, disguised as a beggar, tests a family's hospitality and generosity and leaves them with a magic gift if they pass the test. In many mythologies, only the dogs recognize the stranger's divinity.[12] In Jungian terms, he represents the archetypal Wise Old Man, who offers spiritual wisdom to the personality so we can accomplish our psychological tasks.

The Morgan-Greer card shows a richly clothed man and woman framed in a stone arch. They stand on a pathway imbedded with small multicolored stones, reminding us of the many-faceted foundation necessary for successful relationships. In front of the archway two crossed banners bear the pentacles of the senses. They and the couple represent our masculine and feminine aspects, which together create balance and wholeness. The plume coming from the woman's turban suggests an active ajna center.

In the Aquarian card, the male wears a long cloak in the lavender color of healing and companionship. It naturally envelops the woman beside him since he has his arm around her. A small child beside them looks back over his shoulder. The couple looks through an archway to a distant castle set on high cliffs, which represents the promise of the future abundance of their soul life.

At the very least, the Ten of Pentacles portrays the benefits of following established ways and living cooperatively. It suggests family and/or community responsibility and involvement. We think the card says much more.

As the insight card of the suit, the Ten of Pentacles marks the stirrings of interest in higher service. Now that we have learned the lessons and been through the sensory experiences of cards two through nine, we long for "inner affluence." This card directs us to choose a path of enlightenment and further growth.

It shows the God-Self in its "holy city" and depicts the archetypal Trinity, our inner "holy family." At the same time it suggests that we must step outside the arch to further our perspective. Ultimately the child, representing the potential initiate, realizes this, which propels him into the Page stage.

Shadow elements of this card include: failing to comprehend the wisdom of our life experiences; experiencing feelings of separation or feeling as if we must go it alone; and not acknowledging our inner holiness.

When you draw this card:

- You are likely to become more interested in family or community.
- Things are on hold and you can coast for a while, but new experiences are on the horizon.
- As you enter a new phase of your life, your work will definitely be at a more enlightened level because of the personal and spiritual wisdom you will now want to acquire.
- New tasks await you and you will undertake them from a more mature or widened perspective.

Court Cards

PAGE OF PENTACLES

"I intend to stay busy learning new ideas and skills, and I hope I inspire you to do likewise. Even if our ideas don't work exactly as we think they should, we still can learn from trying. Life is an education. Through study, observation, and experimentation, we develop our potential.

"Take time to discover your real dreams and desires before you make long-term commitments, I say. In career matters, it is important to define your goals and plan how to accomplish them.

"On the other hand, sometimes it serves us to set aside carefully made plans and concentrate our energies on meeting new challenges that arise serendipitously. It takes both kinds of experience to achieve success, appreciate its joys, and develop the confidence to move on to greater things.

"So stop saying, 'Someday I will do that,' and start figuring out just how to do it. I want to inspire you to take the initiative. Consider yourself in the right place at the right time. I do.

"My key phrase is <u>developing creative power</u>."

In the Rider-Waite card, the figure focuses intently on the pentacle that practically floats on his fingertips. He stands in a high green field of lofty aspirations and wears a green tunic denoting new personality growth. Blue hills, which promise the completion of his inner work, rise beyond plowed lands that stand for the work itself. Like his lofty red hat and scarf, the Page is full of passion for and ideas about the pursuit of his goal.

Beginning with the Page, all the Pentacle court cards in the Rider-

Waite deck have yellow backgrounds, representing consciousness, intellectual maturity, and the ongoing process of transformation.

The Morgan-Greer Page wears earthy brown and passionate red garments. In the distance or the East (enlightenment) are the lake of the collective unconscious and the purple mountains of promised maturity. Although part of his pentacle is out of the picture to the left, suggesting the past still exerts its influence, the Page does face North, which is the initiate's position.

The Aquarian figure gazes at a large red pentacle that makes it only part of the way onto the right side of the card. This signifies incomplete plans, goals, or perspective. The Page's brown hat, held in place by a light yellow chin strap (the need for mental perseverance), bears several red feathers and a swath of material flowing from its left side, perhaps to suggest left-brain dominance, or logical thinking.[13]

The Page of Pentacles handles communication in many forms. He is practically inundated with news and new resources, especially where material matters are concerned. The new Page enjoys study, reflection, and "learning on the job." As he changes outward experiences to inner understanding, he tends to be self-absorbed.

This card can signal the need to start out on a new track professionally or change your work style. It urges us to prepare on a practical level for worthwhile service to family and community. Yet inner growth flourishes, too, as our skills and confidence increase.

The Page is dedicated to doing whatever it takes to achieve his goals, and gives scholarship priority over immediate pleasures. Since he is so busy learning, it can take him a while to even realize that his preparation also can serve "higher" interests and goals.

When his "advanced" training involves new sensory input and sensual enjoyment, this security-oriented Page may be thrown off balance. That is a part of his training he doubtless never anticipated, and it may cause ambivalence for a while.

The shadow aspect of this card includes: lowered self-esteem; holding onto illogical or unrealistic goals and ideals; impulsiveness; and being unwilling to study or prepare for what we want.

When you draw the Page of Pentacles, you need to:

- Take inventory to determine what you may have ignored and still need to learn about a current situation.

- Realize that if you are considering a risky situation, either financial or emotional, the only thing you may get out of it is experience, not long-term gain or stability.

- Recognize that you may be in for a "long haul" and prepare to see things through.

- Consider that you still have a lot to learn about your issue or situation even though you think you fully understand it.

KNIGHT OF PENTACLES

"One of my responsibilities is to help you understand the need to make and keep your commitments. I represent structure, organization, and dedication to duty. I am responsible for my actions and serve as an example of how to get a job done. I uphold tradition and urge you to understand the ways that worked in the past, before you consider discarding them.

"I am so dedicated and reliable that some people perceive me as rigid and stubborn, even lacking in imagination. Maybe so. But you mustn't forget that I have entered your life at this time to help you recognize the effect of similar characteristics in your own situation.

"I inspire you to use your talents to benefit your community. Discover your unity with others. Express your caring by sharing your 'know-how.'

"My key phrase is <u>accepting obligations.</u>"

The Rider-Waite card shows an armored person who is ready for business and taking it seriously. He wears a helmet of high ideals with a bushy plume of green leaves to point out the fertility of planning. Its visor is open to offer a clear view of how to proceed. His black horse stands firmly beside a plowed field, suggesting that both Knight and horse are committed to service and hard work.

Green oak leaves, which promise long-lasting growth, decorate the

Morgan-Greer Knight's helmet. His large pentacle acts as a shield. He "wears" the red color of passionate effort and dedication in a scarf wrapped around his armor.

The Aquarian Knight wears a suit of neutral-colored leather showing that he is protected by nature. A pentacle insignia is on the arm. A second pentacle decorates his protective throat piece or chakra energy. In both the Aquarian and Morgan-Greer cards, the Knight's horse is outside the picture, implying that instinctual and sexual energies have been channeled into dedication to personal development or civic service.

Overall, the Knight of Pentacles demonstrates respect for authority and tradition. Although he serves in whatever capacity he is able, his talents lie in his methodical approach to producing material goods and developing creative products. There is no need to ignore material interests while seeking spiritual growth, he reminds us.

Unlike other Knights in the Rider-Waite deck, whose horses are ready to move or are moving, the Knight of Pentacles's horse stands steady. The Knight stares ahead, as if he has lost sight of the real source of strength within himself and has become too identified with his earthly, material functions.[14]

The Rider-Waite Knight represents a time in our lives when we are dedicated to putting all our energy into important life affairs. If carried too far, this can escalate into the workaholic syndrome.

The shadow aspect of the Knight of Pentacles includes: lethargy; lack of discipline, or laziness; the inability to make plans; limited vision; irresponsibility, especially when it comes to carrying out assignments; and always looking for a new start or a new scheme to get ahead.

At the appearance of this card:

- Adopt a practical approach to your situation. Do the obvious first.

- Determine what improvements you can make in your planning and organizational skills. Set definite goals and work toward their completion.

- You may be too single-minded in your understanding of your situation or too rigid in your efforts to resolve it.

- In your zeal you may have lost sight of higher values, or you may have failed to develop inner meaning from your endeavors.

QUEEN OF PENTACLES

"I want to remind you that nature provides all the things we need to enrich our lives and our work. Although we certainly must work with material goods to enhance our lives and the lives of those around us, there is more to work than just labor. In addition to bringing beauty and enjoyment to the lives of others, skillful work, lovingly completed, can raise your level of self-esteem. The beauty and creativity you recognize in the world around you is a reflection of those qualities in yourself. Evaluate the persona you wear, and consider how harmonious you are with your environment.

"It is my energy acting within that inspires you to be compassionate, comforting, and supportive of others. I inspire you to be gracious in sharing your 'know-how.'

"I also encourage you to use your skills and wealth to become self-sufficient, to benefit your community, and to develop a feeling of unity with the world.

"My key phrase is <u>awareness that empowers others</u>."

The Rider-Waite Queen of Pentacles sits on her black and gray throne of wisdom and balance, which is sculpted with cherubs, goats, and fruit. She sits in a field of blossoms; roses climb overhead. They represent her abundant nature.

An orange rabbit, symbol of the earth or fertility, jumps into the card from the lower right corner. In Jungian terms, rabbits often symbolize the mother archetype.

The Queen's gown is the red of passionate feeling and is worn over a white shirt representing purity of intent. Her long, green cap of maintenance—a garment worn by nobility, underneath their crowns, to show that they maintained their spiritual alignment with higher powers or deities—flows like a robe from beneath her golden crown, which is decorated with jewels around the ajna center and at the level of the crown chakra. This is an enlightened woman, capable of gaining access to and using higher knowledge. In the background are the blue waters and mountains of the realized Self.

The Morgan-Greer Queen, facing right (future; consciousness), sits amid an autumn landscape of acorn-bearing oak trees. It is harvest-time. She wears an ornamentally spiked crown over a gem-studded, dark green cap of maintenance, and an orange gem on the second or "personality" finger of her left hand.

The Aquarian Queen of Pentacles faces left toward the past or unconscious. Her crown is decorated with the feminine aspect of divine wisdom at her ajna center and topped with a winged ornament over her crown chakra to suggest her soul connection.

Figures in profile indicate that we are not seeing all of their aspects or characteristics. Together the Morgan-Greer and the Aquarian Queens flesh out the Queen of Pentacles and make her a more whole "person."

The Tarot Queens embody and nurture the growth energy of their suits and then radiate it outward. The Queen of Pentacles epitomizes the knowledge that nature properly appreciated and work performed with the right attitude can result in higher awareness. As one expression of the Earth Mother, she represents the rebirth and regeneration we can experience through our physical efforts.

Receptive to the ministrations of others, the Queen of Pentacles can bring about harmony in times of tension. The authority she earned by developing her own skills gives her an opportunity to help others in their development.

She represents sensuality in many forms, including the enjoyment of sex, as the goats on the Rider-Waite card suggest. Goats are "trickster" figures and imply that the Queen still has the ability to stir up excitement.

The shadow aspects of this card include: being suspicious and conniving; avoiding responsibility; controlling and withholding rather than being generous in our ability to help others flourish; failing to appreciate the bounty of our environment; and finding no redeeming qualities or satisfaction in our work.

When the Queen of Pentacles appears:

- Help or inspire others to reach their potential.

- Consider whether you are being overly nurturing or not nurturing enough, or whether you are sufficiently nurturing to your own inner child.

• Examine what is preventing you from expressing the skills you have. Don't underestimate the value of or wisdom acquired from your experiences.

• Sensual attitudes and feelings may be trying to claim their rightful place in your life. Allow your natural sensitivity to surface.

King of Pentacles

"I am here to demonstrate the harnessing and controlling of earthly energies. You attain my position by paying attention to what you are doing and making good use of your intelligence.

"By handling your possessions in a careful, disciplined manner, you build your own kingdom and rule your life situation. Comfort and luxury are to be enjoyed, but never substituted for feelings.

"Maintain high standards in all your work because it is a reflection of your sacredness. Be a good steward of the earth, realizing that it is the manifestation of spirit, the 'other side of the coin.'

"While you may be tempted by the sensually stimulating, I am here to remind you that relationships and friendships that have ripened with time are your real treasures. Savor them like carefully aged wine.

"My key phrase is <u>the spiritual fulfillment of earthly endeavors</u>."

Like his Queen, the King in the Rider-Waite card sits in his garden, close to nature. A pattern of grapes and leaves, signifying fulfillment and the sweet success of life, ornament his robe, which is so lushly decorated that he almost looks as if he is a growing part of the garden. His golden crown is decorated with stylized roses and lilies, first seen blooming in the Ace of this suit. His red cap of maintenance and the red cowl at his throat suggest the intensity behind his knowledge and his ability to charismatically express it.

Four bulls' heads, an earth symbol, ornament his throne. The background castle shows the security of his position in society. Although the whole effect is lush and relaxed, his left foot, which rests on a stone block engraved with a bull's head, reveals that, underneath his robe, the King remains armored. Apparently he must be ever vigilant, perhaps to guard against giving in to his instinctual nature.

The Morgan-Greer King, dressed more simply, does, however, wear an elaborate gold helmet decorated with green leaves and brown bull horns. Grape vines heavy with fruit twine in front and around him. Like the Rider-Waite King, the sky behind him is the yellow of applied intelligence.

The Aquarian King wears a soft crown. A pentacle floats at the level of his heart chakra, and the bubbly design of divine feminine energies shows on his royal garb. A bull looks over the King's right shoulder, representing the "harnessed strength involved in the King's decision making."[15]

The King of Pentacles represents attainment in the physical realm and reward for diligent effort. He is realistic and uses good judgment in handling money. He also knows how to enjoy his possessions.

As a born leader, he demonstrates high ethical standards, but his steadfastness often makes it difficult for him to consider a different job unless its advantages are exceptionally clear. He acts according to his own high principles, sometimes causing others to regard him as stubborn.

Though his aptitude is in the world of work, the King of Pentacles is aware that work done with the right attitude flows from and enhances the sacredness within. Medieval artisans had their patron gods, and the work of their "ordinary" jobs constituted a liturgy to those gods.[16] No one understands this concept better than the King of Pentacles. You will not hear him speak of this, though. He acts on his ideals, rather than talking about them.

The shadow aspects of the King of Pentacles include: greed; being status conscious; using wealth in corrupt ways or for corrupt purposes; and having a spiteful or distrustful attitude toward those with spiritual goals or intent.

When you draw this card:

- Consider whether you have taken on too little, or too much, responsibility at this time in your life.

- Teach others to develop working skills that reflect outer and inner integrity.
- Realize that you are now secure enough to begin releasing long-standing patterns or habits related to finances and other physical or material aspects of your life.
- Look at how you work. Do your work attitudes and style reflect your deepest human intent?

11 ✸ Swords: Fighting Illusion

Swords family members tend to be independent, goal oriented, and aggressive, but definitely not intuitive or romantic. They are logical thinkers, good communicators, and tenacious truth seekers, although sometimes temporarily blinded to it.

The Swords in all three decks are double edged. "Will you focus on the problem or the opportunity?" they inquire. Will you take action to resolve this situation, or allow yourself to feel like a victim and remain immobilized? Swords are the suit of courage and clarity, as well as the suit that depicts the intellectual concepts we have to develop to find wholeness.

Swords have been described as the "do or die" suit. They point to the mental conflicts we need to remedy and the abilities that will hinder or help us to do that. They put us in position to make decisions, including some that require us to break with past attachments or training.

The entire suit represents the archetypal illusion of opposites or duality. Maturity comes when we stop conceiving of the world as polarized. That is the growth lesson of the Swords. They are associated with the spiritual element of air,[1] and with Jung's thinking function.

Dealing with both positive and negative states of mind, Sword attitudes can be expressed as doubt, overanalyzing, and self-criticism, as well as objectivity and good observation and negotiating skills.[2]

In the Golden Dawn tradition, Swords represent the third letter of the Tetragrammaton, the Hebrew letter Vau—the world of patterns behind matter (the formative world).

All the backgrounds in the Aquarian deck are a multicolored blend of blue, pink, and purple, presumably symbolizing rolling clouds. In the Rider-Waite deck, the background color of the sky offers additional hints about the meaning of the card.

Birds appear on all of the Rider-Waite court cards for this suit. As the "animal emblem" of the court cards, they symbolize the mind's ability to move into the realm of wisdom, especially divine wisdom, and also the aloofness such an attitude can produce.[3]

Numbered Cards

ACE OF SWORDS

"I am the divine gift of reason and logical thinking. I foster intellectual excellence, discipline, and the ability to cut through the clutter of unnecessary details in order to clear a path for progress. My victory crown promises that if you work your way through the experiences of my suit, you will learn the skills you need.

"I make a perfect companion to the Ace of Cups. Together we allow you to tune into your feelings, evaluate information about a situation, and then make a conscious decision. The gifts and skills I offer keep you from becoming mired in your emotions, distorting the facts of a situation, or attributing more importance to it than you should.

"I represent the mind that is capable of detailed analysis. I pierce illusion to discover the truth.

"My key phrase is <u>the power of the intellect</u>."

The Rider-Waite Ace of Swords shows a white hand of energy issuing from a swirling gray (wisdom) cloud of the masked Divine to grasp the sword of equilibrium, which points upward through a golden, jeweled crown. Olive and laurel branches signifying material attainment hang from the crown. Six golden Yods (divine energy) float around the sword, which is positioned against a gray sky of divine balance and above purple and blue mountains of abstract truth.

The sword on the Morgan-Greer Ace is held in basically the same position by a flesh-toned hand emerging from billowing blue (emotions) and yellow (intellect) clouds. The swirling hilt of the sword mimics the upward and downward positions of the hands of The Magician. A red rose of passion is attached to the laurel leaves, and a white or pale blue rose of freedom to the palm frond.

Unlike the other two aces, the Aquarian Ace's sword points downward and extends off the bottom frame of the card. It is bordered on either side by white roses and symbols of the feminine aspect of divine knowledge made manifest. The purple globe that tops the sword's elaborate hilt bears a pattern that represents spiritual support.

The Ace of Swords is the source of mental activity. It is a wellspring of energy that can be mobilized for success. Symbolizing the discipline of mind necessary to advance growth and to get through to the real value of any issue, this card urges us to think logically, organize point by point, and then synthesize the whole.

The Ace marks the beginning of a cycle that can lead to significant intellectual attainment. It also serves to remind us that individual achievements involve conscious awareness of our spiritual bonds to others.

The shadow side of this card includes: an inability to plan; failure to think things through; letting emotions control decisions; being so intellectually removed from situations or persons that feelings are deadened; and rigid adherence to principle.

When you draw this card:

- Your approach to the issue at hand may be too dispassionate or too intellectual.

- Or you may be too emotional about the situation and need to analyze it more objectively.

- Hold your impulses up to the light of objective scrutiny. You are invited to become more rational and conscious.

- Consider how and from whom you learned to make decisions. Are those "lessons" still appropriate for the person you are now?

TWO OF SWORDS

"Here I sit blindfolded, never sure whether I'm defending against new information from outsiders or from my own ability to reason things out. I know there are two sides to every issue, but I'm not sure I want to consider both of them. I might have to change my opinion.

"At times my motto appears to be, 'Don't confuse me with the facts. I've already made up my mind.' I feel balanced and satisfied as I am, although I <u>do</u> get kind of lonely, and tired of holding up these swords.

"Actually I have closed myself off from outside influences in order to patiently resolve my problem. I want to use mental clarity and not be swayed by emotions or the opinions of others.

"One of the conflicts I am called upon to resolve is the integration of conscious will and unconscious motivation. I'll resist, of course, but I know it's a task I must eventually undertake. I do not easily allow my intuition and feelings to have their say.

"My key phrase is <u>false balance</u>."

In the Rider-Waite Two of Swords, a blindfolded female figure, wearing a white gown and yellow shoes of intellectual understanding, sits on a gray stone bench on gray ground (the call for balance). Waite describes her as "hoodwinked."[4] She balances two long swords in arms crossed over her breasts. Behind her is a rippling body of water (emotions) with orange islands (energy centers) in it. She sits in inner and outer darkness with the eclipsed moon suggesting subdued emotions. Intellect rules. She cannot see that the islands of passion, intuition (moon), or the water's unconscious forces are additional sources of strength.

In the Morgan-Greer card, the blindfolded female stands her ground. She wears decorative clothing with an ornate green belt. Its design is almost Celtic in nature, with a buckle bearing three green stones. Although it separates the instinct (lower body) from the intellect (upper body), the circular three-way design of the buckle symbolizes the gathering of creative energy.

The nude female in the Aquarian Two of Swords stands behind large monoliths bearing designs of aspiration and the divine feminine.

The Two of Swords can be a card of procrastination, stalemate and indecision, or the deliberate postponement of a decision. It can signal that weighing options over and over is immobilizing us or that we may need to shut out our rational abilities and trust our feelings. Recognizing that we are blind to certain realities is the beginning of mental awareness. Every choice has its price. The cost of denying our inner promptings or our outer vision is living in a self-limited world.

This card is a graphic depiction of the tension of opposites, which can be temporarily resolved at best, and never by logic alone. New tensions always arise from our reservoir of past experiences and attitudes, as the rippling water in the Rider-Waite card reveals. Time and again we will be tempted to hoodwink ourselves into believing that we only need to achieve balance once, but nothing is permanent, this card reminds us, not even the ability to ignore life issues.

Could we be unnecessarily protecting ourselves from imagined criticism? This card can reflect deep self-doubt. To grow psychologically and spiritually, we must be open to a variety of ideas and information. Have you closed your eyes to a part of yourself?

The shadow of the Two of Swords includes: unchanging opinions; lack of self-control; letting others make our decisions for us; and jumping into action for action's sake.

When you draw this card:

- Consider your options. You do have some.
- Evaluate what seem to be conflicting thoughts or desires. It's time to consider their reconciliation.
- Look for an issue that you'd rather not know the truth about, or suspicions you're reluctant to confirm.
- It suggests that your decision will be one that resolves two or more important issues or aspects of yourself.

THREE OF SWORDS

"Although people perceive me as a sad card, I encourage you to look again. I bear clouds of despair, yes, but usually my heart is not bleeding. I represent false heartbreak and pain that is only temporary. As soon as you understand the reason for your situation, you'll feel better.

"Perhaps you are focusing on past experiences and old wounds long after their emotional content has been dissipated. The intensity of your disappointment may be out of proportion to what is really going on. In time, if you draw upon my logic, reason, and detachment, you will get to the 'heart' of the matter and understand how it fits into the greater picture.

"Accepting and experiencing pain promotes maturity and inner growth. My key phrase is <u>the noble spirit."</u>

The Rider-Waite card shows a two-dimensional heart pierced by three swords. It floats against a background of dark gray rain emanating from three light gray clouds, which intimates that things are lightening up. There is no blood. The rain must be accepted, but the heart remains intact to beat another day.

The Morgan-Greer heart takes on a more three-dimensional appearance, and the middle sword drips blood. The heart floats in a solar burst of yellow light (divine intellect). Although there are billowing dark gray clouds above it, the heart is set against a blue sky of clear thinking.

The puffy pink heart of the Aquarian deck floats against the suit's usual background. Again, no blood. The heart almost seems to be backed by a curtain of purple and gray clouds at the top. Is this merely a performance?

One of the things that the Three of Swords represents is coping with sorrow caused by the loss of something in which we have, or had, an emotional investment. Whether it involves a relationship with another person, an attachment to certain possessions, or a betrayal, this is an experience none of us escapes. When it occurs, we feel "stabbed" in the heart, but ultimately our intellect (symbolized by the piercing swords of reason) helps us make sense of the situation and push the clouds of despair into the background.

Whatever our loss, a time of grieving is called for, but this card suggests it should not last too long, lest we also lose our perspective. Eventually logic must be brought to bear on the matter so we can learn from our pain and apply what we learn to future relationships.

The Three of Swords also represents our keen ability to go right to the core (or heart) of an issue and deal with that rather than superficial appearances or what others say is the problem.[5]

The shadow side of this card includes: jealousy; excessive self-sacrifice; holding onto old pains; and focusing on the problem rather than the solution.

When you draw the Three of Swords:

- Consider where you are today and acknowledge that you are not that same person who was wounded in the past. Use your intellect to release the past, finish what you need to finish, and move on.

- Focus on becoming all that you still can be rather than on what might have been.

- Look for at least three ways to see or define your problem differently, and then consider three possible solutions.

- Look for a rigid attitude or long-held belief that may be allowing you to maintain a false picture.

FOUR OF SWORDS

"Peace, sweet peace. Time out for meditation, introspection, and for trying to understand recent experiences from a greater perspective, or in the light of the divine plan.

"You'll understand your situation better if you don't take it personally. I suggest you concentrate on a more worldly meaning, and on becoming more objective. You can learn something about the way the world works. Allow yourself time to comprehend it.

"I hope I'll inspire you to recognize when you may need a break from the usual struggles and pressures of daily life. After you have done everything possible with your rational approach, you may need to back off temporarily in order to acquire a different viewpoint, release anxiety, or replenish your inner resources. Taking the time to reassess can lead to a new approach, and possibly a shift in priorities or attitude.

"My key phrase is <u>time out for introspection</u>."

In the Rider-Waite card, a yellow (intellectual understanding) effigy of a knight is sculpted atop a yellow tomb. He lies beneath a stained-glass window showing a religious person[6] administering a healing blessing to a supplicant.

In the Morgan-Greer card, we see only the armored head and neck (intellect) of the knight. Brown oak leaves and acorns, representing a change of season, lie above the crown chakra, which gives us access to higher, more mature thought.

In the Aquarian card, three swords hang in a cathedral on light yellow walls of inspired thought. They are mounted between pink orbs of Trinity. A fourth is mounted on the side of the bier, suggesting old patterns buried in the unconscious.

The Four of Swords reflects withdrawal for contemplation and healing. It suggests a period of voluntary seclusion, and the letting go of regular duties and obligations for the purpose of reflecting on the direction and goals of your life. Previous judgments and attitudes are suspended, possibly leading to the death of old ways.

Fours suggest that we need to stabilize our position, to retreat and think things out. It is time for ordering, in this case, internal organizing.

Separating ourselves from the outside world often opens a window to higher wisdom, this card reminds us. Messages may come to us in the dream state, as the Rider-Waite window scene suggests. The position of the swords—three together and one apart—points to a new option resulting from divine inspiration or paying attention to the needs of our body, mind, and Spirit.

In some instances, this card illustrates stunted growth and stalled creative endeavors. The way we think about issues from the past or our reluctance to look at the shadow aspects of our personality (the sword below the Rider-Waite and Aquarian figures) may be to blame.

The shadow side of the Four of Swords includes: withdrawal in order to avoid or ignore problems or confrontations; failure to listen to your inner voice; and using willpower to rush ahead or continue your pursuit even when you don't really feel like it.

When you draw this card:

- Be open to influences and problem-solving possibilities you might not typically consider.
- Don't get sidetracked by blame. Ask yourself what you need to do.
- Take time out to evaluate your present position. How could you handle the situation differently or restore your energy?
- Look inward for the source of your lethargy and trust your exploratory efforts to reveal a remedy.

FIVE OF SWORDS

"Although many people think I am a tyrant or bully, reveling in other people's humiliation, like all of us, I'm not necessarily what I seem to be at first glance. Just because you see me in public acting like I have a great deal of self-confidence doesn't mean I really do.

"Perhaps I sneak around taking advantage of the lull after other people's battles because I have no skills of my own. Other people might say that I am misusing my abilities, but I may not think I have any real abilities or rights except to pillage following someone else's defeats.

"Then again, I could be the epitome of resourcefulness, picking up what others have discarded and profiting by it. I may see the potential treasure in other people's 'throwaways,' and create positive outcomes from negative situations. I believe that 'it's what you do with what you have' that pays off in the end.

"My key phrase is <u>benefiting from others' depleted energy</u>."

In the Rider-Waite card, a man wearing complementary colors—a green tunic over a red shirt—holds three swords and looks over his shoulder at two dejected figures. Their swords lie at his feet to symbolize scattered thinking. A body of moving water (stirred emotions) in the background and distant mountains tell us that mastery or resolution is far away.

All of the figures in the Morgan-Greer card are deep blue, as if reflecting that this is a shadow time. The rising sun suggests new opportunities. The nearest figure is dressed in a hooded cloak signifying concealed ideas or motives. Two crossed swords (crossroads) lie at his feet.

The helmeted figure in the Aquarian Five of Swords wears a pink and gray cloak decorated with ribbons that symbolize the masculine energy of the Absolute. Two crossed swords lie on the light cream foreground. A decision is required.

With its two figures in the far distance, the Aquarian card most clearly depicts a lonely inner struggle and the need to listen to our inner voice. On one level, this card deals with competition and the feelings of victory or defeat that accompany it. The momentary kick of outdoing someone else can be used as a substitute for developing our potential; however, it often reflects low self-esteem. Competitiveness is related to our inner struggle for approval and affection.[7] But neither the need to win nor the fear of defeat promotes inner growth. Thus, the Five of Swords, which looks like some kind of victory, is, in fact, an impasse.

A second way to understand this card is to see the figure in the foreground as prospering from the losses of others. Rather than taking part in their battle, he gathers the swords they left behind. He "wins" through the defeat of others and incorrectly assumes that he has overcome the hostile and aggressive issues of his past.

And what of the defeated whose swords he steals? Fairy tales and mythology tell us that if we don't pay attention to our treasures (energy; creativity), they will be stolen from us by destructive forces.[8] The crucial question to ask ourselves with this card is, "Which figure do I identify with today?"

All fives represent a test, a challenge, a time to reorganize. Will we continue with our same behavior or will we examine it and gain insight? The Five of Swords can also stand for thinking that willpower will always triumph in our inner struggles to "conquer" negative impulses or low self-esteem.

Recognizing and wrestling with the desire to triumph over others or our own inner desires can release growth energy. We have two Major Arcana "five" cards to help us in this test: The Hierophant, the teacher, and Temperance (14 = 1 + 4 = 5), spiritual education.

The shadow side of the Five of Swords includes: an obsession with winning at all costs; projecting our inner feelings on others and scapegoating them; and not taking credit for our own accomplishments.

When this card shows up in your reading:

- Check your motivation for asking your current question.

- Whatever you may think, your conflict is really an inner one and can only be won by attending to the defeated aspects of yourself.

- Consider whether feelings of vulnerability or humiliation are being evoked by your present situation or by unfinished issues from the past.

- Ask yourself, "How important is it for me to win? Will I learn by winning, and what will I close myself off to?" Both are present.

SIX OF SWORDS

"I represent your journey from one stage of growth to the next. I help you look at long-held certainties and decide which to leave behind. I facilitate a higher state of consciousness, even though it may feel like a loss at the time.

"New growth is natural to human beings. Even when we are progressing steadily in our boat of transition, we will stir up things we need to think about.

"I depict the various aspects of your personality (your inner masculine or feminine side, your archetypal inner child, etc.) all working toward integration. Right now your masculine energy is more active, but your inner feminine had the idea. What matters in the long run, however, is moving into a new awareness of how we're interconnected. Without each other, we are incomplete. I also represent the active, passive, and newly developing facets of your inner self.

"My key phrase is <u>making steady progress</u>."

The Rider-Waite card shows a dark-haired boatman transporting a woman and child to the opposite shore. His orange punt holds six swords. He uses the jet-black pole of potentiality. All things remain possible if we remain calm and waste "neither energy nor opportunity,"[9] this card consoles.

In the Morgan-Greer card, the boatman (defined by Prosapio as "Fate")[10] directs the boat toward distant, gray lands. We are moving toward balance and integration.

The helmeted Aquarian boatman[11] guides an elegant gondola across a lake. The pattern at the bottom of the man's coat denotes growing awareness and the power of decision. The flounce on his cap duplicates that of the quail (soul) at the head of the boat.

While presenting a tranquil, somewhat low-key scene, the Six of Swords carries the message that there is always the potential, and the need, for making important changes in our lives. It can represent a gateway to a new perspective or a passage to a higher state of consciousness.[12] The fact that the swords don't weigh the boat down suggests a spiritual or emotional journey,[13] and the growth that results from the struggle between our ego (the boat) and our higher self (the ferryman).[14] The sea ahead will be tranquil if we trust our higher self to guide us.

The Six of Swords can also represent hope and perseverance on our life journey. We keep going toward the future (right side of card), even though we have little awareness of what will happen.

There is a puzzle in this card, as there is in many of the Swords cards. To whom do the six swords belong? Are they the woman's proud possessions? Painful punishments that she takes with her? Or are they the price she has to pay the ferryman, who now owns the swords? Perhaps she has given up her intellectual ideals for a new way of responding. What do *you* think?

At some point in your Tarot studies, take the time to look at all the Swords cards and ask yourself the same question, "To whom do the swords belong?" It may change your understanding of each card.

The shadow side of this card includes: stagnation; postponing action; and letting things happen around us without taking responsibility either for events or their consequences.

When you draw this card:

- Consider transition as an opportunity to expand your inner horizon.

- Ask yourself, "What false ideas do I need to leave behind so I can concentrate on growth?"

- Chart your own course of action by listening to your inner wisdom.

- Adjust your sights a little higher than previously.

SEVEN OF SWORDS

"It's been fun here, but I think I need to take better care of myself. It's time to act alone. I choose what and how much I can handle. Although some people think me sneaky, I hope you will see that I'm shouldering a large burden.

"I am a clever fellow, but I tend to keep my ideas to myself. I have many aspirations, but I need to work them out on my own. I am the one taking a chance and engaged in an act of derring-do. I'm more likely to employ guile than brute force. I can be quite charming, if I do say so myself. When it comes to disarming potentially negative situations, my skill and cunning serve me well.

"My key phrase is rogue scamp."

In the Rider-Waite card, a man carries five swords away from a brightly colored encampment. Two swords remain stuck in the ground. His red hat and matching boots suggest he has strong feelings about the plan he is putting into action. He tiptoes away on a yellow road, which matches the yellow sky, and lets us know that intellectual work has preceded and supports his activity. In the background, three figures are silhouetted beneath a cloud of gray smoke from their fire.

And what do all these images add up to? Most succinctly, a person with a colorful past is using his five senses (the five swords) and his desire (red cap) to develop a better understanding (yellow road) of himself (movement toward the left/unconscious).

The man in the Morgan-Greer card carries the five black swords of his lower (sensory) chakras on his right shoulder. Two silver swords, representing the heart and ajna centers, remain stuck in the ground behind him. He moves downhill away from them, choosing the "lesser" path.

The Aquarian figure heads toward mountains, signifying the completion of inner or higher work. His yellow hat, banded in pink with gray jewels, indicates his crown chakra has been activated. His robe bears the brown and black pattern of the masculine energy of The Absolute running along his spine.[15] This is a man on a spiritual quest for transformation.

In one sense, the Seven of Swords represents courageous, albeit impulsive, effort, which results in partial or temporary success. Old projects are neglected for the actions of the present moment. This card also warns against using deceit in either business or personal affairs.

Spiritually the card suggests that the figure seeks a change in consciousness. Having selected the spiritual ideas he needs, he now focuses on his goal. The card represents a need to clearly define the higher purpose of an endeavor and rely on our physical ability to carry it out.

The shadow side of the Seven of Swords includes: resorting to stealth and deception; using treachery or trickery; denying our own capabilities; and an unwillingness to enlist help when needed (i.e., being too independent).

When you draw this card:

- Think for yourself. Determine what it is you really want.
- Seek more realistic ways to reach your goal or put your ideas into action.
- Examine the role sneakiness or cunning plays in your situation.
- Consider how impulsive action has served you or gotten you in trouble in the past and use that insight in your present projects.

Eight of Swords

"*This is a period of indecision for me. I'm considering so many things before I make a choice that I'm temporarily immobilized. I'm blinded by the opinions of others and also by the attitudes I've developed as a result of my own experiences.*

"*Maybe I'm too withdrawn and introverted. Sometimes I lack the self-confidence to take action or the motivation to make changes. Fear of failure looms large within me and ties me to traditional, established belief systems. I long to take that first step, but I'm too afraid. I feel too vulnerable to share my thoughts with others.*

"*Whether your issue is romance, work, or personal growth, when I appear, take a look at what is really holding you back, especially old ideas or regrets from the past that haunt you. Are you procrastinating or playing down your own abilities due to fear of failure? Waiting for a guarantee can blind you to dealing with life's issues, as it has for me.*

"*My key phrase is* restricted thinking.*"*

The woman in the Rider-Waite card stands in a watery marsh with seven swords set upright behind her and the eighth in front of her and to her right. She is bound in gray wrappings and blindfolded to her options. A red-roofed castle rising out of distant gray cliffs symbolizes the authority by which she feels ruled. Yet the swords do not surround her and the bindings do not restrict her legs.

Eight swords, evenly divided, stand upright on either side of the Morgan-Greer figure. Against a gray sky, blue-gray pinnacles rise behind her. Bound so that she cannot see, hear, speak, or smell, she is sensually deprived and has only her intellect for input.

Wearing a pink dress with black decorations representing the power of decision, the woman in the Aquarian card also stands midway between the swords. Those on her right are embedded in gray rocks representing unresolved issues. Blinded to her decision-making ability, she is unable to see the orange mountains of energy and insight available to her in the background.

The Eight of Swords is a wake-up call. It depicts that state of mind we are in when we refuse to recognize the help available to us. We are so influenced by society and our perception of past experiences that we cannot grow, look forward to the future, or pursue spiritual goals on a more than limited basis.

This is a card of restrictions and indecision that are largely self-imposed and often brought on by a lack of faith in our own ability to handle the problem at hand. As yet unaware of our personal power, we are limited by our rigid beliefs. We're afraid we'll be overwhelmed without the structures and boundaries developed in the past.

We've been trained to believe we are helpless, Pollock notes,[16] and this card shows how that belief oppresses us. We *have* been "hoodwinked." Greer calls it the "Houdini card," because it represents a time when we have backed ourselves into a corner, possibly to force ourselves to come up with a really creative solution.[17]

The bound figure also can be seen as about to give up the darkness of the material mind and have her eyes opened to higher knowledge. It's going to be a difficult initiation, however, if the Nine and Ten of Swords are any indication.

Whenever you draw this card, it's a good time to accomplish something, no matter how small. Walk the dog. Wash the dishes. It will restore your sense of liberation, success, and possibility.

The shadow side of the Eight of Swords includes: accepting other people's ideas of our value and failing to develop our own; failure to acknowledge and wrestle with our inner tyranny; and unwillingness to try anything new.

When this card appears, ask yourself the following questions:

- What are you avoiding? Is there a typical pattern of indecision in your life or only regarding your current issue?

- How does not acting, or being immobilized, benefit you? What's the ultimate payoff?

- What attitudes or ideas are keeping you from taking action or expressing yourself more forcefully or creatively?

- Where in your life *do* you feel, or have you felt, powerful? Draw on that strength and experience and bring it into the present situation to restore your self-confidence.

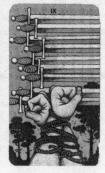

NINE OF SWORDS

"I'm not completely clear as to what is happening. I try to sort it out, but right now it's hard for me to face the future.

"Perhaps without realizing it, I have taken on other people's troubles as my own. I sometimes contemplate imaginary concerns as well. My worries keep me from deciding on a new course of action. I allow them to immobilize me.

"When you feel as I do, shift your emphasis from what you think is being done to you to deciding what you can do. New beginnings are possible when we change our focus or orientation.

"Allowing inner turmoil to take over for too long delays healing. It's time to finish with grief or regrets, to leave our bed of inner imprisonment and reclaim our power.

"My key phrase is despair that leads to healing."

In the Rider-Waite deck, a woman with her face in her hands sits on a pink mattress. She appears to be in despair. The quilt covering her legs has red roses embroidered in the yellow squares, indicating passion backed by intellect, and astrological signs, standing for aspects of her personality, embroidered on its blue squares of awareness. The base of the bed is carved with images, possibly mythological ones. Nine swords are suspended horizontally against a black background and extend beyond the edge of the card. They represent "hang-ups" from the past. In addition, the scene on the base of the bed suggests that a myth or script we live by is an underlying factor in shaping our ideas about ourselves and what's ahead.

The foreground of the Morgan-Greer card displays two forearms, fists clenched, bound at the wrists with brown ropes of past training and old programming. Behind them nine swords are suspended horizontally, tips extending off the card.

In the Aquarian card, a woman sits by a casket, her face in her hands. Her robe bears the pink and black ribbons of the masculine aspect of the Divine, while archways to the divine feminine rise beside her. The Kingdom of the Divine is all around her. She has access to help, but does not yet recognize it. As in the other two cards, the tips of nine horizontal swords, suspended beside her, extend off to the right.

The Nine of Swords refers to that time in our lives when we are temporarily consumed with grief, regret, or remorse. It tells us to examine and sort through ideas, since we seem to have lumped them all together and given them equal value (in the form of nine similar swords). We need to pick out and keep the ones that promote forward movement and let go of those that restrict us. At the moment, our ideas still imprison us, but if we turn inward (hands over face) and reevaluate them, we will be able to refocus our goals based on a broader outlook (seen in the zodiac symbols of the Rider-Waite card).

The Nine of Swords illustrates the feelings of powerlessness and despair that plague us when we convince ourselves that there's nothing we can do to change a situation. After we've done a certain amount of necessary grieving, we must work on shifting our conscious awareness from sorrow and regret to hope and solid plans for the future. This rethinking process will likely occur more than once. The Moon (Major Arcana $18 = 1 + 8 = 9$), which is one of the Nine of Swords' overseeing cards, suggests cyclic activity and long-hidden insights. In addition, The Hermit (Major Arcana IX) shows that wisdom is available to support inner work.

The shadow side of this card includes: blaming other people or circumstances for our own errors in judgment; failure to acknowledge and integrate shadow aspects; and not learning from our grief.

When you draw this card:

- Examine, one by one, all the situations that have contributed to feelings of self-doubt. Then imagine putting them in a yellow balloon and releasing them upward into the gray sky of divine balance.

- Recognize that you are a person of conflicting energies and cycles. If you can hold the tension of this awareness, you will gradually achieve a sense of equilibrium.

- Allow others to contribute their insights to your conscious awareness.

- Reexamine your expectations. Within them lies a source of dis-

appointment. Which ones are unrealistic or as yet unmet because you have failed to communicate to another person?

TEN OF SWORDS

*"Here I lie, looking like I'm done for, but I'm not. Things are not
as they seem at first glance. I am evolving. I'm pinned by the force
of the swords along my spine, in alignment with earthly and divine
forces.*

*"Some people see me as having made a willful sacrifice. I think
that by facing my weaknesses and not deluding myself, I am becoming
a more genuine and insightful person.*

*"I am giving up old ideas and conditioning that have limited my
progress. New endeavors and new opportunities for relationships in
my life lie ahead. But right now I just need to lie here and marshal
my energy. Yes, it's tempting to never move again. However, I will
arise, eventually, 'take up my swords,' and go forward with new
resolve.*

"My key phrase is gathering my reserves."

In the Rider-Waite card, a figure lies on a bank beside water, his
body pierced with ten swords aligned along his spine to open it to
spiritual energies. He is draped with a red cloth reminiscent of flowing
blood. His thumb touches the ring finger of his right (active) hand,
forming the mudra of good fortune or joy, which the Buddhists refer
to as kichigo-in.[18] As he responds with intelligence to his problems,
the black sky of ignorance, so dense in the Nine of Swords, clears to
reveal a yellow sky of conscious intellect and blue mountains that
represent the wisdom of the Self.

In the Morgan-Greer card, the pierced body, wearing the white garment of the initiate, lies bleeding in the snow of frozen emotions. Unlike the Rider-Waite card, the swords are not aligned, signifying the death of old ideas and training. Each has a different hilt, which shows the diversity of enlightened thinking that is possible.

The figure in the Aquarian Ten of Swords does not bleed from the swords piercing him. His is a false or symbolic death, an initiation he must undergo to achieve insight. He lies on barren pink ground, his head turned toward distant brown mountains. As the white sun of inspiration and guidance breaks through the clouds, he blinds himself to "worldly wisdom" in preparation to serve a higher plan.[19] The design on his right sleeve—that of personality-shaping ideas—will become more prominent in the Aquarian Page and King.

The Ten of Swords appears formidable until you understand its message. It shows the pain at the end of a cycle that has brought disruption and misfortune. Yet it simultaneously signals the dawning of things to come. It pictures the realigning of spiritual energy needed to undertake new tasks.

This card represents an extreme blow to the persona. The "wound" feels like the end, but is actually a reorganization that promotes a different way of being and of relating to others.

The Ten of Swords calls upon us to find our own path to enlightenment. It raises the issue of ego interference in listening to and moving toward alignment with our higher self. Japikse calls it the card of "greatest activity, wakefulness, and livingness in the whole Tarot."[20]

All tens reflect regeneration and recommitment. They are often the most complex card in any suit, presenting, as they do, new intentions that have resulted from the preceding experiences of the suit. As such, they also suggest a solution that can propel us forward into the Page stage. In the Ten of Swords, we see this solution reflected in the attitude of joy portrayed by the mudra or finger position we mentioned earlier.

We also have The Magician (Major Arcana I; $10 = 1 + 0 = 1$) as a role model for attending to and marshaling higher energies for the sake of transformation.

The shadow aspects of this card include: remaining in the "poor me" or victim attitude; becoming enamored of and even competitive regarding our pain ("no one suffers as much as I do"); and the inability to face and release our fears and delusions.

When the Ten of Swords appears:

- Reexamine any fixed ideas that may be pinning you down. Who or what is keeping you from expressing your abilities more fully?

- Consider what you need to do to become more genuine, and how you can learn to do it.
- Review your personal philosophy and your place in the Universe.
- The issue at hand is related to spiritual values, and you need to place it in a greater or "higher" perspective.

Court Cards

PAGE OF SWORDS

"I stand here poised for action. I like to check around before I proceed. Since my experience of the Swords pathway and my knowledge of the power of 'Swords energy' are limited, I am alert to possible dangers that may arise. They won't slow me down, though. I'll go ahead in my own way, investigating all the angles and observing the reactions of other people.

"I know more than you think, and right now I'm a little tired of being told what to do. I see myself as determined, dedicated, and impatient to be on my way. I think I ought to be allowed to pursue my own adventures, whether they make sense to anyone else or not. Let me make my own mistakes.

"My key phrase is <u>developing my own understanding</u>."

The Rider-Waite card shows a young man holding a sword that extends off the top of the card into the heavenly realm. The Page pivots on rough terrain. Distant cypress trees bend in the wind. They will repeat on each of the Rider-Waite court cards of the suit, as will the gray clouds of divine overseeing, the blue sky and the flying birds, which demonstrate roving thoughts.

The Morgan-Greer Page stands in profile, wearing military-style clothing. Gray clouds obscure much of the orange sky. Three light brown stone columns standing in the background symbolize stability, while a fourth, which lies fallen, suggests impermanence.

On his right sleeve the Aquarian Page of Swords displays the prominent pink and black interwoven pattern of personality-shaping ideas at work. His rose helmet bears a gray (wisdom) circular decoration over the third eye or ajna chakra. He is definitely "on the path."

The Page of Swords symbolizes an active intelligence, probing the unknown but remaining detached from involvements, for he is not yet ready to make interpersonal commitments. He proceeds intently on his quest to overcome self-doubt and acquire more knowledge of the world. The card reflects both mental and physical agility in search of direction.

The Page is strong-willed and determined to carry out projects in his own way. Although he looks for hidden motives in other people, he doesn't yet have the ability to fathom the full picture.

As the first step on the initiate's higher path, he aspires to connect what he already knows with greater wisdom. He seeks justice and truth, but largely as intellectual concepts since he doesn't yet have the focus or training to incorporate them into his own lifestyle.

The Page wants higher knowledge. Yet needing to develop and strengthen his own keen reasoning powers often makes him impatient to cut through the obvious to the core of a problem.

One shadow aspect of this card is expressed in the saying "A little learning is a dangerous thing." Others include: a false sense of superiority based on limited knowledge; detachment from others because of this "superiority"; assuming that we can force issues or achieve success solely through intellect or willpower; and making decisions based on feelings without regard to reason.

When you draw this card:

- You may need to sharpen your understanding by narrowing your focus, or broadening it to reduce a limited focus.

- Look forward to a period of discovery that will expand your consciousness more than you realize now.

- Consider whether you are attempting to "conquer" or resolve your issue with willpower and the force of reasoning alone rather than discovering what's really going on.

• Determine the present merit or usefulness of previously held beliefs and values.

KNIGHT OF SWORDS

"It's important for me to keep going, but I'll say a few things as I journey along.

"I am very brave, strong, and skillful. My sword points heavenward. Bent on fighting for truth and destroying evil, I welcome any conflicts I encounter. I believe it is my mission to set things right and make the world safer for all. I will inspire you to cut through fuzzy thinking and use the shrewdness of your mind to achieve penetrating insights.

"I have the courage to take action while others are still discussing the problem. Of course, I do tend to rush into things and slay the opposition first. Once I become bored, well, it's time for me to be on my way.

"Some people see me as too impulsive or too callous. I see myself as bold and clever. I also see conflict and change as natural parts of life. Not only should we be ready for them, but we should embrace them.

"My key phrase is <u>the courage to create and defend ideas</u>."

The Rider-Waite Knight leans forward on his galloping gray steed. The Knight's overgarment and the horse's breast collar are decorated with birds, symbolizing both the ride toward wisdom and "flightiness." The horse's collar also bears the butterflies of transformation soon to appear on the thrones of the Queen and King and in the Queen's crown.

The Morgan-Greer Knight, dressed for battle, stands near a burning tower. He wears a studded brown helmet with a light yellow plume, representing the opening of his crown chakra.

In the Aquarian card, the Knight wears a helmet decorated with a quail (the soul) and holds a sword bearing the arched pattern of the power of decision. It is available for decisive action should he need it. His decision-making power increases in strength while the Knight progresses in his training and develops maturity, as symbolized by the increasing prominence and intricacy of the design on the Queen's and King's swords.

The Knight of Swords uses daring and quickness of mind to overcome obstacles and serve righteous causes. In a sense, he represents all the knights of romantic chivalry with their admirable intentions and love of the chase, for which they were so well equipped.

The Knight of Swords can be domineering, pushing his way as the only right one. When it comes time to evaluate the results of his actions, he's apt to have moved on to his next adventure already or be "possessed" by his next idea. He cannot bear being intellectually stagnant and needs constant mental stimuli.

The Knight of Swords "knows" his cause is just because his intentions are based on reason and desire to be of service. Are yours? This card can signal a need to evaluate your underlying motives.

The shadow side of the Knight of Swords includes: recklessly imposing our ideas or actions on others; waiting for others to take the initiative or to set goals for us; being inhibited in action or thought; being unwilling to defend our position; and giving in to others.

When you have this card in your layout:

- You may be acting too impulsively and need to reign yourself in or moving too conservatively and need to add a little gallop to your life.

- Evaluate what would happen if you slowed down and took more time to think about your situation.

- Examine your attraction to the thrill of the chase or your need for excitement. Is there something you're afraid to face? Something you're avoiding by keeping busy or moving on?

- Consider who taught you, or where you learned, about commitment and whether those ideas still hold true.

QUEEN OF SWORDS

"I bring you the fruits of my experiences with the inevitable losses and separation that come with life. Why wallow in self-pity? Use your intelligence to understand emotional situations and you'll transform sorrow into wisdom.

"My sword of logic and reason cuts through the confusion and doubt that arise from misfortunes and seeming failures. I rally inner strength so you can carry on courageously, even with life's inevitable limitations. I embrace challenges with vigor and willingness, transmuting fear into focused energy.

"To some it looks as if I have a natural ability to get things done, but in fact, this is a skill I developed through past activities. I have learned to align my strong will with higher principles, so that I work with assurance. I apply reason to all aspects of life and strive for harmony in all types of relationships. I foster tolerance and generosity of the heart.

"My key phrase is the queen of perception."

The Rider-Waite Queen sits facing right. Her gray stone throne is fashioned with sweeping curved lines and decorated with butterflies and a cherub. It sits on high ground. A lone bird, symbolizing her divine connection, flies in the blue sky above. Under her butterfly-patterned gold crown, the Queen wears a red cap of maintenance. She extends her left hand out, palm up, to receive higher energy. Her head and shoulders remain above the clouds in the clear air of truth.

Large red roses bloom around the Morgan-Greer Queen of Swords, and a stylized rose with a gold jewel in the middle is centered over her heart chakra. It represents the Queen's higher self (central jewel) aligned with the truth of higher reality, which is the ultimate purpose of a secret society, such as the ancient Fraternity of the Rosy Cross.

The Queen's green gown and her golden, leaf-shaped crown link her intimately to the natural growth surrounding her. She looks ahead, focused on her own intentions. Yet she is vulnerable, as indicated by her open collar. The tiny jewel over her throat chakra allows her to speak with "pearls of wisdom."

The Aquarian Queen is dressed in pink, with a decorative accent at her throat chakra. She can express her wisdom. Her long, auburn hair flows along both sides of the card. On her right, it stops at the greatly enlarged (and therefore active) symbols of the divine feminine principle. The hilt of her sword is hidden in a cluster of five red roses representing the senses. She uses the sword to integrate ideas and passion (roses). Its blade bears a more elaborate version of the power-of-decision pattern found on the Knight's sword.

The Queen of Swords represents a mature, logical outlook. Like the young Knight, she enjoys playing with ideas, but in her we see fully developed intellectual skills. She is quick-witted and intense. Having dealt with loss and loneliness, she is able to go ahead with plans for the future in a disciplined manner.

She is capable, a hard worker, and aware of her personal powers. Forthright in her approach, she also can bring mental subtleties to a situation. Her decisions will be well thought out and compassionate.

The Queen of Swords knows who she is and where she is going. She will work tirelessly for "right" causes. She has a quick grasp of problems, finds logical ways to solve them, and can work independently without misgivings. Overall, this card represents inner development achieved by handling emotional distress with logic and courage.

The shadow side of the Queen of Swords includes: being so caught up in the emotionality of a situation that we fail to balance it with rationality; intolerance of others' ideas; rigidity in our viewpoint; being ultracritical; and being self-righteous.

When you get this card:

- Use your intellectual and communicative abilities. Make an objective assessment of the situation and consider alternatives.

- Reevaluate your ideals to determine if you are enmeshed in ones that no longer apply to your situation. What kind of trouble do they cause you?

- Ask yourself how your expectations of yourself and of others may prevent you from changing your situation or acting spontaneously.

- Evaluate your current position. Is it really based on high ideals? Or are you opposing someone else's position to protect and defend yourself against feeling too vulnerable?

KING OF SWORDS

"I represent mental and intellectual authority, and I know it. I stand for law and order. I am disciplined in my behavior and expect others to be, as well. Because my judgment is sound, I am comfortable asserting my will and helping others with their problems. I am widely known as a seasoned advisor.

"My confidence comes from experience in analyzing situations and then taking action. I know my abilities are superior, so I expect others to follow my lead. They should realize I would not take needless risks. My very presence inspires others to develop their own strategic abilities.

"Some have called me crafty. Others have called me unfeeling and lacking in compassion. But all my decisions and actions stem from high standards. I always act with integrity.

"My key phrase is <u>intellectual leadership</u>."

The Rider-Waite King of Swords sits on an armless gray throne, the back of which is embellished with nude figures and symbols of transformation, such as crescent moons and butterflies. His golden crown, decorated with a cherub, represents mental energy in the service of the Spirit. Like his Queen, he sits on high ground. Two birds fly in the higher realms of divine wisdom, giving him the choice of thought or action.

The Morgan-Greer King of Swords faces left. He holds an upright sword and three stalks of wheat symbolizing creativity. Oak leaves bearing acorns and berried laurel clusters seem to float around him. His is the sword of justice linked with the ability to bring ideas into material manifestation.

Also shown in profile, the Aquarian King holds a sword bearing the strong black pattern of decision-making power. Over a gray cap of maintenance studded with buttons, he wears a brown helmet-crown, studded with a jewel over the ajna chakra. His pink shield bears his insignia crown above the pattern of personality-shaping ideas seen earlier on the sleeves of the Ten and the Knight. His sword and the large gray-green plume on his helmet both extend off the card and into spiritual realms.

The King of Swords symbolizes the power of authority earned through disciplined mental effort. He represents shrewdness in the service of common good. His manner is cautious but commanding, and sometimes like a military dictator's.

In personal relationships he takes patriarchal values for granted. Forthright, aggressive, and determined to maintain his position of strength, the King of Swords acts on high principles and for what he believes is the good of all concerned. Those under his influence may view him as domineering, though.

Shadow aspects of this card include: cruel or bullying behavior; corrupted authority; using intellect for personal aggrandizement or dominance of others; ruthlessness in our quest for power; pride; arrogance; and lack of compassion.

When you draw this card:

- Consider the role your judgmental or tyrannical attitude plays in shaping the situation.

- Don't allow others to push you into a decision. Take all the time you need to think through your situation.

- Determine whether or not you are being too stern or adamant about the situation or your role in it. Or, conversely, do you need to exert your willfulness more?

- Your situation might benefit from some organizing and the application of strict rules or limits.

12 ☀ Cups: Feeling Your Way

After the material grounding portrayed in the Pentacles and the logic expressed by the Swords, we move on to the Cups, the emotional pathway. Members of the Cups family are ardent, sensitive, and known for their strong feelings.

Cups emanate enthusiasm, passion, and conviction. Yet they can be perceived as irresponsible, unrealistic, or lacking discipline, especially when they use one of their favorite phrases, "I just feel like doing it."

Cups shed light on the emotional side of our questions. They speak of emotional responses to situations, some positive, some negative, and many with little basis in external reality.

In the Golden Dawn tradition, the suit of Cups represents the second letter of the Tetragrammaton, Heh, the creative world, the realm of pure idea. They are associated with the spiritual element of water,[1] and with Jung's feeling function.

Cups offer valuable insight for learning to trust and respond to feelings without being ruled by them. They teach us to connect outer awareness to inner awareness, and take action based on that integrated perspective.

The themes and lessons of this suit are expressed in and through relationships, with the feelings that arise in those relationships helping us to achieve a better inner relationship with ourselves. The cards in this suit mirror our struggles and successes with emotional fulfillment. All the Rider-Waite court cards have water in the background, which refers to emotions and especially to the rise of emotion from the unconscious.

Numbered Cards

Ace of Cups

"*I bring you a change of direction and new beginnings. This is a gift from the universe. I am blessed to be the carrier.*

"*I bring the capacity to love and the gift of Divine Love. I offer the opportunity for feelings of self-fulfillment in any area of your life. I am the stimulus for soul development through relationships. I inspire you to reach a new level of emotional contact.*

"*My dilemma, and one that will soon become yours as well, is that the gift of emotional expression encompasses all feelings, including rage, fear, and resentment. The good news is that learning to recognize and acknowledge those emotions paves the way for you to learn to control them rather than being at their mercy.*

"*You can adopt new ways to accept and shape the resources that surround you differently. With my encouragement, you will even learn to refine raw feelings until they express exactly what you want to say, until they form the inner poetry of your soul.*

"*My key phrase is* the power of emotions.*"*

In the Rider-Waite card, a radiant white hand emerging from the gray cloud of the Divine holds a golden chalice. Five streams of water representing the senses spout up from the cup[2] and flow down to a lake below on which water lilies of purity float. Blue droplets in the shape of Yods (divine energy) also fall into the lake. Water is the element of this suit as well as a symbol of the collective unconscious. Directly above the cup, a dove signifying Spirit holds a Communion wafer bearing the "cross potent," ancient symbol of sun gods.

The flesh-toned hand in the Morgan-Greer Ace also grasps a golden cup overflowing with five streams of water. In the foreground one eight-petaled pink lotus of cosmic harmony is in full bloom. To its left is a bud standing for potential, and to its right a seed pod of fulfillment. The pale blue dove with wings extended to illustrate exalted spirituality hovers behind a glowing ball of energy in the center of the cup.

The Aquarian card is dominated by a large russet chalice decorated with the triangular pattern of Trinity interspersed with the V-weave pattern that represents personality-shaping ideas. The Divine Sun emanates from the cup. The card suggests that, in this suit, emotional experiences brought about by the higher self will be interacting with the persona for spiritual development.

The Ace of Cups's message is this: Emotions can facilitate the expression of spiritual ideals in our daily activities. If we need to understand and deal with a problem, this Ace stimulates the unconscious to bring forth new approaches from the Spirit, rather than the ego. It tells us we have the potential for unbounded joy when we lovingly attend to the physical, mental, and spiritual aspects of life. It encourages us to look for new forms of artistic expression and to use our imagination to see things in a "new light."

This card signals the onset of an intense period of inner growth. All Cups embody the feminine element of receptivity, and the Ace opens our eyes to new teachings and our minds to new ways to apply what we learn.

Shadow aspects of this card include: failing to realize the bounties that life offers; not recognizing that we are part of a greater universe; and getting caught up in the importance of our own being.

When you draw this card:

- Open your eyes and your heart to the beauty and bountifulness of your situation.

- Look for ways to express your abilities with more feeling.

- Expect a new cycle of self-love and appreciation. It will enable you to work with confidence and empower others with whom you interact.

- Work to acknowledge and accept *all* the emotions you experience in relationship to yourself and others. This can be a struggle.

TWO OF CUPS

"*I demonstrate the healing and nourishing power of cooperative and constructive unions. I represent the joining of abilities to produce something greater than one alone could create.*

"*I urge you to appreciate rather than compete with others. Respect the masculine and feminine strengths each of you contribute to a relationship.*

"*In your daily activities, partnerships and relationships offer advantages and opportunities to better understand the human situation. Be aware of them and discover a variety of ways to interact.*

"*When I am active in your life, you have the capacity to express compassion for others and to understand their feelings. However, you must guard against one of the difficulties that comes along with empathy—the desire to 'fix' others' hurts, partly to lessen our own discomfort with their situation. It's a constant dilemma and challenge.*

"*My key phrase is* <u>the two sides of emotionality.</u>"

The Rider-Waite card shows a young man and woman pledging their troth. Between and above their cups, the caduceus of the Greek god Hermes, a symbol of the healing power of relationships, rises toward a winged (spirit) red (passion) lion's (sexuality) head. In the distance, green undulating fields surround a red-roofed house, possibly their future home.

The man, whose yellow clothes show that he represents actions and logic, leans toward the woman and reaches out with his right hand to touch her golden goblet. She represents emotion (blue clothes), sensitivity, and compassionate understanding (red shoes).

In the Morgan-Greer card, a young woman and man raise their golden goblets to each other as they gaze into each other's eyes. She wears a green wreath, while her companion wears a red headband over his ajna chakra. His green cloak is fastened at the throat chakra with a gold clasp, showing the value of his spoken word. Behind them patches of indigo foliage rise against a pale yellow sky, their shapes suggesting the promise and fertility of dreams and imagination.

The man and woman in the Aquarian Two of Cups also raise their goblets to one another. His glove bears the bubbly design of the feminine aspect of the Divine. They both wear pink headgear that crosses and activates the ajna center. His cloak is clasped at the throat chakra. She could be pregnant.

Japikse says the pale, almost invisible, yellow outline on the inside border of the card suggests that pledges can only be made to our higher self, not to others.[3] To violate that inner pledge is to violate an aspect of our soul.

The Two of Cups is a card of relationships and partnerships of many kinds. It often represents long-term friendships based on mutual ideals and principles. It echoes The Lovers (Major Arcana VI), bringing the creative power of love to bear on everyday events. At a higher level, it urges us to acknowledge our inner masculine or feminine aspects. This opens a channel for our higher self to express itself more actively and fully.

The personal growth instigated by this card comes from identifying opposing emotions without trying to diminish one or the other of them. Both are a part of us and serve us in some way. Likewise, spiritual growth results from accepting both our separateness and our integration with the Great Oneness.

Shadow aspects of this card include: the inability to commit to a situation, romantic or otherwise; stubbornness that prevents us from making the first move toward resolution; possessiveness in a relationship; and denial of both feminine and masculine aspects of our personality.

When this card appears:

- Take time to reevaluate the benefits of your commitments to others.

- Consider that ideas you once opposed could now have some merit or even offer an appropriate solution for your situation.

- Expand your perspective to include an understanding of another person's viewpoint. Although you still may not agree, taking the time to see things through someone else's eyes will enrich your inner life.

- Begin the process of identifying opposing dimensions of your personality and how they manifest in your relationships.

THREE OF CUPS

"I am the ritual of celebration. I remind you of things that have worked out well and life's problems that have been solved by joining forces with family and friends.

"Take time now to recognize your accomplishments and honor the people who have helped along the way. Cherish your associations. Good results are seldom achieved alone.

"Psychologically you are becoming more aware of your emotions, including some opposing ones. That's certainly a victory of sorts. Bask in its glow while you can, because there's more work to be done.

"My energy allows you to take a break and enjoy yourself for a while. You'll need to guard against the desire to play, play, play all the time, though. I'm tempting that way.

"My key phrase is <u>the abundance of the Self.</u>"

In the Rider-Waite card, three young women raise their cups, most likely as a toast to their friendship and mutual support. They wear the colors of the three basic alchemical elements—blue for salt, yellow for mercury, and red for sulfur—needed to begin "the Work" of change or individuation.

On the Morgan-Greer card, three women gaze outward. The central woman wears a band of flowers over her ajna center, signifying natural wisdom. The woman on the left wears a garland of blossoms, which represents the blossoming of our inner nature or wisdom. And the woman on the right wears a wreath of leaves and berries associated with the fruiting of the Spirit when we acknowledge the Divine in our nature. They stand together in the same triangular pattern as the cups are placed in this card and the Rider-Waite card, suggesting the acknowledgment of the Trinity in nature and in ourselves. Emotional growth fosters spiritual growth, this card implies. Together they represent the balance required between higher wisdom, sensuality, emotions, and self-confidence that is necessary to bring conscious and unconscious knowledge together in action.

The three women in the Aquarian card hold orange cups, the center one bearing the interwoven pattern of personality-shaping forces. The woman on the left has a pendant over her throat chakra. The center woman's face and body are partially concealed by the goblets and bodies of the other two. The third woman, her back to us, wears a blue-gray shawl that displays the pattern of aspiration and decision making. She wears a red headband of spiritual wholeness over her ajna center. An enormous yellow flower located behind the women suggests immense spiritual potential and the presence of divine influence.

The Three of Cups represents the observance of a happy but temporary conclusion to a dilemma. It signals a time for shared merriment and celebration. Make room in your life for joy, is this card's message. The work of inner growth does not always have to be serious. Laughter has great healing power.

The three figures are linked to the mythological concept of the triple goddess. They are representative of the three aspects of femininity (maiden, mother, crone), who, personified, dance around the cauldron of life, the sacred vessel of transformation. The oldest depiction of these is the Norse Norns, who established the cosmic order and guarded Yggdrasil, the world tree.

On the surface, the Three of Cups looks like a simple and carefree card, yet it is actually a very spiritual one as indicated by the position of the cups as well as the locations of flowers and jewels over the ajna, crown, and throat chakras. It is a signal that emotional and spiritual change has begun in our lives, or needs to. True celebration comes with the awareness of the Trinity that resides within us and makes it possible for us to access our higher nature.

The shadow aspect of the Three of Cups includes: failing to honor the contributions of others to our good fortune; overindulgence; placing too much emphasis on comfort or success; feeling jealous of the success of another; and failing to acknowledge our inner nature.

When this card appears:

- Let others know of your successes; and rejoice in theirs, too.
- Don't spread yourself too thin. Conserve some energy for finishing projects and enjoying the tasks you have undertaken.

- Lighten up. Don't be so serious about your situation, and you may get a new perspective.

- Reevaluate the role spirituality has (or hasn't) played in your life.

FOUR OF CUPS

"I'm not ready to make up my mind. Frankly, I don't know whether I want to do <u>anything</u>. I've had to put up with some unhappy experiences in the past, so now I'm going to take some time off, even if it means ignoring opportunities.

"I'm not sure how I feel about the future. It seems sometimes as if there's something missing in my life. I don't know if it's a higher purpose, but I do know I have to find my own way. I wish I could just do, feel, and believe the way others seem to, but I can't. It just isn't me. Maybe if I sit here and listen to my inner feelings, I'll figure out what I want or need. Once I get settled, though, it's tempting to simply sit forever and never do another thing.

"The trick is to know when to wait and when to move. That's why my key phrase is <u>finding the balance between action and inaction</u>."

In the Rider-Waite card, a young man sits crossed-legged under a tree. He looks at three cups lined up before him, and appears to be ignoring a fourth, which is offered to him by a hand emerging from a small puffy cloud to his right. He wears a long green vest indicating growth over a red shirt of passionate action and protectively folds his arms across his chest.

In the Morgan-Greer card, a youth peers out from vines at a hand holding a cup. He looks beyond three cups set in lush greenery. The figure is reminiscent of the medieval Green Man, the masculine aspect of Mother Earth and fertility. This card suggests the abundance and growth that can occur when emotions are acknowledged.

In the Aquarian card, a youth faces three brown cups decorated in the V-weave pattern of personality-shaping ideas. Their oddly stacked arrangement on the left side of the card suggests a piling up of feelings from past experiences. In the lower right side of the card (the future), the feminine aspect of the Divine begins to appear, but the young man is turned away from it at this time in his life. A yellow-gloved hand, clasping a small fourth cup, descends from an orange cloud in the upper left-hand corner of the card. Will the boy accept more personality-shaping ideas from the culture and others, or will he turn toward the future and begin to develop the inner feminine aspects of his character?

The Four of Cups represents dissatisfaction with what is presently occurring in our lives, and uncertainty about how to make a change for the better. Whatever is in the offing does not appear to be the answer, although it may be tempting. ''Is it really the solution?'' we wonder. More emotional awareness seems like the last thing we need.

This is a stalemate or impasse card, a time out. We're not yet ready to make a decision. Of course, the time can be used to discover our intentions.

If we want to act from our hearts and not just meet the expectations of others, we may need to withdraw for a while and tap into our inner wisdom. However, knowledge doesn't come from introspection alone. Perhaps you're familiar with the Zen idea that the path to enlightenment is found in the everyday activities of chopping wood and carrying water. Well, action also leads to personal and spiritual development. Thinking and doing—this card challenges us to balance the two.

The shadow side of this card includes: letting apathy and withdrawal become a way of life; failing to make our wishes known; allowing others to speak for us; having difficulty taking action because we're afraid to fail; resenting help or input from others; and blindly doing what's expected of us even when it's not what we really want to do.

When the Four of Cups is drawn:

- Make an honest assessment of where you stand and why you are keeping yourself from joining in with others in your life.

- Don't wait for someone else to provide solutions. Listen to your higher self for guidance.

- Accept and enjoy the "cups" of emotional strength you have, even if you decide not to accept the helping hand or new opportunity that's offered to you.

- Look for the "higher purpose" in your next task or relationship, and you'll make life an everyday experience of the Spirit.

FIVE OF CUPS

"I'm so disappointed. My feelings were just not reciprocated, and I feel as if I've lost my chance for happiness. I guess I should try to salvage what I can, but I don't think I'm ready yet.

"No one knows better than I that we all need a period of grieving after loss. We can wallow in grief and self-pity, which I sometimes think feels rather good, or we can use the time for emotional cleansing and letting go of unrealistic expectations. Like all my siblings in this suit, I represent both possibilities. I warn against doing too much or too little grieving over losses and disappointments.

"Look to those cups still standing. Take stock of your present alternatives. When you experience a sense of lost opportunity, revise your goals and priorities. Search within for your own values and follow their lead. Remember you still have two cups left.

"My key phrase is <u>facing your fear of disappointment.</u>"

In the Rider-Waite card, a figure of indeterminate sex wearing the long, black cloak of ignorance looks down at three fallen cups and disregards the two standing cups that remain. Beyond, a blue river of time, life, or our psyches flows under a white bridge.

In the Morgan-Greer card, the person focuses on three cups spilling wine, oblivious to the two goblets sitting on a rock in the right foreground.

The Aquarian figure turns away from the two orange cups in the lower right corner, focusing instead on the three overturned ones. The ground is edged with black reeds, apparently blowing in the wind of the unconscious. Their presence implies that unseen water lies beyond them. Birds (divine messengers) circle in the gray-white sky.

Like all fives, the Five of Cups represents an upset, in this case an emotional one. How will we handle it? Fives test us, sometimes bringing out the worst in us, but also helping us activate the previously untapped strength and resolve found in the two standing cups.

This card reflects grief related to real or perceived losses, including old wounds that continue to affect our present relationships. Regret for things we "might have done" is prominent, possibly accompanied by a feeling of hopelessness because we can never recapture the chance or redo a wrong. Our despair temporarily prevents us from realizing what we *can* do now.

We need to recognize that what seem to be failures in life often offer necessary learning opportunities. Dwelling too much on the past prevents us from seeing the greater picture. We need to analyze our mistakes, determine what of value remains, and let the rest go. Identify overlooked opportunities and begin anew, this card advises. Turn your back on worry and look to the standing cups for inspiration.

Although this appears on the surface to be a card of regret and discouragement, fives bring the opportunity for a change of attitude. In the Rider-Waite and Morgan-Greer cards, there is a home or haven (the castle) in the future. The Rider-Waite card implies that the water of life flows on and that in the future (right side of the card) this time in your life will be regarded as "water under the bridge." Our figure will draw from the standing cups, cross the bridge of transition, and turn the experience of loss or grief into something useful for inner growth.

The shadow aspect of this card includes: indulging in regrets rather than getting on with life; waiting for wrongs to be righted by others; maintaining the posture of a victim; and failing to learn from our experiences or acknowledge what is left after a loss.

When the Five of Cups appears:

- Take stock of how past disappointments affect your approach to current problems. What can they teach you, and how can you apply what you learn to your present situation?

- Look around for new avenues of self-expression and joy.

- Identify the attitudes—especially long-standing negative ones—

that keep you from getting on with your life or stop you from trying things you have long wanted to do.

• Set things right in your world. Make your apologies to others and to yourself. Put aside old regrets. If living with them has been habitual for you, expect to feel some temporary loss.

SIX OF CUPS

"I am the feelings of abundance and satisfaction that come after hard work. I am pleased with my efforts to make my dreams come true, and want to share my success with others. I also want them to enjoy my sense of fulfillment. Having finished my grieving, I am once again ready to bloom with joy and confidence.

"Lately I've been remembering experiences from my past. I'm beginning to understand how they have shaped my character. Some are satisfying simply to remember. Others have new meaning for me now that I'm an adult whose perspective is tempered by the experiences of intervening years.

"I encourage you to think about how much you *may still operate under influences of the past. Accept your experiences as stepping-stones toward acquiring new insights and wisdom. Take time to smell the flowers and attend to the needs of your inner child.*

"My key phrase is using memories and feelings creatively.*"*

In the Rider-Waite card, a boy and girl stand amid golden cups filled with star-shaped flowers and greenery signifying abundance.

The Morgan-Greer boy and girl look at each other over goblets overflowing with large white lilies and greenery. In both of these decks, the boy offers the girl a cup filled with flowers.

The Aquarian children wear orange cloaks that merge with the color of the shelf, where pots filled with various flowers and greenery sit.

The Six of Cups speaks of wholeness following introspective work. It represents our link to the past and tendency to idealize it, remembering only the good parts. This card also addresses how creativity blooms when we acknowledge our inner child.

In Jungian terms, sixes represent the union of inner masculine and feminine attributes. The card represents a temporary resolution to the tension of opposites. Since it is only the six of the suit, however, there is more emotional work ahead.

Review the past to see if it still has relevance, this card advises. Attend to whatever unfinished business may be holding you back. Don't let nostalgia divert your energy from the tasks at hand.

Rachel Pollock sees the Rider-Waite scene as a dwarf giving the gift of memories to the future, the child.[4] In mythical and fairy-tale symbology, dwarfs stand for aspects of ourselves that we've never fully developed or personifications of creative impulses or energy.

The Egyptian dwarf god Bes protected people from the dangers of the unknown and was the protector of roads, byways, and transitions—often signified by the symbol X, or the cross of St. Andrew, which is carved on the pillar in the Rider-Waite card. It represents a crossroads, decisions needing to be made, and the union of opposites in Jungian terms.[5] Its prominence on the card suggests that change has occurred or is on the threshold.

Another meaning of the St. Andrew's cross is the union of the upper and lower worlds.[6] Mythologically this links the card to the goddess Hecate, who descended into the underworld to rescue her daughter Persephone, and to the death/rebirth motif.

This card also deals with the innocence and joy needed to integrate love of the world and love of the Divine. This usually involves major growth work and soul-searching, and results in a definite change of attitude. So while the card celebrates one level of fulfillment, it also shows that an inner creative struggle is about to begin.

We are about to make a decision that will take us to a new level of emotional understanding and development, represented by the Page strolling toward the East in the Rider-Waite card. Certainly a time of trial and initiation is at hand, as we are about to see in the Seven of Cups.

The shadow side of the Six of Cups includes: a fixation on former triumphs; fear of taking on new challenges; stubbornly clinging to old ideas; refusing to change our ways; and hoping our dreams will come true without effort on our part.

When this card shows:

- You may need to revisit the memories of childhood, and, perhaps with the help of a therapist, determine how they shaped your personality. Then leave the garden of childhood and grow up.

- Welcome new activities and areas of expression, especially ones that nurture your inner child.

- Pinpoint your one-sided, black-and-white attitudes and consider the consequences of enlarging your viewpoint. Can you handle it?

- Evaluate how you express or withhold love and make an effort to be more loving, especially in service to your community or humanity.

SEVEN OF CUPS

"I'm here to remind you that you can have it all. You don't have to settle for anything yet, because there's so much abundance to choose from.

"I encourage you to look beneath the surface glitter of the riches you feel you must have. Do they really suit you? Is that object obtainable? Is that relationship one you want to live with? Is the house, vacation, or corner office you yearn for someone else's image of success? Line up your options in front of you as I have done and take a careful look.

"You can learn more about yourself in this same manner. If you look a little deeper, you'll see that my cups contain elements of your

being that need to be acknowledged, examined, and dealt with or honored. You'll find hopes and fears, shadow aspects, and plenty of surprises. Sometimes I'm surprised myself when I see all that has gone into the formation of my personality.

"My key phrase is <u>getting to know me</u>."

In the Rider-Waite Seven of Cups, a man, symbolically in the shadows, faces seven golden cups floating on gray clouds. Various fantasy objects bubble out from them. A blue, smiling woman's head represents sexuality; a cloaked angel, spirituality; a yellow snake, energy or wisdom; a blue castle, adventure. Brightly colored jewels promise wealth, and a green victory wreath, success—although the skull design on its cup indicates that success is short-lived. A blue dragon symbolizes untamed emotions. The top three cups form a triangle, reflecting the mind (human head), body (kundalini energy of the snake), and Spirit (the radiating angel), which has yet to be fully recognized, as the covering over the angel signifies. The bottom four cups hold items associated with the material plane.

The bronze cups in the Morgan-Greer card hold similar items except there is a mask (public image) and no angel. The wreath is different as well. Oval and tied with a red ribbon, it isn't a victory wreath like the one on the Rider-Waite card. It is the wreath from The World card, which is a card of inner and outer Spirit, and thus replaces the Rider-Waite radiating angel.

In the Aquarian card, the cups' contents suggest the need for spiritual development (the rod), the personality (diving mask), the ego (head), the development of the Self (mandala-shaped, yellow flower), fruitful transformative experience (fruit/butterfly), healing (snake, the animal form of Asclepias), and spiritual fulfillment (rainbow).

On one level, the Seven of Cups represents wishful thinking and illusion carried to an extreme—an excess of ideas and imagination. In this sense, it is a castles-in-the-air-pie-in-the-sky dreamer's card. So much to choose from, we may postpone decisions and delay actions while simply waiting for our dreams to come true.

When seen in a positive light, this card refers to creativity—the ability to dream up ideas and plans, possibilities and opportunities, for the future. However, the inherent problem remains. We can't seem to focus on one of those ideas or take the next attainable step to make our fantasies come true.

The seven cups have been associated with the ways we indulge ourselves, the things we are addicted to, or reach for when we are frustrated or depressed.[7] They have been compared to "popular fads and fashions," or the glamorous ways the world views success.[8] The card challenges us to resist those influences and make choices based on our deepest feelings instead.

The Seven of Cups offers us the opportunity to explore our fantasies, dreams, hopes, and fears; to acknowledge their place in our lives; to choose those that may be possible in our present situation; and then to bring them into fruition. Remember, sevens offer tests and temptations. They are part of our shadow. We need to recognize, but not get caught up in, them.

Although we have suggested some of the things we think the cups might symbolize, the best way for you personally to work with the card is to ask yourself what ideas or personality traits the contents of each cup bring to mind.

In fairy tales, seven often represents the inner evolutionary process. It is the tension between the sacred number three and the human number four,[9] between the God-Self and the ego. Psychologically the Seven of Cups challenges us to recognize that all the ingredients of the cups are components of our personalities. Can we acknowledge and integrate the aspects of ourselves shown in the cups? Or will we continue to stand outside the picture, believing they all belong to someone else?

One aspect of soul work, says Clarissa Pinkola Estés, is to "recognize treasure as treasure, no matter how unusual its form, and to consider carefully what to do next."[10] The Seven of Cups calls for soul work and the recognition of both our negative (shadow) and positive aspects. Clearly it is a pivotal card in our personal and spiritual development.

The shadow side of the Seven of Cups includes: delusions of grandeur; social isolation; indecision; daydreaming; waiting for fantasies to come true; and refusing to acknowledge all the aspects of your personality, remaining shallow and undeveloped.

When you draw the Seven of Cups:

- Analyze the real problems in your present life. You're ready to confront them.

- Identify the false assumptions you have made about plans for the future. Concentrate on creating a realistic and specific plan. Take stock of your skills and abilities. Then determine how you can best fit them into your plan.

- While you may want to enjoy the immediate pleasures of a new relationship or partnership, avoid getting so caught up in its blissful aspects that you overlook potential problems and other practicalities.

• Make up your mind about something, no matter how minor, today.

EIGHT OF CUPS

"I know it's time for me to make a move. I have been fortunate thus far. I would not change anything of the past, but I feel a need to leave behind conventional things and try something new.

"I express your sense of imbalance and a desire to reestablish harmony in your life. It may be time to change direction, abandon previous plans, or go off on your own. My energy helps you know when to walk away from a situation.

"I represent your search for insight, meaning, and a more authentic way of being. Introspection is needed during this time of transition. Withdrawal may facilitate it. So let us embark on a path of our own making and seek the higher wisdom required at this stage of our lives.

"My key phrase is <u>taking time for me</u>."

In the Rider-Waite card, a man with a staff walks away from eight cups of past contentment. A mountain of abstract principles and higher truths looms large. A full-faced moon, which is partially eclipsing the sun, suggesting a period of inner awareness, oversees his progress.

In the Morgan-Greer card, a figure wearing a red cloak with a hood, representing concealed thoughts, strides into the canyon of the Self.

The Aquarian figure, like all the others, heads toward the right (future destiny). His tan cape spreads to form a wide train on which his eight cups are arranged. It will be quite a challenge or sacrifice to leave them behind and continue his journey. The issue is whether or not he has incorporated Spirit into his personality, in which case he will experience no loss.[11]

The Eight of Cups symbolizes a conscious detachment for the purpose of exploring our inner state. We may have to abandon present plans for a short period of time, or forever, in order to make progress of a different kind. We'll find greater fulfillment if we break with things that have lost their relevance for us, this card implies. It urges us to turn inward for evaluation, healing, meditation, and any other work we must do to restore our inner equilibrium.

Continue exploring what is real for you, the Eight of Cups advises. Be open to new concepts and practices. Read, or reread, philosophy books or the works of inspirational writers. Become your own teacher.

In the Rider-Waite and Morgan-Greer cards, the cups are stacked to form a group of three and a group of five in order to recognize the inner Trinity and the outer world of the five senses. They suggest that the figure is going away in order to integrate the two. However, their equal placement may also signify that the person already has the answer—he is already imbibed with Spirit—but doesn't yet realize it. In the Zen tradition, he will follow a path to find himself only to come full circle and return to where he started.

The shadow side of the Eight of Cups includes: failing to allow time for study and introspection; lack of awareness of others' needs; emotional withdrawal; filling others' needs to a point of being overwhelmed or drained; and overindulgence in whatever we feel passionate about (sex, drugs, work?).

When this card appears:

- Become aware of what it is you want to leave or to *avoid*.

- Consider how your past attitudes and actions have brought you to your present situation. Can you allow yourself the soul-searching necessary to make new plans?

- Identify any regrets or feelings of loss you may have and consider how you can live your life differently from this point on.

- Look for ways to incorporate spiritual exercise into your daily life. Make every day more sacred through meditation, focused activity, study, prayer, or any other action that strengthens your inner life.

NINE OF CUPS

"I have overcome difficulties and reached a stage of satisfaction, if not total fulfillment. 'But is this all there is?' I sometimes wonder. Is the ability to sit here smug and self-satisfied what I've worked so hard to get? I certainly thought it was while I was struggling.

"Some people tell me that I'm afraid to turn around and actually see what's in my cups; that I use my feelings of success to avoid delving any deeper into my personal and emotional development. Maybe that's so.

"Then again, I could be turning away from the material world so that I can begin to seek spiritual enlightenment and wisdom. I'm not totally prepared to do that, though. I think I'll just sit here a little longer and see what comes along.

"My key phrase is <u>enjoying the good life</u>."

The Rider-Waite card shows a man who has feasted to satiety.[12] He sits in front of an arch-shaped counter, on which the nine cups, signifying abundance, are displayed like trophies. Although his arms, crossed over his heart chakra, close it off, his red hat suggests that his crown chakra is open. Apparently he has access to higher wisdom, but is too involved with his pleasures to open his heart and do the emotional work. This could change, since he cannot ignore the open crown chakra for long.

In the Morgan-Greer card, the man is ruddy faced and smiling. We see only his upper body, emphasizing the need for heart or soul development over the taste for sensual pleasures he has already developed.

The bearded man in the Aquarian Nine of Cups wears a shirt that displays the interwoven design of personality-shaping ideas. A red ornament fastens his shirt at his throat chakra. The white inverted V-shaped area behind him is edged in orange, which shows that he is aspiring toward the spiritual. Behind it, nine cups sit stacked on four shelves.

The Nine of Cups speaks of enjoying the fruits of our labor. It suggests physical and emotional satisfaction, as well as a measure of victory over the material challenges in life. We have reached a point when we have much to offer and share with others. We feel secure psychologically as well as materially.

Still, we can't expect to sit there on that bench indefinitely. The semiarchway shape of the counter symbolizes a starting point for inner growth. There is life behind that curtain, and it calls to us.

With The Hermit and The Moon as the Nine's overseeing Major Arcana cards, the "fat and sassy" Nine can't be completely shallow. He probably has done *some* inner work already and realizes there is more to do. He's merely taking a break before being nudged forward again to face the next stage in his development.

The shadow side of this card includes: feeling so self-sufficient that we isolate ourselves from others; failure to give credit to those who assisted us; lust; greed; laziness; aimlessness; and overindulgence.

When this card appears:

- Evaluate your motives and expectations. Consider taking your talents in different directions than you have previously.

- Examine what it has taken for you to arrive at your present situation and prepare for the next cycle with enhanced insight.

- Your sense of security and satisfaction may add some much-needed balance to your life.

- Take stock of what you have and ask yourself how you might use it for more than your own simple enjoyment.

TEN OF CUPS

"I am the kind of happiness most people want to achieve. I represent not only emotional fulfillment, but the potential for physical and spiritual development, as well. Love and wise use of the imagination spawn new commitments to expand my own life and those of others. For me, having good friends and a loving family is paramount.

"As you observe and celebrate your earthly joys, resolve to pay even more attention to the guidance you have been receiving. As you bring more love and harmony into the world, the lives of those who interact with you will change also.

"Find ways to provide inspiration and set examples for those still struggling to find their way. Help them realize that dreams don't just happen. The pot of gold at the end of the rainbow is filled through our labors.

"My key phrase is <u>realization of my desires</u>."

The Rider-Waite card depicts a husband and wife, arms upheld toward ten cups in a radiating rainbow (peace; harmony; God's covenant) arched across the blue sky. Beside them, two children dance together. They wear the orange and blue colors of the divine aspects of masculine and feminine Spirit.

In the Morgan-Greer card, two right arms—one masculine, one feminine—intertwine to hold a single golden cup. The landscape is lush and fertile. Nine additional cups, arranged in a descending line, pass through a brilliant rainbow, which extends off the card into the future.

The Aquarian man and woman face each other and are bordered by the ribbons of the masculine aspect of divinity. From a large central cup, a rainbow flows off toward the future. Like the Morgan-Greer rainbow, it also can be seen as flowing from the divine realm into our earthly cup.

The Ten of Cups symbolizes what much of humanity would like to have: a secure, strongly loving family, material comfort, and the ability to live in harmony with nature and neighbors.

A surge of joy comes with shared happiness, and the Ten of Cups celebrates this and also validates "coming home" to friendships and other havens from worldly strife.

While the Nine of Cups represents the happiness and success of material possessions, the Ten of Cups refers to inner satisfaction from having lived up to our ideals. It can also illustrate the harmonizing of personality goals with those of the higher self. The Morgan-Greer Ten in particular suggests the inner satisfaction that comes from reconciling masculine and feminine aspects of our personalities.

Of the four Tens, none more obviously hints at our potential for greater wisdom than the Ten of Cups. What could more perfectly portray the higher promise of the spiritual path we may reach by attending to our emotions than ten cups floating in a rainbow? Indeed, Iris, the goddess of the rainbow, was the personification of a bridge between heaven and earth. Alchemists considered her the feminine transformative aspect of our basic nature, the *prima materia*. In short, the initiation is about to begin.

The shadow side of the Ten of Cups includes: neglecting to cherish the very real gifts of the heart; ignoring the needs of those close to us; denying that we are all part of the physical and spiritual human family; and getting caught up in unrealistic dreams.

When you draw this card:

- Find a new way to express your gratitude for the love and satisfaction you receive from your relationships with others.

- Consider expanding your horizons, possibly by involving yourself with a larger part of humanity.

- Don't be surprised if you have a new sense of connection with Spirit greater than yourself.

- It may be time to acknowledge the gifts of your heritage.

Court Cards

PAGE OF CUPS

"I thought I knew all about emotional expression and emotional control until I entered this initiation. Now I find that what came before was baby stuff.

"I feel like the fish in my cup, out of my element, and not sure I'll survive. I am working to identify and deal with my emotions. My teachers, the King and Queen, call this differentiation. Alchemists considered it a crucial early stage in the process of turning base materials into gold. Right now I'm not sure they'll ever get any gold out of me! Looking back at how innocently and confidently I began to follow this path, I almost have to laugh.

"Recognizing and understanding emotions is never simple. There are some pretty murky depths to muddle through. I'm certainly not used to the intensity. I didn't even know I <u>had</u> some of those feelings. Sometimes I'm so overwhelmed by them that I feel as if I'm drowning.

"My key phrase is <u>the complexity of emotions.</u>"

In the Rider-Waite card, a youthful courtier standing on the yellow ground of intellectual understanding contemplates the blue fish of unconscious energy and material rising from his cup. The lad wears a blue hat with the ajna center clearly marked and a blue tunic decorated with what are usually identified as white and red tulips.[13] The Page stands in front of rolling blue water (the unconscious).

The Morgan-Greer Page wears a blue hat similar to the one worn by the Rider-Waite Page. It represents the awakening or stimulation of intuition. A blue fish also rises from a golden goblet. Two red tulips coming from below the table represent the rising and flowering of unconscious passion.

The Aquarian Page wears a tan cloak and an orange beret with an elaborate flounce. A red scarf trails from the beret as if it were flowing with passion and aligns with his spine or chakra energies. His head is turned toward the rising fish. Behind him two red tulips grow.

Sometimes the swirling scarf is seen as representing the inability to control the downward energies of spirit that seek to be manifested and suggests that we have mistaken emotional fulfillment and psychic glimpses for "profound" spiritual experiences.[14]

The Page of Cups represents a combination of the "gung ho," somewhat egotistical ("I've made it this far, I must be pretty smart") attitude of a young student and that of a serious person who is loyal and willing to be of service. Either one of these attitudes can rule at any given moment. The Page is trustworthy and sensitive to the needs of others, but his ideas need grounding. He won't be able to carry them out until they're in more realistic terms. Waite describes the card as "pictures of the mind taking form."[15]

Fish, which Jungian analysts equate with unconscious material, can represent the Self, our guiding inner force. The cup and the fish together promise an active phase of transformation—and a fruitful one for those of us who can temper our ideas and fantasies with practical skills and sensibilities. In the Page phases of our own lives, we begin to take emotional risks in terms of revealing who we are or how we feel. And it's pretty scary when we do. We may be facing certain hidden emotions for the first time, and learning how we feel about our feelings as well.

The shadow aspects of this card include: unwillingness to be open to any spiritual ideas or greater truths; lethargy; restlessness; and wanting change, any change, immediately.

When you draw this card:

- Look around. Be open to helpful suggestions and stimulation from many sources: people, inspiring books, visual and audio media.

- If you have been waiting for someone to compliment you or reconcile with you, wait no longer. Take the first step yourself. Give up the waiting game.

- Although you want to express your inner state more frequently, take care with whom you choose to do it.

- Remember this. You are experiencing emotions that everyone experiences, and few of us deal with or express them any easier or more comfortably than you do.

KNIGHT OF CUPS

"I offer my cup to you. It symbolizes my guiding principle. But you should think carefully before accepting it. This is serious work.

"I continue to learn that emotions are not the simple things I originally thought they were. As a Page, I learned to identify and not be overwhelmed by my emotions. Now I am discovering how I express each emotion through my statements and actions. There are levels and layers to them, and contradictory feelings, too. You have to sort them out or, most often, simply acknowledge and live with them.

"I'm here to remind you that to become an explorer Knight and live the emotional life, you'll need to learn what role various emotions play in your life, and how they serve you or others.

"People say I represent strong emotion, love in particular. This path certainly is about love, all right—learning to love all of yourself, which is my key phrase."

In the Rider-Waite card, a Knight, mounted on a gray horse to symbolize the mastering of one's instincts, rides forth, holding out a yellow cup in his right (action) hand. The visor is up on his blue, winged helmet. Over his armor, he wears a tunic decorated with red fish and waves.

The Morgan-Greer Knight also wears a winged helmet with an upraised visor. A linked clasp with a wavelike design holds his cloak around his right shoulder. In the background are blue cliffs denoting successful accomplishment, and closer to him, a prominent yellow one representing challenges, the path.

Two red tulips grow behind the Aquarian Knight. They are in the same location as they were in the Aquarian Page of Cups. This Knight also wears a winged helmet. He does not hold his cup, though, suggesting that he does not yet have a firm grasp on his quest.

The Knight of Cups is dedicated and focused, but at times too single-minded. Riding forth to meet and embrace his destiny, he brings us messages of and opportunities for emotional expression. He has used his strength to improve himself and tries to inspire others to take the same path for their own good.

When you draw this card, you have a strong personal appeal to others, but your intensity may overwhelm them. Sometimes you become too emotionally involved with people or projects and forget to weigh options, or consider alternatives. You need to guard against self-deception, self-inflation, and the sway of others' emotional exhortations.

Mythologically all the Knights in the decks are connected with the "knights of old," especially those of the King Arthur legend (Galahad/Lancelot, Percival) who sought the Holy Grail, symbol of divine knowledge and the growth of the Self. The winged helmet of the Knight of Cups also links him to Mercury/Hermes, messenger of the gods. It associates this Knight with the alchemical concept of *mercurius*—"the 'spirit-substance' that lurks unseen in the core of our psyche"[16]—and psychologically ties him with the unconscious and the Jungian principle of individuation.

This Knight is definitely on a quest for wholeness and knowledge of the archetypal mysteries, but his armor suggests that he may be protecting himself from some of the input he needs. He is still emotionally wounded and seeking answers outside himself. Sometimes his armor protects the world from him. Knights often think they know more than they actually do; however, they *are* willing to take risks and do what's necessary to follow their dreams.

The shadow aspects of the Knight of Cups include: self-absorption and withdrawal from the mainstream to concentrate on emotional and sensual satisfaction; narcissism; acting out our emotions; a need to move from one situation or relationship to another in order to avoid boredom; and desire for power or knowledge—or using power and knowledge—as a means of controlling or manipulating others.

When this card shows up:

- Strive for a balance in your emotional and mental activities.

- Examine your motives for helping other people. Do they really want to be rescued?

- Slow down, get off your high horse, and look at the situation from a different perspective. If you can't do it alone, ask someone for input.

• Identify any feelings, attitudes, wishes and fantasies—possibly carried over from your family of origin—that might need to be resolved or revised in light of your present circumstances.

QUEEN OF CUPS

"I am the soul of this suit. I want to share my thoughts with you, so you can be more aware of your feelings and better understand the emotional path to spirituality.

"At this point in your journey, you can acknowledge and confidently express your own inner state as well as comprehend other people's feelings. You no longer feel uncomfortable or overwhelmed when they express their emotions, and you may even encourage them to do so. Your own inner strength, compassion, and illuminating insight allow you to nurture and draw out the best qualities of others.

"I must caution you, though. Your empathy may convince people that you are the perfect mother whose only concern is for others. Thanks to this perception <u>and</u> your own somewhat dreamy and elusive nature, you may rarely feel free to express your own inner state.

"My key phrase is <u>emotional imagination and understanding.</u>"

The Rider-Waite Queen of Cups sits on a throne decorated with a huge scallop shell and cherubic mermaids. She contemplates a large ornate gold cup decorated with a cross at the top, winged figures on two sides, and a red jewel. The land or sand beneath is covered with multicolored pebbles representing her connection to people and the earth. The water flowing near her feet and merging with her patterned mantle shows that she is in touch with her unconscious. Her blue and white mantle, decorated with waves, is clasped at her throat chakra by a red brooch, pointing out her ability to clearly communicate emotions.

The Morgan-Greer Queen is presented as a "Lady of the Sea." She wears pearl-drop earrings and a crown of pink and rose shells set on a base of pearls. She is positioned against the backdrop of a large scallop shell, which links her with Venus/Aphrodite, goddess of love and passionate experience. Venus was also considered a wise judge and counselor, and is the equivalent of the Egyptian goddesses Hathor and Isis, whose symbol, the crescent moon, is part of the ornament that hangs from the Queen's collar.

The Aquarian Queen appears before a backdrop of red and orange lightning (divine energy). Her cup floats in front of her, a pale pink rose of love resting at its base. Her ajna (crown jewel) and throat (red fringe) centers are open for insightful communication.

The Queen of Cups represents the feminine qualities of emotional integrity, loving nurturance, and wisdom applied in constructive ways. She is the quintessential female authority, one form of the cosmic mother.

Passionate, loyal, and warm, she is supportive to those she believes in. She is emotionally full and a natural authority, in command of herself and able to put her talents into practice, aware of her feelings and unafraid to express them openly—when she gets the chance. Many of the people she encounters would rather unburden themselves to her than hear how she feels.

The Queen's great sensitivity is often expressed in artistic talents. Her appearance in a reading signifies that we have those talents, too, and ought to find ways to express them in our work or in other activities. This card also suggests the potential for deep spirituality. It is a signal to seek ways to express divine love in our own lives.

The shadow traits of the Queen of Cups include: becoming so immersed in our own introspective thoughts that we neglect others around us; jealousy; unfaithfulness; scorn; moodiness; obstinacy; and unattainably high ideals.

When you draw this card:

- Determine how strongly your feelings may be influencing those around you and your situation/issue.

- Share insights and ideas with those who request them or, in some cases, those you think can profit from hearing them.

- You can begin some shadow work, if you desire. Although you may have caught a glimpse of this work previously, you are now developmentally ready to undertake it.

- Trust your feelings and allow them to guide you in creating what you've been dreaming about.

KING OF CUPS

"I am the active spirit of this suit. Some think I'm merely fortunate to be in this position of authority. The truth is that I have studied and worked hard to gain mastery of emotional energies and use them wisely.

"Like me, you have developed into a person of many talents and great insight into others. You have the skills to understand other people's feelings and to express your own articulately. Professions in which you advise or teach others are perfect for you. Watch out for your tendency to assume the imperious attitude of a king, though. Don't hold yourself aloof.

"Expect to be a leader. You have the experience to offer sound advice to others. Be considerate when dealing with others. You already know your power and have no need to reduce theirs, even though they may regard themselves in competition with you.

"My key phrase is <u>highest emotional responsibility</u>."

The Rider-Waite King's throne of gray (wisdom) stone (security) floats on rolling waves. In his left (feminine) hand he holds a short, gold scepter, symbolizing masculine authority.

It bears a stylized lotus design that is duplicated below on his throne and again in his crown. This is generally considered a feminine symbol and shows that the King is aware of his feminine aspects and not afraid of his emotions. Mythologically it links him with the Egyptian queen goddess Isis, with the concept of the watery origin of the world, and with the pillars in Solomon's Temple (see The High Priestess, Major Arcana II). The lotus can also stand for the four elements[17] (earth, air, fire, water) as well, which suggests that the King is in control of those four life processes and has access to the four characteristics of God.

The King also holds a gold cup (feminine) in his right (masculine) hand. Clearly this is a card of masterful balance. The King of Cups combines the wisdom of the feminine and the masculine. An ornamental fish pendant hangs over his heart chakra. In the background, a red ship rides the waves, and a blue fish, possibly a dolphin, leaps from the water.

The Morgan-Greer King wears a blue robe—signifying communication abilities—beneath a yellow cloak of intellectual understanding trimmed in red to show the passion of his convictions. His cap of maintenance and matching cowl resemble fish scales, and his crown is comprised of serpentlike coils.

Over a white cap of maintenance, the Aquarian King wears a purple crown studded with buttons, indicating an active crown chakra. On his breast, at the heart chakra, is a translucent amulet. Against the white background, jagged points of black and orange suggest that he directs emotions upward to the level of Spirit.

The King of Cups represents someone who expresses mental power, accepts social responsibility, and is qualified to lead others. He is truly accomplished on the emotional path.

Because he understands and accepts the complications of his own and other people's emotions, it is his choice whether or not to get involved, which is why the Rider-Waite King's foot does not touch the water. He is stable, levelheaded, a healer, and a teacher. Responsibility is often more important to him than creativity.

The shadow characteristics of the King of Cups include: bigotry; intolerance; being so caught up in our own feelings of importance that we become oblivious to the legitimate needs of others; hedonism; arrogance; dishonesty, especially in playing on the feelings of others to get what you want; and if taken to its extreme, swindling others.

When this card appears:

- Remain levelheaded. This is a card of self-mastery, not of ruling over others.

- Clearly explain your view or position on the situation or issue.

- If someone in your life obviously wants your help but may be too proud or stubborn to ask for it, take the first step.

- Evaluate how satisfying your life is—or isn't. Really get in touch with your feelings. Are some changes needed?

13 ☼ Wands: The Spirit Soars

Wands represent the revelation of the Spirit through intuition, the "development of the creative imagination ... and the dangers of too much imagination without common sense."[1]

Members of the Wands/Rods family place high value on the meaning of an experience. They have learned to trust themselves above all else and to listen to their inner voice. Facts and details take a backseat for them. They consider small talk irrelevant. They are interested in expanding their own awareness and that of others. Their experiences show us how to live for the joy of living.

In the Golden Dawn tradition, Wands represent the first letter of the Tetragrammaton, the Hebrew letter Yod, the archetypal world of pure Spirit. They represent Jung's intuitive function, and the spiritual element of fire.[2] Fire is associated with the alchemical stage of *rubedo*—the "cooking" phase of transforming raw material into the perfected Self.

In our opinion, each card in the suit shows the conflict or choice between striving to think of an answer or opening up to inspiration and receiving one. We are shown experiences and struggles that test our ability to trust and communicate with our higher self.[3]

Although phallic or masculine in shape, all the wands are blooming or budding, and their fertility indicates they have feminine attributes as well. They symbolize the integration of the masculine and feminine.

Mythologically, Wands—or Rods as they are called in the Morgan-Greer and Aquarian decks—are related to the Maypole, a phallic staff implanted in the feminine womb/earth on May Eve or May Day to celebrate "fertility magic"[4] and the return of spring.

Traditionally, the Maypole tree was a cypress,[5] and the Maypole itself represents the world tree or *axis mundi*, framework of the cosmos. In the Morgan-Greer deck, however, all wands are oak, which is associated with Zeus, the king of the gods of Mount Olympus.

The fact that they bear acorns and green leaves simultaneously rather than exhibiting fall colors as they should has prompted New Mexico psychotherapist Richard Prosapio to regard them as "magic" or supernatural, transcending the forces of nature. "They . . . remind us [that] when we embark on a spiritual path (seeking higher awareness) . . . there are indeed powers that exist beyond our efforts to explain them."[6]

Beginning with the Five of Wands, all the backgrounds in the Rider-Waite deck are blue, the color of Spirit or the celestial realm. The Ace and Two have a gray background, signifying higher wisdom, while the Three and Four have yellow backgrounds, referring to conscious intellect.

Numbered Cards

ACE OF WANDS/RODS

"*I am here to help you begin a new phase in your life experiences. I think of myself as a lightning rod for creativity and wisdom. The energy I bring is less destructive than lightning, but it can strike as swiftly and change attitudes as dramatically. My divine gift is the ability to combine conscious intention, understanding, and emotions so that you can develop a spiritual way of life.*

"*I urge you to listen to every aspect of yourself, all of it—your goals, work, hopes and fears, physical and mental tensions or symptoms, imagination, fantasies, and dreams. Together they provide spiri-*

tual wholeness. When you acknowledge them, you can be more authentic.

"My energy provides the ability to understand how the experiences of the other cards contribute to living a fully soulful life.

"My key phrase is the power of budding inspiration."

The Rider-Waite card shows a white hand radiating cosmic energy as it reaches forth from gray clouds of spiritual truth to present a budding wand. The eight Yod-shaped leaves floating around it represent forces of nature, "bursts of elemental energy."[7] Below, a river flows through the yellow-green land of mental growth toward purple mountains (the Path). A distant castle, symbolizing both our aspirations and the center of civilization, reminds us of all we have had to do to become open to inspiration. Trees dotting the landscape signify fertility and the pathway to the Divine. They all grow on the right (future) side of the stream, suggesting that we are moving toward our spiritual nature. The stream of emotions carries us there, taking us from our past attainments (the castle) into the future (off the right side of the card). Our natural growth potential and the artificial accomplishments of humankind are both separated *and* connected by the river.

The Morgan-Greer Ace of Rods is a short length of sprouting oak symbolizing the growth of spiritual knowledge. It appears above a lake surrounded by lush green trees representing growth and renewal. The soul or God-Self is in line with nature and the cosmos.

Springing from the curving patterns of the feminine divine, the flowering Aquarian Ace of Rods is one of the most beautifully striking cards in any deck. The card reminds us to reevaluate our beliefs and assumptions, making use of the wisdom available to us. It allows us to understand the spiritual principles behind appearances.

Flourishing without earthly roots, the Ace of Wands symbolizes creativity and self-expression nourished by divine essence. It adds a spirit of optimism, purpose, and increased awareness to our experiences and renews our sense of connection to the universal source of all energy and knowledge.

The Ace of Wands inspires us to appreciate the wide spectrum of experiences available in life and to use them in our own search for meaning. A channel for communication with the spiritual is always open to us. Intuition can come to us even when we aren't looking for it.

This card provides the transforming power of the suit, spurring us to begin a new cycle of spiritual development, creativity, and self-awareness. It represents the intuitive mind, the mind that knows that it needs more and seeks what it needs to know. It may trigger a *first* awareness of the higher Spirit or the God-Self within. It can also motivate us to advance further in the quest for spiritual wisdom.

The shadow side of this card includes: shallow thinking; not trusting your own insight to give you needed information; not realizing that you have access to inspiration and creativity or the power to tap into them; and not acknowledging your inner or higher self.

When you draw the Ace of Wands:

- Evaluate the role intuition plays in your life. Do you listen to and trust your hunches?

- Expect to move in a new direction, one that will take you to a more creative or spiritual level of experience or understanding.

- Ask yourself if you need to be more focused. How many of your projects are unfinished or never started? Which ones should be tackled again and which simply discarded?

- It suggests you are, or will soon be, changing your self-image based on the thinking or creating you will do.

TWO OF *WANDS*/*RODS*

"Even in these opulent surroundings, which I have acquired and maintain by my diligent efforts, I am restless. I can hear my future and the world beyond my domain calling for me to do something more. Perhaps you've experienced this restlessness too.

"I represent the aspect of divine energy that infuses you with the desire to express yourself through your creations. I motivate you to

find new outlets for your abilities and ideas. You may need to clarify your own spiritual direction at this time, or turn onto a different path, perhaps by combining divergent philosophies.

"I have succeeded in the past, and will again. There are always more ideas and worlds to explore. I want to inspire you to pursue your own enterprises with courage and determination as well as compassion, truth, and authenticity. Your intuition will tell you what is needed to proceed. I bring you the confidence to make the choices that are best for you.

"My key phrase is <u>the inner stirrings that lead to creation.</u>"

In the Rider-Waite Two of Wands, a richly dressed man holding a globe in his right hand looks out to sea (his inner self) from a gray stone parapet of worldly accomplishment. The upright wand in his left hand, which shows that he is receiving inspiration, rests on a block emblazoned with crisscrossed roses of desire and lilies of truth. From its position to his left (the unconscious), this heraldry calls for him to awaken to and acknowledge higher or inner truths.

He holds a globe in his right hand, suggesting he is the mundane aspect of the King (who holds the world orb in his right hand and a scepter in his left). As lord of the manor, or king of his world, he surveys his earthly area of dominion, and possibly dreams of a greater one. His red hat tells us that his crown chakra is activated. He also faces northeast, the direction of the initiate.

The cloak of the man in the Morgan-Greer Two of Rods is clasped by a red and yellow brooch at his heart chakra, signifying the ability to infuse passion and understanding into new plans. His shield duplicates the heraldry of the Rider-Waite card. This card speaks of choices and potential new partnerships, so aptly represented by the hand of an unseen person in the lower left corner of the card.

The figure in the Aquarian card holds a blossoming rod in his gloved left hand, which bears the bubbly pattern of the divine feminine, accessible to him for help in making choices. His pink sphere represents devotion to the Divine. His shield also duplicates the heraldry.

This card promotes preparation. The two rods represent two different aspects, or views of the situation, and a suggestion to consider other possibilities before taking action. Like other twos, it calls our attention to the seeming polarity between the mundane or worldly (the globe) and the spiritual (the wand). We must learn to live with both.

The Two of Wands refines the goals inspired by the Ace, providing an opportunity to analyze our situation and evaluate our progress. It awakens memories of past successes, stimulates optimism about further endeavors, and builds self-confidence. Do your homework, this card urges. Find a balance that will help you complete your spiritual tasks. As the ruler of your inner and outer worlds, you must respond to wake-up calls for new or changed action. If you don't, you will become a mere dreamer, trapped by your possessions and unable to venture beyond the walls of your manor except in your memory and imagination.

The shadow side of this card includes: spiritual stagnation; dogmatism; being mired in discontent or dissatisfaction, unable to move forward; failure to recognize your fear of the unknown; remaining in the fantasy world of success without gaining the necessary training or experience to make your dreams come true; and boredom.

When you draw this card:

- Recheck any recent plans you have made to determine if you are truly comfortable with them.
- Don't be surprised if you have a "feeling" about something important in your life, even though you can't explain it logically.
- It is likely that you have begun, or soon will begin, to honor the role of spirituality—you may call it ethics or principles—in your life.
- You may begin to recognize or search for a new purpose in your activities.

THREE OF WANDS/RODS

"I stand here contemplating my achievements and involvement in various ventures. I bring you the assurance that success is possible. We must not rest on our laurels too long, though. There's more to be accomplished. I nudge you to make new plans and investigate new areas of interest.

"If you ask yourself what you really want to do, and listen to the answer, your work and relationships will progress with more ease and joy. I suggest that you look at how far you have come and evaluate the work you have done. Then decide whether and how to pursue other enterprises. Past successes instill the confidence and openness to try new things.

"I also inspire you to look within. See yourself more clearly, accept what you see, nurture yourself, and determine how you want to be in the future. These are the tasks I set before you.

"My key phrase is <u>exploring the inner and outer unknowns.</u>"

In the Rider-Waite card, a man stands on a cliff (nature's peak) overlooking a yellow sea, watching three ships sail. They represent exploring our unconscious nature. There are three wands planted firmly in the ground around him, and he grasps one of them with his right hand (conscious choice; destiny). This suggests that he is well grounded and prepared to engage in the spiritual work that awaits him in the distant purple mountains of spiritual aspiration, which he faces. By looking to the East, he takes in the potential power needed to inspire new projects and growth.

The man wears a red robe of physical power over a shirt of blue, the color of emotional energy. A short green mantle symbolizing growth covers his left shoulder, and a black and yellow checkerboard sash representing choices crosses his back and right side. Except for the narrow white headband, which likely crosses his ajna center, his head is uncovered, indicating an attitude of candor.

Under an orange sky of available spiritual energy, the Morgan-Greer figure looks into the distance or the future at yellow mountains, which represent new areas of thinking.

The Aquarian figure, who also stands amid three rods, wears a brown helmet studded with pink jewels to attract spiritual wisdom to his crown chakra. The pattern of arches on the back of his brown jacket represents aspiration.

The Three of Wands embodies the integration of various talents and energies. It encourages us to acknowledge previous accomplishments as well as explore new possibilities. Partial success can spur us to take on greater projects, it suggests. We can stand on the threshold of life at any age and accept the challenge to plumb new depths within ourselves and to take on new tasks or roles.

Seek and accept the help you need, the Three of Wands tells us. Interact candidly with others whose interests are similar to your own. This card urges us to be open and genuine in our personal dealings and to pool talents and resources for the good of everyone involved.

The checkered pattern on the sash in this card shows up in the works or designs of many mystery schools. It serves as a reminder of polarity. Like the chessboard, the pattern calls to mind the steps or "moves" available to each of us depending on our position in life, training, or spiritual initiation. Just as chess pieces are limited in the moves they may make, we frequently have limitations placed on us. Our next move is always determined by the knowledge and level of experience we have attained.

Shadow aspects of the Three of Wands include: an inability to see the greater picture; failure to appreciate what is close to home; not being realistic about our own abilities; and being unwilling to try new things until someone else proves their worth.

When you draw this card:

- Remind yourself of your successes and transfer that confidence to whatever you are currently engaged in.

- Where necessary, adjust ideas and plans based on new input and the overall picture.

- Seek inner guidance to align your priorities with higher will. You express spiritual energy through everything you do.

- Look for patterns in your behavior. What is their significance? What do they tell you about your inner state of being?

FOUR OF WANDS/RODS

"*I want to share with you the joys of achievement. I have success-fully carried out the ideas I was merely considering when I was a three. Now it's time to celebrate.*

"*I offer you a place to rest, a time of contentment. I represent your progress and the harvest reaped from your ideas. For just a while, you can leave the seriousness of your daily life behind and be playful and carefree.*

"*Having established a strong foundation of confidence, I am open to inner guidance and ready to leave the security of the old castle walls. If I were a myth, I'd portray the successful union of the masculine and feminine for earthly fecundity. Psychologically speaking, attaining that union <u>within</u> gives birth to productive spirituality.*

"*My key phrase is <u>fruitful creation</u>.*"

In the Rider-Waite Four of Wands, two maidens carrying bouquets and wearing garlands in their hair approach four tall wands that stand on the yellow pavement of correct thinking beneath a bright yellow sky of divine inspiration. Red ribbons tie (union) a garland of flowers and vines between two of the wands. In the background, a red-roofed, gray castle (the Self) serves as a secure place for inspired passion—symbolized by the women's blue (inspiration) and red (passion) mantles—to spring forth. A bridge similar to the one on the Five of Cups extends from the castle off the right side of the card. The Four of Wands shows us what can happen if we resolve the grief depicted in the Five of Cups, and develop our inner wisdom (the castle).

The Morgan-Greer card is one of three cards in this suit that has no human attributes. Four rods frame a castle (the Self) built on a hill. A thick garland of grapes, fruit (fertility), and roses hangs between the two back rods. The castle and surrounding landscape are ocher, under a yellow sky, representing new ideas in formation.

The two front rods in the Aquarian card are tied with cords that support a spray of red roses (feminine love) with a pink orchid (male potency) in its center. When our inner masculine and feminine energies unite, we have the sacred marriage that strengthens the Self (background castle).

This is the last card to have a yellow background in the Rider-Waite Wands. The remaining cards all have blue backgrounds. Spiritual influence will become prominent, but for now we can celebrate the joy gained by reviewing and restructuring our former beliefs and patterns of thinking.

With the Four of Wands, the physical, mental, and emotional Trinity within becomes an outward, earthly expression. We experience the flowering of understanding and the rejuvenation of our energies. We have the opportunity to celebrate the completion of successful endeavors, or to relax before responding to the restless energy that is already pushing us to identify and plan for future accomplishments.

The shadow side of the Four of Wands includes: failure to discard methods or concepts that no longer offer solace or satisfaction; not allowing ourselves to experience joy in our progress; and never having a sense of completion.

When you draw this card:

- Acknowledge your current successes, and create a way to honor or enjoy them.
- Consider creating something you've only thought about before. Make a dream come true.
- Adjust your perception of yourself or the role you play in the situation in question.
- Have a party and invite us.

FIVE OF WANDS/RODS

"I enjoy this camaraderie and mock competition. I gain insight by playing one idea against another. Tossing around different strategies makes me more open to creative energy and better able to alter my priorities. I argue and negotiate with people because interaction is exciting and challenging. If I keep 'sparring' with my associates, we might put our wands together to erect a five-pointed star of power. Since we are tapping into new abilities and resources, our struggle is to have a successful outcome. Sharing power increases it.

"I would be remiss, however, if I did not tell you that I am also struggling to put the aspects of my personality into some kind of order. As always, understanding ourselves is the deeper issue, and 'can we handle the confusion while we sort it all out?' the more meaningful issue.

"My key phrase is <u>the struggle and challenge of inner and outer growth.</u>"

In the Rider-Waite card, five youths, brandishing long rods, joust in sport. Three look upward, indicating that they are more interested in spiritual ideas than personalities.

In the Morgan-Greer card, five rods are grasped by five hands, each clothed or decorated differently, to portray divergent opinions and ways of thinking.

In the Aquarian card, three youths holding rods surround a fourth youth, also holding one. The fifth rod is held by an unseen person (the unconscious). Though each youth is dressed differently, they all wear a glove of the same dark brown color, to show that they have a similar interest in and "grasp" of the situation. The two young men on the sides wear green shirts of new growth, while the central figure sports a cloak decorated with a gray band of higher wisdom that runs down the line of the spinal chakras. His red hat and the dark spot on his forehead mean his crown and ajna centers are opening. The remaining youth has a red headband over his ajna center.

The Five of Wands promotes the sharing of ideas in a creative group effort. As the midpoint in the sequence of ten, it reflects the need and willingness to continue with ideas and goals established earlier, as well as the importance of wrestling with changed plans or new directions.

This card also warns us that disorder and tension can result when conflicting values or competing needs aren't reconciled. It symbolizes the inner, and sometimes outer, battle we all engage in as we strive to reformulate plans and improve our behavior.

Confusion between human and divine laws can bring inner chaos for a time, too. It is an almost universal side effect of our early attempts to open and receive guidance from the higher self. The Five of Wands reminds us not to look for a quick fix. Each wand is a facet of ourselves, and its energy needs to be used constructively, not denied.

The shadow aspects of the Five of Wands include: thinking we can do everything alone; not taking time or making the effort to see another's side of an issue; and following a leader without thinking through our actions.

When you draw this card:

- Evaluate how your expectations about the process or outcome of your issue/situation change as you consider negotiating or compromising on it.

- Look at one of your projects. Would it be more successful if you got others involved in it? Or, conversely, could it be floundering because others *are* involved?

- Seek support for your changing ideals or philosophy from a like-minded group.

- Examine and, as necessary, reorganize or revise your priorities.

Six of Wands/Rods

"I made it. I did it my way and now ride high, bearing the important news of my victory. I expect to make new conquests from a position of leadership.

"As I move into the future, reviewing my successes, I give credit to my loyal workers. We are an example of what can be accomplished with focused teamwork. Good fortune seems to have smiled on our undertakings.

"I enjoy the view from this higher perspective. I receive creative ideas even as I ride and will continue working diligently and with care on future tasks. Let me encourage you to review your accomplishments and enjoy the satisfaction of work well done.

"My key phrase is <u>sweet success</u>."

In the Rider-Waite card, a mounted horseman wearing a laurel wreath of victory on his head carries a wand with a second wreath attached to it. He is accompanied by wand-bearing footmen whose presence at his left side signifies teamwork and a sense of community or belonging. The green cover on his horse suggests he can trust in the fertility of his instincts.

In the Morgan-Greer card, a richly robed warrior carries a rod with a laurel wreath laced to it with red ribbon. Five additional rods are behind him. His golden helmet and red plume suggest he is a man who passionately operates from highly spiritual ideals.

In the Aquarian card, a woman dressed in the pink of Divine Force rides an elaborately bridled black horse. Her hot pink hat is decorated with gray dotted circles to attract spiritual understanding into her crown and ajna centers.

The Six of Wands represents putting our abilities to the best possible use and gain for humanity. Victory is the result of effort and cooperation, this card reminds us. It reflects the satisfaction and self-confidence that not only result from creative efforts, but also will fuel future efforts (heading toward the right). The Rider-Waite card emphasizes joint efforts more so than the Morgan-Greer or Aquarian cards, which focus on personal triumph.

The struggle that began in the Five of Wands ends in success here.[8] This card shows satisfaction with the present situation, optimism for the future, and belief in oneself. The rider sits easily, balanced, and in harmony with his surroundings—which is one property of the number six.

The card also can reflect the dichotomy between higher truths and human instincts (represented by the horse). Each of us is a spiritual warrior on a quest to discover hidden aspects of ourselves, symbolized by the Rider-Waite and Aquarian figures appearing only in profile.

The shadow side of the Six of Wands includes: impulsiveness; looking for shortcuts to success; trying to get by without putting forth effort; deceit and betrayal; and lack of confidence and low self-esteem or, conversely, too high an opinion of ourselves.

When you draw this card:

- Give yourself a pat on the back for your persistent and valiant efforts to overcome recent obstacles.

- Be ready to move on to a new challenge.

- Cooperative efforts may be necessary to resolve your issue.

- Give appropriate credit to those who have helped you in some way.

Seven of Wands/Rods

"Even in this advantageous position, which I reached by my own efforts, there is still more to contend with. I must remain vigilant although I have already proven my worth.

"I thought the success shown in the Six of Wands was all I needed and that I had achieved enough. I was ill prepared for conflict and competition—so much so that I left home wearing two different shoes. I am an example of learning the hard way.

"Thank goodness I have the ability to sort through new ideas and incorporate the beneficial ones into my work behavior or self-image. I have more than one way to define myself.

"I also have the stick-to-itiveness it takes to complete worthwhile projects and inner work. When I set my sights on something, I seldom get sidetracked.

"My determination to face future challenges, whether they come from within or without, has earned me my key phrase: having the courage of my convictions.*"*

In the Rider-Waite card, a young man stands alone on a hill, defiantly brandishing a wand against six others that rise up before him from below the frame (the unconscious).

Like the Rider-Waite figure, the bearded man in the Morgan-Greer card holds his rod diagonally. A pink brooch clasps his cape together at his throat chakra.

The Aquarian figure holds his rod horizontally. His brown gloves have the small bubbly pattern indicating access to inspiration from the divine feminine. His throat and solar plexus chakras are open and connected, showing that he can speak his convictions.

The Seven of Wands illustrates courage in the face of opposition. Following our initial success (as seen in the Six of Wands), we may go through a period of refinement and adjustment. The Seven of Wands warns us that our ideas may be pitted against the demands or ideas of others. It can represent the attitudes of a self-made person, or one who works alone and feels threatened when called upon to work with or include the ideas of others in his plans. It captures the anxiety we feel when we join forces with our peers, only to find competition instead of cooperation. "Where have all our supporters gone?" we wonder. The Seven of Wands also points to a tendency to become defensive in situations or relationships wherein we feel we have to prove ourselves.

"Who or what is at the unseen ends of the rods?" you ask. One view is that they represent hidden aspects of yourself, which you may have difficulty seeing or accepting. They are now attempting to get your attention.

Another view is that each of the rods represents one of the seven chakras. Their awakening or rising energies can result in chaotic and confusing action initially. The young man's wand crosses his heart chakra, closing off the heart to new input.

This, then, is a card of fighting self-awareness and change. By his action the person in the card says, "I will not open my heart to this. I am not ready." The impetus for change has already begun, however, for as a seven, the wands also represent the seven stages of alchemical transformation.

Shadow aspects of the Seven of Wands include: giving in to the wishes of others against our better judgment; being wishy-washy in stating our position; being unwilling to reassess our position; not standing up for what we believe in; not wanting to prepare or educate ourselves for what we need to do; and taking on more than we can handle.

When you draw this card:

- Evaluate your present position in terms of your original purpose or ideals. Does it still benefit you? Is it still necessary to maintain a protective stance?

- Identify some of the ways you are *not* prepared to handle your present situation. How *could* you become more prepared?

- Consider whether you are acting from a position of strength or defensiveness.

- Take some small action—clean out a messy drawer, finish a project left hanging, do a load of laundry—that will help you feel more capable.

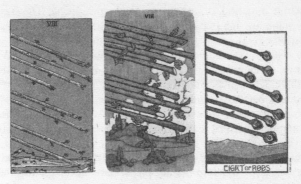

EIGHT OF WANDS/RODS

"I am movement. Sometimes I rush forward, leading some to be-lieve that I arrive too hastily, without proper thought and preparation. Others think I am too single-minded. They'd like to see me expand my interests instead of focusing all my energies in one direction.

"My world seems endless and inspired. I am filled with possibilities. Right now many choices await me, and I don't want to be limited.

"I'm also trying to figure out who I am. Which ideas are truly my own? Which don't fit me? Perhaps I've carried some too long and need to toss them aside.

"Of course, I am also anxious to arrive at my destination. I am so eager to create my future and reap its rewards that it's hard for me to slow down. I fly over the river of time. It flows. Who can really say which of us moves too fast? There's so much yet to do.

"My key phrase is <u>up in the air</u>."

In the Rider-Waite card, eight parallel wands in groups of four, two and two, sail over open country, against a blue sky. They are separated into this distinct pattern to show us we need to sort out and organize our ideas for future efforts.

The scene in the Morgan-Greer card is similar, only more colorful. In addition, the eight rods flying over lush countryside are evenly divided.

The eight Aquarian rods fly through a white sky, over low-rolling, barren land. They may represent archetypal thoughts or forces, which, when attended to, make the mind sacred.[9]

The Eight of Wands represents rapid movement or change, a rush of ideas or energy. The wands's trajectory—downward from the divine realm toward consciousness and from left to right (the future)—signals philosophical, religious, or spiritual growth. To achieve it, however, we must take the bounty of ideas coming our way and organize them, making them our own. They are not yet fixed (grounded) within us.

When things are "up in the air," we often want to settle them quickly. This card reminds us to take our time, to evaluate and prioritize before moving forward. Try some inspirational reading, discussion with others, and seeking guidance from a higher source.

Waite says the card pictures "motion through the immovable,"[10] which is nearing the end of its course. The wands' direction shows focus in "accessing our potential and finding and living our personal destiny."[11]

The shadow side of the Eight of Wands includes: ignoring a troublesome situation and doing nothing to remedy it; lethargy; putting off necessary action; and formulating plans that "never go anywhere."

When you draw this card:

- Clearly delineate your purposes and goals. Set some priorities.
- Figure out where there may be too much chaos in your life or, conversely, too much organization and rigidity. Can you find a middle ground?
- Evaluate how important tradition is in your life so you can give it a place that is appropriate for you.
- Resist the temptation to plunge right in with a new burst of energy. Take time to develop an overall perspective so you won't feel overwhelmed.

NINE OF WANDS/RODS

"I have to follow my own path, find my own way, as we all must. I am the one ultimately responsible for my destiny, so I can't help but take an active role in shaping it.

"This means I must examine my past experiences and the patterns of thought resulting from them, especially those that limit me. Until I recognize them and stop succumbing to them, I will remain wounded.

"Some of the negative attitudes I bring from my past show up as a tendency to be overly cautious, lonely, self-absorbed, or entirely too inhibited. I wonder if I ought to throw away the conventional and do something truly innovative.

"My dream is to acquire greater insight about myself and humankind and to express my ideas more freely. I hope I don't get scared or shut myself down before I fulfill the destiny described in my key phrase: finding my way."

In the Rider-Waite card, a bandaged figure holds one wand and looks to the left where he may glimpse unconscious energy, his feminine aspect, or his past. Eight wands stand behind him in the green growth of his development. If he would only turn around, he would see the opportunities available to him.

In contrast, the Morgan-Greer figure is a bearded military man dressed in yellow armor and a flowing red cloak, which shows that he is protected from passion by intellect. A red plume attached to his yellow helmet at the crown chakra appears to be blowing back as he moves forward to take action.

The lad in the Aquarian Nine of Rods, who does not appear to be moving, wears a white hat studded with purple jewels.

Although the Rider-Waite Nine of Wands is often associated with someone who is inflexible, "imprisoned" by his ideas (the wands), and stuck, the Morgan-Greer card more accurately depicts the interpretation we prefer—that the person shown has reached a level of accomplishment. The rod he holds represents his selection from the many options that flew his way in the preceding card. He has chosen to face his past or the unconscious material represented by the left side of the card. He will learn to cope with it. The remaining rods represent ideas that he must recognize in order to heal and know himself more fully. They also protect us from moving too fast or encountering more than we can handle. This can be seen most clearly in the Aquarian card, where it appears that the boy is going to have to make his way *through* the wands.

In the Morgan-Greer and Aquarian cards, the figures are dressed for the struggle. Indeed, the Aquarian youth may be a little too protected. In the Rider-Waite card, he is more aware of his wounds and more wary. His situation isn't hopeless, though. As the Rider-Waite figure lingers on the gray walk (need for balance), his understanding grows (green boots). The green hills in the background suggest his inner work will be successful.

The shadow aspects of this card include: being immobilized by our doubts; reluctance to face and resolve issues from the past; and wanting to live in the past.

When you draw the Nine of Wands:

- Look to your past for unfinished business of an emotional or spiritual nature. How can you put it to rest?

- Examine how you're thinking about the issue at hand. Are you following old patterns? Where is your thinking distorted? Do you need to broaden your perspective?

- Consider the possibility that you may be prepared to do battle over an issue that has more to do with your past experiences than your present circumstances. Rather than rushing into the fray, try to truly understand the other person's point of view.

- You may need to take some time for healing before making a final decision regarding your issue/situation.

TEN OF WANDS/RODS

"*Does it look as if I've taken on more than I can handle? Don't worry. Now that I've chosen to continue my journey on the path of Spirit, my burden doesn't seem too heavy. I have finally gathered my thoughts and am headed in a direction that is right for me.*

"*Determination is one of my qualities I want to pass on to you. If you have set your mind on something, get in there, take responsibility, and take action, I say. Keep your goal in sight and move toward it step by step. Even when you can't understand why you have to engage in a particular task, or when you feel quite alone, push forward. People like you and me listen to an inner belief. We trust the training learned from past experiences and try to help others by expressing higher values in both our words and our deeds.*

"My key phrase is <u>perseverance toward higher service</u>."

The Ten of Wands is an insight card, giving us a glimpse of how things can be. This is depicted most clearly in the Rider-Waite card, where a man carrying a bundle of ten wands walks toward a red-roofed house, representing where his future Self resides. The wands, which represent his conceptions of what he'll find by following his intuition, are crossed (signaling that a crossroads or turning point has been reached). Both the house and the walkway leading to it are ocher—the color of intellectual decisions. Green land and trees promise growth and fulfillment. Ocher tights covering his legs indicate that he has chosen a direction, and his brown boots show how solid or grounded that decision is. The figure's red tunic suggests the passion behind his decision, which has yet to be integrated into his personality. His purple shirt hints at the heights that he can achieve on the path of wands. His yellow hair identifies him as the solar son moving toward his future initiation.[12]

The Morgan-Greer youth seems to be carrying out a task rather than glimpsing the future, although the maroon bands across his back do suggest a crossroads. The red and a white feather of truth that decorates his brown beret points to the passion and purity of his future path (the right side of the card).

The Aquarian figure, also heading toward his future, wears a hot pink helmet, encircled with jewels that cross his ajna center. The cap's shape and the jewels show that he aspires toward spiritual service with unsullied (white undercap) dedication (pink helmet).

The Ten of Wands represents a time when we are intensely focused on our goal. The weight of the wands gives us some inkling that it could be difficult to make our dreams come true, but we don't realize the full extent of what we'll need to do. The fact that we finally have a "true" direction is gratifying enough to lighten the load for a while. We realize that we exist to serve Spirit rather than the other way around.

The person in this card also might be seen as "weighed down with commitments."[13] He has taken on more than he can handle and is, therefore, blinded to what he needs for himself. In this case he will receive insights to help him decide how to release or divvy up his heavy load. His task will be to learn how to say, "No."

The shadow aspects of this card include: rebelling or fighting against responsibility; procrastination; and failure to set priorities or make choices for ourselves.

When you draw the Ten of Wands:

- Ask yourself if you're approaching the matter at hand stubbornly or with dedication. What role does each play?

- Look for places where your tendency to jump in and assume responsibility may be preventing others from developing important skills.

- You either need to persevere in resolving your situation or, conversely, you are blindly pushing for a resolution where none is likely.

- It's time to make a new commitment to resolve or finish your question/issue.

Court Cards

PAGE OF WANDS/RODS

"*I stand here trying to fully grasp the commitment I've made. Sometimes this inner work seems lonely and barren. I wonder what I'm doing here. I long to get out 'there' and get going. That's when I pull my hat low so I can block out distracting worldly images and more easily turn inward. I am training my mind to listen to my soul. I am learning to trust the ideas that come to me.*

"*Because my devotion to duty, my studies, and other solitary pur-*

suits leave little time for anything else, I'm often identified as a loner. But that's just a temporary stance, and not my basic nature.

"Eventually we all have to take off our hats and face our futures. But I'm not ready just yet. My new knowledge is still too intellectual and not yet an integral part of me.

"My task is to stay focused and learn to listen to my inner self, which is why my key phrase is <u>following my heart</u>."

The Rider-Waite Page of Wands, in his yellow tunic over red tights and yellow cape lined in red, has begun to intellectually understand (yellow) the lessons he is being taught, and his energy (red) is more controlled. His gray hat sits on his head lightly to show that both his crown chakra and his ajna center have been awakened, but their wisdom has yet to be incorporated into his soul. His yellow boots are trimmed with a flamelike design we will see again in the King of Wand's crown.

The salamander design on his tunic will be repeated on the Knight's tunic and the King's robe and throne. In legend, the salamander is the guardian and vital source[14] of fire, the suit's element. Some of the Page's are close to becoming uroboros, the mythical lizard/snakes who swallow their tails and transform themselves. In Jungian terms, they symbolize the Self, which here is not yet completed. The pyramids in the background are not well formed—another sign that the Page is an initiate in the land of ancient and secret wisdom.

The Morgan-Greer card's mountainous desert landscape suggests that the Page's journey toward higher ideas will be a difficult one.

The Aquarian Page's garment has a brown band down the center, aligning with the spinal chakras and awakening kundalini energy. His russet hat with its grayish feather of higher truth covers his face. He has turned inward to set his inner world in order. In addition, the seven cattails growing in the background suggest that, unlike the other Pages, he stands near water and has access to the unconscious.

Pages in all suits represent the potential for inner growth in one who is still relatively naive or untutored, and the Page of Wands is no exception. The card's appearance in a reading signals restlessness, vague creative stirrings, an urge to do something new or different. The trick is to stay still and inwardly focused long enough for those feelings to take an identifiable form, thus the Page's immobile posture. Although these inner rumblings may not amount to anything initially, once we learn to recognize and honor them, something *will* develop. A new task, direction, self-image, or self-definition will emerge eventually.

The shadow aspects of this card include: being uninterested in checking out new ideas; refusing to take risks; and acting impulsively.

When you draw the Page of Wands:

- You may be called upon to take some kind of risk in the near future, possibly related to your role in your question/issue.

- Realize that you do not have all the knowledge or insight you need. Take care not to get too dogmatic.

- Spiritual ideas are beginning to play a greater role in your life. Those related to your situation need to be clarified.

- Trust feelings of restlessness or dissatisfaction to point you in a new direction. Give the issues behind those feelings time to surface and illuminate your next move.

KNIGHT OF WANDS/RODS

"Wow! I think I'm getting the hang of this spiritual stuff, and it really excites me. Few people bring more enthusiasm to their tasks than I do.

"I'm the one who encourages you to get all fired up about your ideas and do what it takes to make them come true. My fiery nature makes the unexpected happen and startling new ideas pop into your mind. Sometimes I will entertain notions or initiate actions that seem unconventional, but they will never be unethical.

"Yes, I can be so devoted to a task that I will push until I find a way to accomplish it, and so relentless when pursuing a goal that I come off as self-centered or egotistical. I'm really not, though. I just get so excited, and I forget that others aren't equally so.

"My key phrase is <u>unexpected change or challenge</u>."

Riding a horse whose orange color captures the fiery splendor of a mind infused with Spirit consciousness, the Rider-Waite Knight of Wands wears armor trailing red flame-shaped material to show he is a man of action. His yellow overgarment is decorated with salamanders (symbol of the fire element) not yet in the uroboros stage. Three pyramids are distinct in the background.

The Morgan-Greer Knight wears yellow gloves bearing the salamander design. A yellow, winged, lizardlike creature decorates his helmet.

Both the bubbly design on the Aquarian Knight's brown armor and its pink and black duplicate in the lower right corner represent the active presence of the feminine aspect of God. She protects and inspires the young Knight. The arrow motif on his glove points in the direction of his journey,[15] which is clearly an inner one (facing left). He's headed toward awakening the inner or spiritual feminine.

The Knight of Wands is an active, energetic person, unlikely to hold back what he knows. He eagerly charges forward, mobilizing intellect and instincts—mind and body—to accomplish his task.

His great energy dissipates quickly, though, and as soon as it does, he will look for another exciting situation, which makes him a somewhat erratic personality. His fire burns hot and heavy for a while. Then he needs to move on and light another fire. His great strength is his enthusiasm. It is contagious and inspires others to act morally and spiritually. His task is to learn to temper his excitement so he can *choose* to be steady in some situations and "fired up" in others.

Shadow aspects of the Knight of Wands include: depression; withdrawal; boredom; lethargy; lack of discipline to pursue our goals; and waiting for someone else to do "it."

When you draw this card:

- You may be feeling too cramped or restricted by your situation. Try expanding your perspective.

- You may be feeling restless. Look around for new challenges.

- Qualities such as exuberance, excitement, and a sense of adventure are attempting to surface. Acknowledge them. Allow them to take their rightful place in your personality or situation.

- Your enthusiasm or the exuberance of someone involved in your situation may be a bit overwhelming. Set some limits.

QUEEN OF WANDS/RODS

"I am the force that makes dedication to a spiritual path possible. I have learned to combine and draw inspiration from both the spiritual and the material realms.

"The deep conviction that something is right for you and the reassuring sense that a situation will be all right are signs of my influence flowing through you. I inspire intuitive thinking. I am never interested in superficial relationships.

"Unlike the young Knight under my tutelage, I do not scatter my energies. I have tamed my exuberance and direct it toward a few important projects or people to whom I am devoted. In my heart I carry a vision of how they will turn out. My efforts on their behalf are constant and undiminishing.

"My key phrase is <u>manifesting the spiritual potential</u>."

The Rider-Waite Queen sits on a yellow throne bearing a heraldry of lions and sunflowers. Lions are carved into its base as well. The throne is situated on a gray platform of balanced wisdom with three pyramids of spiritual achievement visible in the background to its left. In her left hand the Queen holds a sunflower. Her crown is decorated with green leaves of natural growth.

She wears a yellow gown with checkerboard trim along the V neckline that points at the solar plexus chakra (expression of vital energy). Her grayish robe is clasped at the heart chakra by a red pin in the shape of a cat's head. A black cat, representing domesticated instinctual energy, sits at her feet. It suggests that the Queen's playful energy is close to consciousness. It also highlights her independence. She is sure of and true to herself.

The Morgan-Greer Queen of Rods also wears a yellow robe and holds a sunflower. Green vines entwine around the top of her crown, which bears the V-shaped design of Spirit Immanent and the inverted V of Spirit Transcendent (see Note 1, Chapter 6).

The Aquarian Queen wears a pink robe bearing lines of energy that align with her spinal chakras. The gray design in the center of her tan crown carries this alignment off the card into the divine realm. She is the earthly extension of spiritual energy. She holds a purple (will perfected in God) sunflower. The symbol of God in its center duplicates the one she wears around her throat. At the base of the card are the designs of the divine feminine.

The sunflower as a mandala represents our God Spirit, our Self. It is an emblem of spirituality, illumination, and divine riches. It carries the sun's alchemical representation of "philosophical sulfur"—the fiery element that is the soul of nature.

The Queen of Wands fully recognizes that her personal power flows from her strong connection with her inner God-Self. She trusts this connection and draws on it for support and guidance. She represents "the deepest essence of who we are."[16]

The presence of heraldry on the Queen's throne tells us she is able to understand on several different levels what is happening in a situation and recognize the implications of the attitudes or actions expressed.

The archetypal "keeper of the hearth," the Queen of Wands motivates us to create beautiful surroundings and decorate with things that are important to us. As the lions and cat on the Rider-Waite card indicate, she is the perfect combination of wild and domesticated feline energy. She has both under control.

The shadow aspects of this card include: a lack of confidence; miserliness in our actions or attitudes; feeling weak or incompetent; self-righteousness; selfishness; and having little appreciation of spiritual qualities or needs.

When you draw the Queen of Wands:

- Recognize and live by the qualities of loyalty and constancy.

- Either you or someone else involved in your situation is being too strong-willed, which makes it difficult to reach a compromise.

- You may be ignoring a mentor who could give you good ideas and strong support.

- You are allowing another to have too much control over you and need to take charge of *your* situation.

King of Wands/Rods

"I am clear about who I am and my ability to express myself. I trust my well-honed intuition and often base my actions or decisions on it. I am the highest expression of creative imagination.

"Like my Queen, I have the need and the discipline to make my visions reality. I am less interested in helping others realize their vision, though, and I certainly do not work behind the scenes as she often does.

"I prefer to infuse you and others with the excitement of <u>my</u> vision and inspire you to work toward it for me. I take charge early and shape situations to conform to the way I think they should be. I meet challenges head-on, and with supreme confidence and determination overcome them.

"My key phrase is <u>master of creative imagination</u>."

The Rider-Waite King of Wands sits on a yellow throne, its back bearing designs of lions and the uroboros. The latter also appear on the King's yellow robe, signaling that the transformation is now complete. The King wears a red cap of maintenance beneath a yellow crown with flame-shaped decorations, which are duplicated on the edge of his yoke, and at his wrists. A salamander rests on the gray platform beneath his throne. He wears a lion pendant at his heart chakra.

The Morgan-Greer King of Rods wears a brown cap of maintenance studded with yellow. His crown chakra is open to divine inspiration and his golden crown has a red jewel situated over the ajna center. The red edge of his robe follows the spinal line of chakra energy.

The Aquarian King of Rods wears a winged helmet with a gray jewel over his ajna center. His gray cap of maintenance is studded with red stones. The decorations on both the helmet and cap of maintenance indicate his spiritual centers are activated.

Confident and determined, the King of Wands knows what he wants and goes after it. Like others, male or female, who possess this powerful personality trait, he can also be intolerant of those who are not equally confident or goal directed. Waite describes him as "dark, ardent, lithe, animated, impassioned, noble," and says the card always signifies honesty.[17]

A passionate leader with a penetrating mind, he easily influences others, and his fiery spirit is infectious. He carries and communicates well-thought-out values, and often serves as a role model of spiritual strength.

When we are driven by our own vision, assume a leadership position, or strive to improve our own life situation, we are actively expressing King of Wands energy.

The shadow side of the King of Wands includes: being dictatorial, hot-tempered, arrogant, or bigoted; and behaving as if we should always get our own way.

When you draw the King of Wands:

- Acknowledge or use your leadership abilities.

- You, or another, are being too domineering.

- Allow your creativity to flow unrestricted, so new ideas and modes of action can develop and become clear.

- Clarify your current position or, conversely, make sure you are not being so single-minded that you have lost sight of the other alternatives available to you.

PART FOUR

MAPPING IT ALL OUT

14 ✹ Learning the Lay of the Land

The following table provides step-by-step directions for how to proceed with a Tarot reading. Where applicable we indicate those steps that require more explanation and the chapters in this book that include the necessary additional instruction.

Table 3
How to Conduct a Tarot Reading

Step	Chapter
1. Set up the area where you're going to do the reading.	Chapter 3
2. Choose the deck you're going to work with.	Chapters 3 and 4
3. Decide how you're going to respond to reversed cards.	Chapter 3
4. Formulate your question.	Chapter 3
5. Select the layout you want to work with.	Chapter 14
6. Choose the style(s) of reading you will do.	Chapter 15
7. Shuffle the deck as you concentrate on your question.	
8. With your left hand, cut the deck into three piles and then restack it into one.	

STEP	CHAPTER
9. Turn over the cards one by one in the pattern of your chosen layout.	
10. As each card is turned over, speak or write your understanding of its message.	Chapters 5-13
11. Consider and interpret any patterns or interrelations you think important.	Chapter 14
12. Summarize your understanding of how the reading responds to or answers your question.	See summaries of the readings in Chapters 16 and 17.
13. Enter a copy of your reading and your interpretation in your Tarot journal.	Chapter 2 and Appendix Journal Forms

A Tarot layout (or spread) is a map for asking certain kinds of questions and placing the cards in specific positions to arrive at your answer. The question you create and the amount of information you want helps you determine which layout to use.

With any layout, you begin by shuffling your cards while concentrating on your question. With your left hand, cut the cards into three piles and then restack them into one pile.

Turn over the first card and place it in the appropriate position indicated in the diagram of the layout you have chosen. Decide what its message is in relation to your question. Then turn over the second card and do the same. One by one, continue turning over the number of cards required by the layout and placing them in the order prescribed by the layout diagram.

Once you understand the meaning of the card itself, an important question to ask yourself at this stage of the reading is "How can I make the most of this information?"

In this chapter we teach you six spreads. The first, the Cross of Awareness, gives you detailed background information on the issue or situation at the root of your question. The others give you five additional ways to get a new perspective on events in your life.

Cross of Awareness Layout (10 cards)

The Cross of Awareness layout (see Figure 4) is based on the Celtic Cross, one of the oldest layouts in existence, and one of the most frequently used. We have modified the names and meanings of the positions to help you more effectively consider what's happening with respect to a current situation or issue.

Appropriate kinds of questions for in-depth exploration with the Cross of Awareness fall under the heading of "what more do I need to know or consider" about a given person, situation, or issue. Typical kinds of questions might include:

- What complications could occur if I take a new job I am being offered?
- What opportunities for growth does this [job, relationship, etc.] hold?
- What prevents me from getting more serious about this [man, woman, project, etc.]?
- What will I have to confront about myself if I take this [job, vacation, training seminar. . .]?
- What do I need to know about myself in order to make this a more successful [relationship, work situation, vacation. . .]?
- What lessons are in store for me if I dive into this project, job, or relationship?

Get the idea? Your questions are focused on clarifying your understanding of the situation and uncovering what you need to know in order to function in it more satisfactorily or successfully.

Position 1, Here & Now, offers you information about present inner or outer aspects of your situation. It says something about who you are or where you stand with respect to that issue or situation. It also can indicate strengths or weaknesses that you bring to the situation.

Position 2, Challenge, shows difficulties you may have to overcome in order to successfully resolve the situation at hand. It can also identify what in your life is generating conflict. If the Here & Now card seems to refer largely to your inner attitudes, the Challenge card may indicate actions you need to take to balance your inner state.[1]

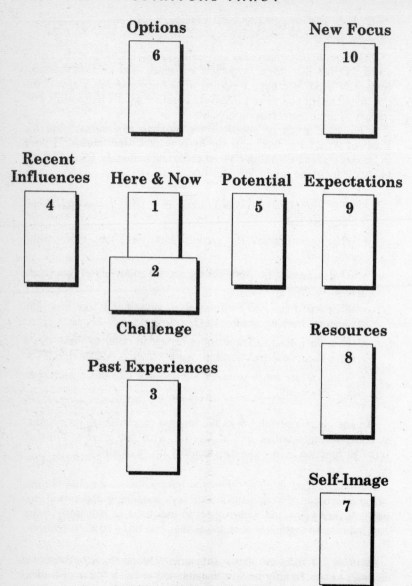

Figure 4
Cross of Awareness Layout

The Here & Now card and the Challenge card always interrelate. One cannot be fully understood except in relationship to the other.

Position 3, Past Experiences, points out past events, attitudes developed in your past, or previous actions on your part or others' that exert influence on the matter you're concerned about now. They are what's *behind* the situation, and you need to understand how they have contributed to your present situation. What role have they played? These typically long-standing memories, beliefs, or feelings can be either negative or positive, and you may need to modify or let go of them in order to resolve the issue.

Position 4, Recent Influences, is similar to Position 3 except the events depicted on the card are likely to have occurred more recently and be more recognizable. In some instances, cards in this position indicate a long-standing past attitude or memory that you have recently become aware of or started working to resolve. It can also suggest a current lesson being worked on or a recent "lesson learned."

Position 5, Potential, refers to the possible changes that may occur as a result of wrestling with your question. Cards in this position also can depict energies to be drawn on or attitudes that will develop as you work to resolve the matter.

Position 6, Options, can suggest where you are headed, a possible next step, or new opportunities open to you. Alternatively, it can indicate, given the preceding cards, what may happen if you do nothing. The cards in this position sometimes suggest the next "lesson" in your life and how your present situation is preparing you for it.

The four cards to the right of the greater cross, often called the staff, give information about the "pathway" for resolving your situation.

Position 7, Self-Image, cards may suggest how you see yourself in the situation or in relation to the issue at hand. They can illustrate your ideas and attitudes about yourself under the circumstances you're asking about. These feelings can be positive, or they can be fears that undermine you in the situation. On rare occasions, cards in this position are a message from your higher self indicating what traits need to be developed.

Position 8, Resources, points to places or situations that offer you important information or a fresh perspective. It may identify people who are likely to relate to you in ways that will provide additional insight. The cards can also alert you to books, media information, or other written or visual sources of helpful ideas.

Position 9, Expectations, illustrates some of your expectations for the matter being examined. It brings fantasies to light, including those previously hidden from your awareness. Traditionally this position has been called "Hopes and Fears." By considering shadow aspects, one card can give you both types of information.

Position 10, New Focus, suggests where the energy of the reading is trying to go. It may depict an "outcome" or outgrowth of the cards, (i.e., the new stage of your development). Or it may suggest a new direction for your journey. Sharman-Burke and Greene suggest that its influence may extend for the next six months.[2]

Micro-Cross Layout (2 cards)

The Micro-Cross layout (see Figure 5) consists of the first two positions from the Cross of Awareness layout. The positions have the same meanings in both layouts.

Used as a "daily" reading, the Micro-Cross layout allows you to get in touch with your inner state of being. It can identify your prevalent attitudes and that day's possible challenges or opportunities.

The Micro-Cross layout also can be used to give you a fast update on a situation for which you've already done a Cross of Awareness layout, or to ask for insight on any situation when you don't have time for, or want to do, a full reading.

The first way to use the Micro-Cross layout is simply to draw cards without formulating a question. When you do this, the two positions/cards in the layout define *the issues of the day.* The upright position—Here and Now—asks the question "Where do I stand now?" and the card you draw depicts your inner state of being.

The Challenge position asks the question "What's in my way at

Here & Now

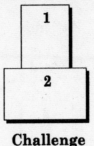

Challenge

Figure 5
Micro-Cross Layout

this time?'' and the card drawn suggests at least one thing that you will need to confront for the sake of personal or spiritual growth.

A second way to use the Micro-Cross layout is to create a question in the same way you would for the Cross of Awareness. The two cards you draw give you a quick summary of your attitude toward the situation you've asked about and at least one thing you will need to deal with before you can resolve the matter.

Triad Layout (3 cards)

The three-card layout is sweet, simple, and fast. That may be why it is so popular and used in so many creative ways. Here are four of the options we've come across. In each, three cards are laid out one at a time from left to right to form the three-card row seen in Figure 6.

(1) In this common method of divination, the left card represents the *Past*. The center card represents the *Present*, and the right card represents the *Future*. Your question is inherent in the layout. Whether or not you actually formulate the questions, you are asking, ''Where am I in my inner life right now?'' ''What happened in the past to influence today's position?'' ''What will I need to deal with in the future?'' We like Mary K. Greer's idea that once

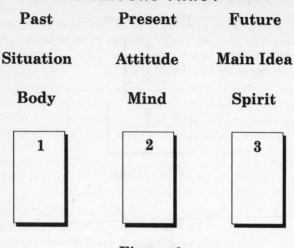

Past   Present   Future

Situation   Attitude   Main Idea

Body   Mind   Spirit

Figure 6
Triad Layout

you have your time perspective, you can "take your life in your own hands," move the same cards around in any way you wish and create a new reading to consider new possibilities.[3]

(2) The Triad spread also answers yes/no questions. To use it for that purpose, select three cards from a shuffled, fanned-out deck, being careful to pick up and turn over all three in the same way. Two or three upright cards count as a "yes" answer, while two or three upside-down cards signify a "no."

If you use the Triad layout to answer a *yes/no question*, the type of question you ask is one that can be answered "yes" or "no." While we do not think asking these kinds of questions is a helpful way to use the Tarot, we also recognize that there will be times when "yes" or "no" is the only answer you'll be interested in. Do not ask the question over and over until you get the answer you want, however. The Tarot does not take kindly to that sort of manipulation. So ask only once and lay out the cards only once.

If you're dissatisfied with the answer you get, use a more extensive layout to explore ideas such as "What's in my way at this time?"; "What's keeping me from getting what I want?"; "What do I need to learn from my 'yes' or 'no' answer?'' This longer reading may give you insight into any inner obstacles you need to clear up. Then, as you change your world, subsequent answers to your questions will change also.

(3) To use the Triad layout for insight and growth rather than divination, Gail Fairfield, author of *Choice Centered Tarot*, suggests using the three-card layout to answer the question ''What's happening now?'' It gives you a quick take on the inner attitudes active in your life today, the learning experiences you may have. The left card depicts the *present situation*. The middle card presents your *attitude* toward the situation; and the third card shows the *main thing* that you must keep in mind.[4]

(4) Mary K. Greer[5] uses the positions from left to right to stand for the *body* (physical body, environment), *mind* (thoughts, attitudes), and *spirit* (ideals, goals, aspirations). For this reading, you create a subquestion to a basic first question that is formulated in the same fashion as Cross of Awareness questions. That subquestion is ''What do these three aspects of myself have to say about [your basic question]?'' You finish the reading by connecting all the cards into a sentence that has the format ''My body wants _____, my mind tells me _____, and my spirit urges me to _____.''

Daily Opportunity Layout (4 cards)

The Daily Opportunity spread serves the same purpose as Fairfield's three-card layout, and offers several additional insights. It highlights the past or ongoing influences that have led you to today, the day's potential, its challenges, and the opportunities for personal development the day will bring. It's a great layout to use while you're traveling to add awareness to your sight-seeing activities. The question inherent in the layout and reading is ''What do I need to be alert to today?'' or ''What inner work will likely be stimulated today?''

To use the Daily Opportunity layout, shuffle and cut your cards into four piles. *Do not recombine them into one deck.*

Fan out the first stack with the cards facedown. From anywhere in the array, select one card and place it in Position 1 of the layout, as shown in Figure 7. Do the same with the second, third, and fourth piles, placing each card in its corresponding position on the diagram.

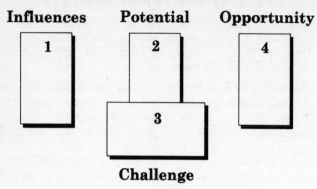

Figure 7
Daily Opportunity Layout

Position 1, Influences, suggests at least one event or attitude from the recent or distant past that affects today's situation. If the connection is not immediately clear, reflect on the card during the day. Memories or ideas may emerge to explain its influence

Position 2, Potential, addresses one aspect of your situation as it is now. It can point to an attitude that needs to be considered, as well as actions that can be successfully undertaken today.

Position 3, Challenge, shows difficulties you may encounter. They may involve actual events or inner conflicts.

Position 4, Opportunity, suggests a new course of action or way of being that may become available to you as a result of the inner work you do today. It can also reflect a possible outcome of actions taken during the day.

Fountain of Creation Layout (5 cards)

The Fountain of Creation layout gives you a look at some of the psychological factors that may be influencing your situation. It helps you gain insight into how this experience can further your growth and what processes may now be at work in your life because of it. Appropriate questions for the Fountain of Creation layout are of the type that ask:

- Where am I headed?
- How can I make the most of my situation in terms of my inner, spiritual growth?
- What lessons is my situation offering me?
- What influences do I need to be on the lookout for?

To use this layout, shuffle the cards and place them in the positions and in the order shown in Figure 8.

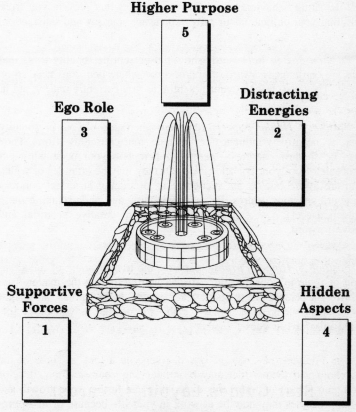

Higher Purpose

5

Distracting Energies

2

Ego Role

3

Supportive Forces

1

Hidden Aspects

4

Figure 8
Fountain of Creation Layout

Position 1, Supportive Forces, identifies the people, events, or actions that are influencing you now or soon will be. Some are familiar. Others are just beginning to play an active role in your life.

Although they may exist in your present environment, they are more likely to represent inner strengths (attitudes, ideas, feelings) that can serve you well in your current situation—if you are receptive to them.

Position 2, Distracting Energies, points to situations or issues that may keep you from accomplishing your goals. Like Supportive Forces, they may come from people or events in the world around you or from your own inner attitudes. Cards in this position often highlight self-defeating behaviors or continuing conflicts that prevent you from fulfilling your obligations or fully expressing your joy and satisfaction.

Position 3, Ego Role, cards show the present personality traits that you are consciously aware of and/or areas where decisions need to be made. They also refer to your potential as you currently understand it.

Position 4, Hidden Aspects, represents the facets of your personality that can negatively influence or sabotage your conscious efforts. They may be shadow energies—qualities inherent in your personality but concealed from your consciousness. Or they may be attitudes of which you are aware but do not recognize as producing an effect contrary to your conscious desires. By acknowledging and understanding these hidden aspects, you can release dammed-up creative potential and move forward.

Position 5, Higher Purpose, captures the true meaning of the situation or issue in your question. It may help you view the matter from a different perspective or suggest a "lesson" to be learned, an insight to be acknowledged, or a new "path" to consider as you move forward in your life quest.

Star Guides Layout (6 cards)

The Star Guides layout helps you evaluate potential projects or enterprises and requires the same kinds of questions as those for the

Cross of Awareness layout. It offers guidance through five approaches, each of which culminates in the insight revealed in the sixth position.

Shuffle and cut the cards the usual way. Then place them in the positions and in the order shown in Figure 9.

Position 1, Facts First, takes the approach of the Scientist, who considers the known facts of the situation, including your own abilities and goals. It can identify possible starting points or give clues as to what needs to be investigated before making your decision.

Position 2, Sage Advice, expresses the approach of the Philosopher, the voice of experience. Sometimes thought of as conventional wisdom, the advice from a card in this position is similar to what you'd hear from someone who has observed people traveling a similar road, and who speaks from a neutral position. Cards in this position can point out precautions to think about.

Position 3, Dragons to Slay, is the province of the Warrior. Its card tells you what stands in your way now, or may get in your way as you proceed, including both external challenges and internal conflicts.

Position 4, Right Use of Talents, reflects the approach of the Mystic, and highlights religious or ethical considerations. Cards in this position advise you to use your abilities for the highest expression of your principles and the greatest good for all involved. It asks, "How does this project fit with your code of values?"

Position 5, More Possibilities, approaches the matter using the transformative methods of the Magician. "What new and different results might you get by rearranging and recombining elements in the situation?" it asks. It also suggests ways to improve the picture and new areas to consider before taking action.

Position 6, Crucial Insight, is to be read as tying together the first five cards and producing an "aha" reaction, which may or may not be the hoped-for "answer." It's the key that may unlock the door so you can proceed with the project. It also can signal that more preparation is needed or encourage you to wait for more fortuitous circumstances.

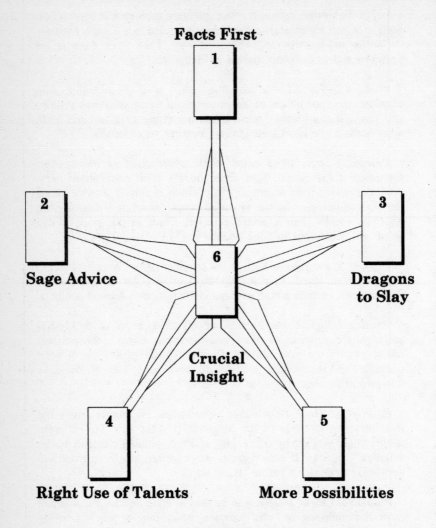

Figure 9
Star Guides Layout

PART FIVE

READING THE MAP

15 ☀ What Do I Consider?

You've selected a spread, shuffled the deck while concentrating on your question, and laid out your cards. What's next?

The first thing to consider is each card's meaning relative to its position in the layout. The location can alter the meaning slightly or even dramatically. For instance, the Six of Cups in the Here & Now position suggests that you could be mired in nostalgia and unable to get on with your life. The same card in the New Focus position would be telling you to get in touch with your past experiences and use their insight to further future activities.

More subtly, the Seven of Swords in the Challenge position may mean that you need to work on some situation with a clear mind, or use your cunning to accomplish some task, or face the truth about something. When this card is in the Resources position, however, it would indicate that someone you have been counting on will not be there for you, so you will need to rely on your own astuteness.

To get a better sense of the impact position has on a card's interpretation, you might select a card you have gotten to know fairly well and think about what it might mean in each of the Cross of Awareness positions.

In addition to the placement of individual cards, there are a number of other factors you'll want to consider in order to add depth to your readings.

The Predominance of Certain Cards

Four or more Major Arcana cards in a 10-card layout (or an abundance of Major Arcana cards in a spread of fewer cards) indicate a reading of powerful magnitude. Intense emotional experiences or changes are occurring.

Few Major Arcana cards show that you are acquiring and assimilating Minor Arcana experiences that prepare you for future transformations. The absence of a Minor Arcana suit suggests that an imbalance exists. You are lacking in the kinds of experiences associated with the missing suit, which can be positive or negative, depending on the other cards in the layout.

Four or more Minor Arcana cards of the same suit suggest that your perspective concerning your question is linked to the meaning of that suit. For instance, a predominance of Pentacles might suggest that material concern takes precedence for you or that you are attempting to resolve your issue in a businesslike manner. Swords could say that you want to or think you should search for the truth behind your issue or that it is mainly an intellectual one for you. Cups show that the resolution of your question is tied to your emotions or to a relationship issue, while Wands indicate that, whatever else it may seem, at the heart of it, your issue is a spiritual one. Depending on where the cards fall, and the rest of the cards in the layout, a predominance of cards from one Minor Arcana suit can be a positive force, showing skill and potential, or a negative one, showing rigidity in your approach to problem solving.

When four or more court cards appear in a 10-card spread, chances are that you are at the beginning of a growth cycle.[1]

Position Interrelationships

Connecting the information from cards in various positions also can deepen your understanding of the message of the reading. This is especially popular with cards in the Celtic Cross layout, or our modification of it, the Cross of Awareness. One of the best position interrelationships to consider is the crucial three-way interaction. Eileen Connolly says that often the reason for the reading, or the problem, lies in the interrelationship between the first three positions—Here & Now, Challenge, and Past Experiences.[2]

If you consider the Challenge as applying to *both* of the other positions (rather than just to the Here & Now position), you can quickly get to the heart of the matter you've asked about. Why? Because the Past Experience card often shows the reason for your present circumstances as they are depicted on the Here & Now card.

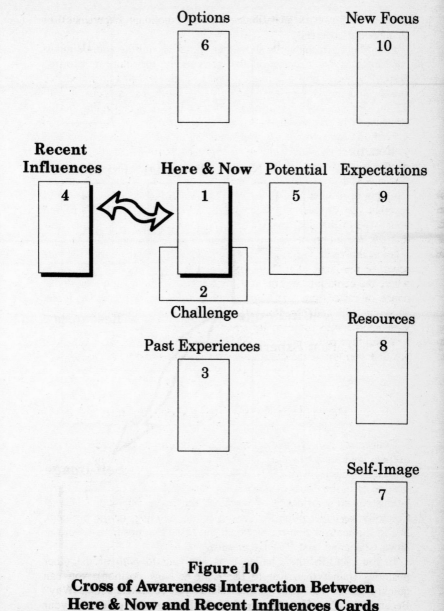

Figure 10
Cross of Awareness Interaction Between
Here & Now and Recent Influences Cards

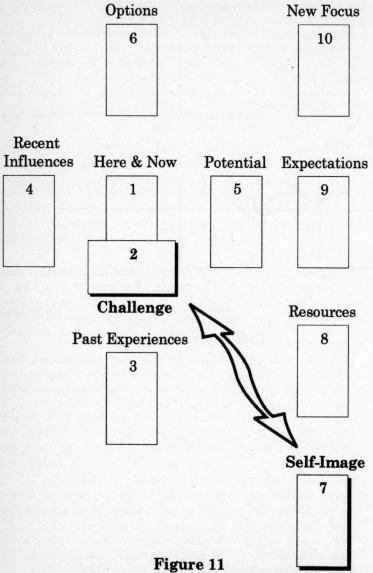

Figure 11
Cross of Awareness Interaction Between
Challenge and Self-Image Cards

The Challenge then highlights which of those past influences you may need to use, release, or learn from in your current situation.

Here are seven additional Cross of Awareness interrelationships that can give your readings more depth and you more insight.

To enhance your understanding as we progress through them, you might want to consult a layout you've prepared for yourself or re-created from a previous reading. If so, stop now and lay out your Cross of Awareness.

(1) *The interaction between Here & Now (1) cards and Recent Influences (4) cards* offers insight into some of the things that have occurred recently that have *actively* influenced your present situation. They helped shape the question you're posing now. In particular, look for the card in the Recent Influences position to reveal attitudes or behaviors that may not have been too clear to you at the time, but now, with this reading, begin to make sense. "Aha!" you may say as you compare these two cards/positions. "So that's what was really going on."

(2) *The interaction between Challenge (2) and Self-Image (7) cards.* The card drawn for the Challenge position may be regarded as a benefit worth going after or a dilemma you don't want to face. Your definition of the Challenge, and whether you're more likely to rise to or run from it, depends to a large extent on your Self-Image card.

Like the Here & Now card, the Self-Image card can be a comprehensive reflection of how you perceive yourself, but is more likely to express only one aspect of yourself, and often a shadow aspect. The question to ask yourself while looking at the Challenge/Self-Image interrelationship is "Since I feel or see myself as [*Self-Image card*], how am I likely to deal with my [*Challenge card*]?" If you don't like the answer, come up with alternative courses of action.

(3) *The interaction between Past Experiences (3) and Self-Image (7) cards.* This connection reveals how one or more experiences from your past may have shaped your Self-Image. What part did they play in building or knocking down your confidence and convincing you of your strengths and weaknesses? How actively is the situation depicted by the Past Experiences card still influencing your Self-Image today?

(4) *The interaction between Past Experiences (3) and Recent Influences (4) cards.* Recent Influences, especially those stemming

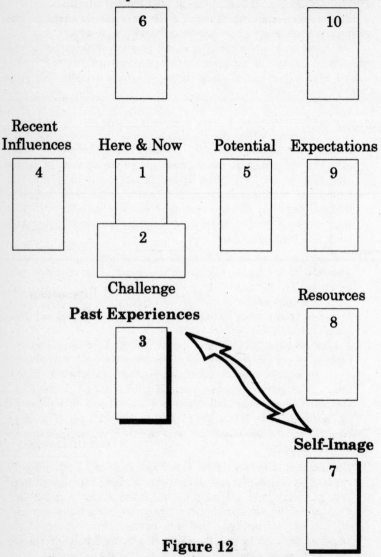

Figure 12
Cross of Awareness Interaction Between
Past Experiences and Self-Image Cards

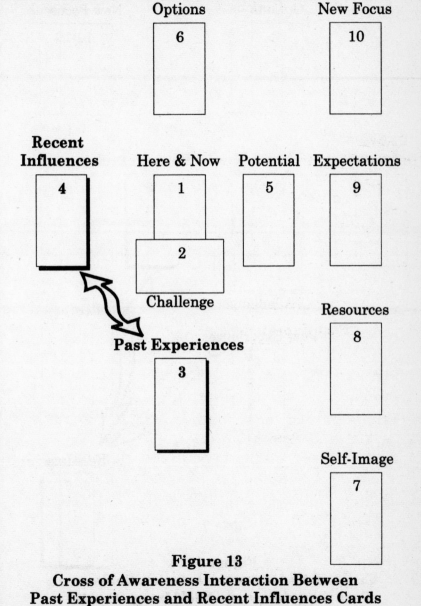

Figure 13
Cross of Awareness Interaction Between
Past Experiences and Recent Influences Cards

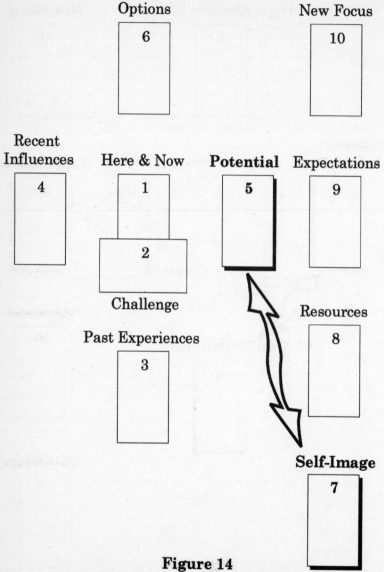

Figure 14
Cross of Awareness Interaction Between
Potential and Self-Image Cards

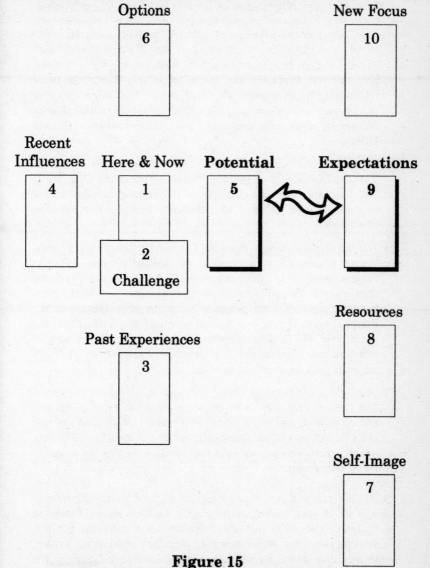

Figure 15
Cross of Awareness Interaction Between
Potential and Expectations Cards

from your own actions or attitudes, can be shaped by Past Experiences too. If the cards in the two positions are in the same suit, it's likely that the experiences reflected in those cards are quite closely and still actively connected. If they are of different suits, and the Recent Influences card falls further along the sequential progression of Pentacles, to Cups, to Swords, to Wands, the interrelationship shows growth. This also may be the case when cards of different suits show problems that have been wrestled with previously (Past Experiences) and then resolved (Recent Influences).

(5) *The interaction between Potential (5) and Self-Image (7) cards.* You can have the most positive Potential card in the deck, but if you don't see yourself as capable, or if you have an inflated view of yourself, then you may have difficulty bringing that Potential into fruition.

(6) *The interaction between Potential (5) and Expectations (9) cards.* What you expect from a situation will often affect your ability to bring it about. Thus, this interrelationship can point out expectations you should pay special attention to when you want to enhance or unblock your potential to obtain what appears in the Potential card. If ever you want to consider reversals, this is the position in which to do it, because a reversed card can suggest that you have expectations that you have hidden from others or may not even be aware of yourself.

(7) *The interaction between Options (6) and Expectations (9) cards.* The Options card may show that there are a variety of things you can do to turn your expectations into reality. Or it could say that even though you have "great expectations," there is really only one direction open to you—and one direction on which you should focus your energy.

Certainly you will not want to look at each of these interrelationships in all of your readings just because we have included them in this chapter. The cards that show up are what make the position connections important. Sometimes their meanings build on each other. Sometimes they don't. So just take a quick look at the cards in the positions we've mentioned here, and if similarities in number, suit, colors, or symbols seem to signal the presence of an influential connection, explore those interrelationships.

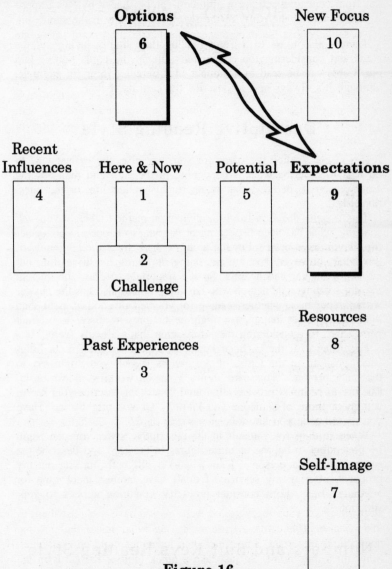

Figure 16
Cross of Awareness Interaction Between
Options and Expectations Cards

HOW DO I SAY IT?
....

There's also *more* to a Tarot reading than simply laying out the cards and considering the connections among the cards you've laid out. Cards can be read in a number of different *styles*,[3] for example, although it's always best to describe the card itself first.

Descriptive Reading Style

If you are reading the cards for someone else, the easiest way to do it is to describe what is happening in the card and then ask the other person if, or how, that relates to his or her life, or the question asked.

This is quite different from the divination method wherein you *tell* someone what has been happening or is going to happen in his or her life. If you have been following along with us since the beginning of this book, however, you are not using the cards for divination, but rather for insight and healing. So it's important to draw the querent into the reading. The person who has the problem also has the answer within. Your task, whether reading for yourself or another, is to shed light on the places that answer might be and present a new or different perspective for considering the information that's already there.

For instance, if the Eight of Pentacles appears in the Recent Influences position in the Cross of Awareness layout, you might say to the other person, "This card shows a person working industriously. The results of his efforts are all around. Does that describe your recent actions or those of someone you know?" Or you might ask, "Have you or someone you know been working hard?"

When reading for yourself in the descriptive style, you can begin by pretending to be one or more figures in the card and describe the scene in the first person: "I am a worker diligently turning out my products, offering my services. I don't have interest in or time for anything else." Then consider how that condition applies to your situation.

Numbers and Suit Keys Reading Style

Another relatively simple way to read the cards is to describe the scene, and then to refer to the meaning of the suit and the numerological meaning of the card.

For instance, if the Four of Cups is turned over in the Challenge position of the Cross of Awareness layout:

(1) Begin with your description.

"A young man sits under a tree, contemplating three cups, while a fourth cup is offered to him, seemingly from the heavens."

(2) Then refer to the suit and number meanings.

"Cups is a suit of strong feelings and emotions. It usually reflects situations involving your relationship with yourself or another. Fours refer to setting things straight, and to inner organization. They offer the opportunity to release the past and build on new ideas. So I must need to get in touch with my feelings about [the issue raised in the question] and to decide what I want to do. Setting aside some time to meditate or weigh the pros and cons of the situation would probably help too."

Now, try this yourself for the Eight of Pentacles in the Recent Influences position.

Here is at least one thing we might say:

"Pentacles are a suit of work and productivity. Eights call for a choice and possibly the reorganizing of priorities. So it would appear that I have recently been reconsidering how my work fits into my lifestyle, and perhaps how much importance I should give it in light of my other interests."

Exactly what you say, of course, will be tempered by the question raised for the reading and the position the card is in.

Evoked-Feelings Reading Style

A third way to understand the cards is by tuning into the *feeling* behind the card's scene as it pertains to the person for whom you are reading. This is a more difficult method than the first two, especially if you don't consider yourself particularly intuitive or haven't worked with your own feelings before. We recommend practicing on yourself quite a bit. Then practice with a friend you know well or one you can trust to give you accurate feedback.

To continue your reading of the Eight of Pentacles in the evoked-feelings style, you would add to your monologue one or two sentences about the way you feel.

> *[description as above in Numbers and Suit Keys Reading Style]. . . "I am tired of working alone even though I turn out good work."*

Or

> *"My work all looks the same. I am disappointed in my efforts."*

Or

> *"I am proud of the consistency and high quality of my work."*

If reading for another, after describing the scene or the numbers/keys interpretation of the Eight of Pentacles, you might ask,

> *"How do you think this person feels?"*

Or, depending on the issue being examined,

> *"Have you been feeling burdened by work or tasks?"*
> *"Has someone overwhelmed you?"*
> *"Are you feeling extremely pleased or confident about something you've accomplished recently?"*

The Gift and the Challenge Reading Style

A fourth way to read the cards is by describing the gift each card offers and the challenge it presents.

For instance, if The Moon card is drawn, you might say,

*"This card offers me the opportunity to get more in touch
with ideas that I may not have given much credence previously."*

*"It challenges me to acknowledge the new insights that may
emerge from my dreams or memories, even though they may
confuse me at first."*

To use this style, you have to know more about the card meanings
than you did for the previous reading styles. You'll become more
comfortable with it as you become more and more familiar with your
cards. But try it now anyway with the Two of Swords.

We might say,

*"The challenge with this card is to examine my attitudes,
especially stubbornness or defensiveness, and determine how
they are affecting my present situation.*

*"Although this card suggests I am in a difficult position, the
gift of the card is that it reminds me that I have the logical
ability to cut through illusion once I realize how it is affecting
me. I already sense on an intuitive level the need for balance."*

Spiritual or Personal Lessons
Reading Style

This way of reading involves considering the "lessons" or "messages" of the card as they apply to your growth or spiritual work.
We simply could not improve on this style of reading, created by
Mary K. Greer, and introduced in *Tarot Mirrors*, so we present it
with her permission.

Unless people specifically ask a question that suggests they are
ready for this information, or specifically ask for this kind of reading,
you probably will not do many readings of this nature for anyone
except yourself—and certainly not until you are quite familiar with
this reading style.

The major question you ask about each card, relative to its position,
is "For my highest good, what do I need to learn from the experience
this card represents?" A corollary is the question "Why is it happening and for what purpose?" Its meaning will change or be expanded
on by the other cards drawn; therefore, one card can seldom be considered the total answer.

Because this reading style is quite subjective, your experiences with it may differ considerably at different times and when different issues are being pondered.

For instance, when the Five of Wands is drawn, its spiritual or personal lesson might be:

> *"It's time for me to share my ideas with more people and get feedback from them ... because I need to learn that their criticism or opposition is directed at my ideas, and not at me personally."*

The important information in the message is the part that follows the *because*. Up to that point, the advice could be appropriate for many people. The lesson after it is different for each individual. "It is a sort of personal 'aha!' experience," says Greer. "Once you 'get it,' the original advice almost becomes unnecessary because the realization transforms *all* your interactions."[4]

Depending on the other cards drawn, and where you are in your life, the Five of Wands might be saying,

> *"It's time for me to take more leadership responsibility ... because I need to learn to stand up for myself and learn that what I say and do can make a difference."*

Or

> *"It's time for me to stop being the leader and let others have a chance ... because I need to learn that things will not fall apart if I am not in charge and that I can now relax."*

If the Eight of Swords is drawn, how would you respond? Stop now and consider your response. We might say,

> *"This card is telling me to look at how I am inhibiting myself and to stop blaming others for my failure to proceed... because then I have the opportunity to do something about my behavior."*

Or we might say,

> *"It is in my best interest at this time to take more risks and tell X [someone important in personal life] more of how I feel*

about the recent decision he made... <u>because</u> I need to learn that true friends don't desert you when you express your opinions.''

MORE POSSIBILITIES

Daily Focus Card

The more you work with Tarot cards, the more you will see how they apply to your life. We like to draw one card each morning and then watch for the ways the card's message expresses itself in the day's experiences.

To ensure that the information you receive is clearly focused, ask any of the following questions as you shuffle the cards for your daily draw:

- What energies will be manifesting themselves in my life today?
- What characteristics do I need to focus on or develop more fully today?
- What inner strivings are active in my inner being today?

At the end of the day, consider how its occurrences related to the card's meaning. Does looking at the day's events this way help you more fully understand them or perceive them differently?

The Traveler's Tarot

While traveling, we pull cards to suggest what we need to be alert to that day. On a trip to England to visit sacred sites, we each carried our own decks and performed a daily Tarot ritual following breakfast.

The person designated to go first pulled a card from his or her deck to determine what would be working in his or her life that day. The other two then pulled single cards from their decks to determine how they were to assist the designated person in attending to the message of his or her card. We repeated this process for each of us, and at the end of the day, evaluated how our behavior and our reactions to places we visited had been expressed by the cards.

Intuitive Layout

Richard Prosapio, author of the *Intuitive Tarot*, suggests that rather than using a layout created by someone else, you trust "the spirit within" and, by picking the number that pops into your mind, intuitively decide how many cards you need to answer your question.[5]

Draw them from the deck. Lay them out left to right. After you understand them, be sensitive to whether your higher self thinks you need to draw additional cards.

Dreams and the Tarot

Don't be surprised if your Tarot work or meditations begin to influence your dreams and vice versa. Dreams are another medium for the expression of archetypal energies, and measure your progress toward individuation. A dream may clarify how a particular Tarot card relates to your life or give you new ideas about the message it's trying to get across. The insights you gain from a Tarot reading also may be repeated or expanded in subsequent dreams.

After you have been working with the cards for a while or have spent some time meditating on a card, you can even ask your higher self for a dream that gives you more information about how that card is expressed in your life, or how its energies affect your life.

Although some of the images in your dream may be identical to those on the card, it is more likely that your dream will include its own symbols that elaborate on how a card's energy—let's say The Magician's—affects your psyche, your life experiences, or your spiritual growth. They are your *personal* Magician symbols.

Incubating dreams—seeking solutions from them—has long been a form of dreamwork, and there are a number of elaborate schemes and rituals for accomplishing it. However, the most *crucial* element is to spend a sufficient amount of time preparing yourself for the dream. When the dream you're incubating involves a Tarot card, your preparation might include: studying the card; meditating on it; attempting to live the card in your life or defining how it's active in your life; and reading or reviewing what others have said about it. For a brief, intensive period of time, you immerse yourself in every imaginable aspect of that particular card.

Then, on the night you want to ask for a dream, write your request (How does The Magician express itself in my life?) on a piece of paper. In the morning, write down your dream(s) in as much detail as you can. How does it answer your question? If the answer is not clear, continue thinking about your question and how the card fits into your life. Then repeat the procedure for the next two or three nights.

If you don't get an illuminating dream immediately, don't be discouraged. Although many people do have a clear insight the very next day, some research suggests that dreams occurring five to seven days after an incubation request may be more useful and to the point.

You can also understand your dreams by selecting a Major Arcana card that closely resembles your dream image. "Meditation on this tarot figure will provide a subtle tuning and realignment of energy that permits a fresh look at the situation that triggered the dream,"[6] writes psychiatrist Irene Gad.

Drawing one card for each item, person, or event in the dream and then rephrasing the dream using the cards' meanings can also be fruitful in understanding your dream, according to Gail Fairfield.[7]

PART SIX

SAMPLE JOURNEYS

16 ❂ Opening the Door

In the next two chapters we present readings we did using the various layouts introduced in this book. All readings were done during the time we were writing the book (October 1994–June 1995).

Signe's Card Perception and Expression Reading

Signe was having difficulty writing about the suit of Cups. Although the discipline of writing every day was becoming easier, the work was not flowing as it had previously and she was not having as much fun with it as she had earlier. Her question for the Tarot was:

> How can I resume my joyous perception
> and expression of the cards?

She used the Rider-Waite cards in her reading. They appear in Figure 17.

POSITION 1, HERE & NOW: THE CHARIOT (MAJOR ARCANA VII)

NUMBERS AND SUIT KEYS READING: This is a card of charging ahead victoriously (seven) and depicts Signe's present state ... charging firmly, even compulsively, ahead, focusing on the discipline of getting the job done, whether she enjoys it or not.

Options

New Focus

Recent
Influences

Here & Now

Potential

Expectations

Challenge

Resources

Past Experiences

Self-Image

**Figure 17
Signe's Cross of Awareness Reading**

CARD MEANING READING: Signe is moving forward despite her doubts about her recent writing, and her sense that discussing emotions (Cups) has to be serious, whereas other suits do not necessarily have to be.

The charioteer has his heart protected. He is strong and armored against the emotions raised by the Cups. Perhaps Signe is not drawing on her feminine intuition the way she did in her earlier writing.

Instead she has been using her "head thinking," which she understands as being part of her masculine energy. She has been trying to filter the Cups' emotional material through her intellect.

Signe's reaction to this card was "My masculine side is not happy. The suit of Cups is soft and watery. You step on them. They spill out all that feminine stuff."

GIFT AND CHALLENGE READING: The gifts of the card are strong motivation to change, especially in the direction of the spiritual. The challenge is to stop harnessing her emotions and imagination.

POSITION 2, CHALLENGE: KING OF CUPS

NUMBERS AND SUIT KEYS READING: Cups express the emotional side of an issue, and that is precisely Signe's problem. She has been plunging ahead, ignoring her feelings about the meanings of the suit and about her work. She needs to pay more attention to her feelings and to use them in the service of her writing.

Signe needs to reward herself for the discipline she has already achieved and not take the project as seriously as she has been. She needs to allow herself to be more jubilant.

CARD MEANING READING: Signe's challenge is to recognize that her masculine side does have emotions. She needs to trust and draw on both her masculine and feminine aspects in order to expand on her descriptions of the meanings of the cards. Joy and interest will return to her work as she recognizes and accepts her feelings about the cards and writes from that awareness, as well as from the intellectual knowledge of their meaning.

GIFT AND CHALLENGE READING: The gift of this card for Signe is confidence to know and express her feelings. The challenge is not to think that because she has reached a higher level of know-how than before, the situation is resolved.

POSITION 3, PAST INFLUENCES: SIX OF SWORDS

NUMBERS AND SUIT KEYS READING: Swords are a suit of keen logic and analytical ability. As a double three, sixes suggest that Signe obviously has had some previous success in learning to operate logically; however, sixes also speak of self-discipline and suggest that Signe has developed that skill as well and can apply it to the resolution of her question.

CARD MEANING READING: Signe says that the figure she identifies with in this card is the man who is guiding the boat. Signe got along in the past by behaving logically and sensibly, and only dipping into the waters of her emotions now and then.

GIFT AND CHALLENGE READING: The gift of the card is the ability to change focus and gain a new perspective. It challenges Signe to maintain tranquillity during times of stress and not to go to extremes.

POSITION 4, RECENT INFLUENCES: ACE OF PENTACLES

NUMBERS AND SUIT KEYS READING: Aces represent potential while Pentacles refers to working to make gifts tangible. If it weren't already obvious, Signe's recent work has prompted the reading.

CARD MEANING READING: Signe's writing is so different than it has been on previous projects that she doesn't know where it's coming from. She has been amazed and astounded. This card represents the mysterious source of the material that is coming to her and the energy with which she has been able to work.

GIFT AND CHALLENGE READING: This card offers Signe the ability to be definite and focused about the task at hand, along with a new surge of energy. It challenges her to use its energy for more than the task at hand, and not to fall for a premature sense of security about her ability.

POSITION 5, POTENTIAL: STRENGTH (MAJOR ARCANA VIII)

NUMBERS AND SUIT KEYS READING: The potential to overcome her problem is available, but the battle is not going to be won with willpower.

The card's number, eight, suggests the opportunity for inner reorganization.

CARD MEANING READING: Because of the lion, this is sometimes referred to as the Leo card, and Signe is a Leo. She does have the ability to express feminine strength, especially if she can reconcile her attitudes about masculine and feminine functioning.

GIFT AND CHALLENGE READING: The gifts of the card are reconciliation of Signe's higher and lower selves, and being more attuned to her inner nature. She is challenged not to suppress her emotions to the point of killing her spontaneity.

POSITION 6, OPTIONS: TWO OF WANDS

NUMBERS AND SUIT KEYS READING: Twos calls for a choice and some kind of balance between two positions. Wands steer our growth in the direction of imagination and spirit. Signe's choice will definitely result in growth for her, not only in creating the book's contents but in her own spiritual work.

CARD MEANING READING: This has always been one of Signe's favorite cards. It says to her that "the world is your oyster," and that she doesn't need to be so limited. The two wands represent a choice between when to draw upon masculine logic (the lilies of truth) and feminine wisdom (the roses of passion).

GIFT AND CHALLENGE READING: The gift is the power of choice. The challenge is to confront the desire for stability with no change and consider its cost—boredom or a false sense of security.

POSITION 7, SELF-IMAGE: ACE OF CUPS

NUMBERS AND SUIT KEYS READING: Aces signify the readiness to change and to begin to grow in a different direction. The suit of Cups suggests that this new direction will involve more honoring of emotions.

CARD MEANING READING: What a wonderful card to draw in this position! Clearly the creative energy of emotions is going to be accessible to Signe, and she is ready for it. She may never regard her emotions in the same way. She'll value and have access to both logic and emotion without having to devalue either.

GIFT AND CHALLENGE READING: The gift of this card is the opportunity to recognize and express her emotions. The challenge is to acknowledge resistance, especially toward experiencing negative feelings, hopes, or doubts.

POSITION 8, RESOURCES: SIX OF PENTACLES

NUMBERS AND SUIT KEYS READING: The six suggests that Signe has, or will have, the discipline to accomplish the next step, which is related to inner growth and to changing her work with the book. We wouldn't be surprised if, from this point on, Signe attracts additional ideas and support.

CARD MEANING READING: Signe's inner masculine (the merchant) now becomes generous and gives spiritual sustenance (gold coins) to previously neglected aspects of herself. When this card was turned over, Signe said, "Ideas are going to fly to me to help my readings, especially those I do at church. I'm going to be able to do readings differently."

Signe must also take care that her physical needs are met during the writing of the book.

GIFT AND CHALLENGE READING: The gift of this card is the ability to share resources and receive assistance. The challenge is to give freely with no conditions and expectations, and to receive what is freely given with no inner score keeping.

POSITION 9, EXPECTATIONS: KING OF PENTACLES

NUMBERS AND SUIT KEYS READING: Signe expects both to do the work (Pentacles) it takes to master this situation (King), and to master it. The downside is that she still expects, at some level, to do a lot of the work by male logic. She'll think it through.

CARD MEANING READING: One of Signe's recent worries has been about whether we are going to get the book put together in time to meet our deadline. She also feels that after the wrestling she has done with her writing and the material for this book, she will now feel more free to talk to people and do workshops. She will be able to see herself as an authority. As she dons the King's cloak, her inner and outer growth will speak for itself.

GIFT AND CHALLENGE READING: The gifts this card offers are mastery of emotional information and outward accomplishment. Its challenge is to not get mired in emotions.

POSITION 10, NEW FOCUS: SEVEN OF PENTACLES

NUMBERS AND SUIT KEYS READING: Signe will become an "initiate" (sevens) in the ways of the emotions. She will work (Pentacles) for it, and it will work for her. It will also change the way she focuses on her writing and her Tarot work.

CARD MEANING READING: This card suggests that when the deadline has been reached, Signe will look back over her accomplishments and contemplate her work with satisfaction. It is a card of work and of victory, so it shows that she can go from this reading, employ patience, and use her skills (toiling) to make her expectations a reality. She no longer needs to worry about whether or not we will meet the deadline.

GIFT AND CHALLENGE READING: The gifts of this card are the ability to evaluate her experiences and the patience to wait for results. It challenges Signe to move through self-doubts about the value of her work and her skills.

SUMMARY: In her reading Signe has two Major Arcana, two Cups, one Sword, one Wand, and four Pentacles, a good representation of all the suits, with a special emphasis on work (Pentacles). This makes sense since her question was about her work and her way of working.

Because both were aces, we compared the cards in the Recent Influence (Ace of Pentacles) and Self-Image (Ace of Cups) positions. The Ace of Pentacles shows that Signe has recently experienced joy in her work. The Ace of Cups shows she has the emotional capacity to experience that again, especially if she looks at her writing as a gift that is to be expressed naturally. The nature of the soul is to express joyfully.

Looking next at the two Major Arcana—The Chariot in the Here &

Now position and Strength in the Potential position—we see that Signe has the discipline (Chariot) as well as the compassion and gentleness (Strength) to handle her future writing in a gentle and joyful manner.

Considering the relationship between the cards in the Here & Now (Chariot), Challenge (King of Cups), and Past Experiences (Six of Swords) positions once again highlights Signe's inner battle between the royal masculine and the impoverished feminine—a battle, by the way, that is typical of many people in our culture. Who is needed to resolve the situation? Why, no less than the master of emotions, the King of Cups.

Signe has new discipline (The Chariot) to handle her emotions (King of Cups). Whereas in the past she merely skimmed over her emotional world (Six of Swords), now she can gently and firmly rule the waters of her emotions (King of Cups).

Sandra's Shadow Work Reading

Sandra became interested in shadow work while she was researching and writing *Cloud Nine*, her book about dreams. In addition to that research, she has continued reading and attending lectures about the shadow. She also had two significant dreams pertaining to her shadow work during the months immediately preceding this reading.

Consequently Sandra asked the question,

What do I need to consider to
advance my shadow work?

She decided to work with the Aquarian deck. The cards Sandra drew appear in Figure 18.

POSITION 1, HERE & NOW: THE TOWER (MAJOR ARCANA XVI)

NUMBERS AND SUIT KEYS READING: Sandra is ready for major new work on her personality, and the seven ($16 = 1 + 6 = 7$) suggests that she has already begun the process and is an initiate.

CARD MEANING READING: The Tower's appearance reinforces the fact that Sandra is already involved in her shadow work and experiencing some emotional upheaval. In this new cycle she will have to face

Options

New Focus

Recent
Influences

Here & Now

Potential

Expectations

Challenge

Resources

Past Experiences

Self-Image

Figure 18
Sandra's Cross of Awareness Reading

some beliefs about herself that she has not faced before, and maybe throw them out, along with some old roles she has adopted along the way.

When this card was turned up, she said, "How appropriate. I was just writing about the shadow aspects of this card last week."

GIFT AND CHALLENGE READING: The gifts of the card are flashes of insight and intuition, and liberation from restricting attitudes. The challenge for Sandra is to allow herself to feel vulnerable and fearful as new material emerges.

POSITION 2, CHALLENGE: THE CHARIOT (MAJOR ARCANA VII)

NUMBERS AND SUIT KEYS READING: As a challenge, seven cautions that there will be tests and temptations. Sandra's challenge will be to pass the tests or avoid the temptations, such as intellectualizing her ideas or being superficial about the material that will emerge. She must not get sidetracked.

CARD MEANING READING: Sandra must keep going even when she thinks she has been "victorious." There's still more to come. The card also cautions Sandra not to get too cerebral about her shadow work, but instead to learn to draw upon spiritual energy to help her examine old debris stored in The Tower (Here & Now card).

GIFT AND CHALLENGE READING: The gift of the card is the ability to harness her energy toward her purpose. The challenge is to not give in to the feeling of being at the mercy of her instincts or inner nature.

POSITION 3, PAST EXPERIENCES: THE STAR (MAJOR ARCANA XVII)

NUMBERS AND SUIT KEYS READING: Eights (17 = 1 + 7 = 8) suggest that even though Sandra has achieved a certain amount of balance from her past work, she also made decisions and set priorities that are preventing her from experiencing the fullness of life. These definitely have a major effect on her need to do shadow work at this time.

CARD MEANING READING: The Star is Sandra's personality card (see Chapter 4), which makes this reading and this position especially important. Past therapeutic and healing work has led Sandra to this point. It provides her with the preparation and inspiration to take the next step.

Whether she realizes it or not, spirit has been influencing her (the V shape of the horizon). As those shadow experiences of the past emerge, Sandra will understand some of the basic principles of shadow work (jagged design in star) and specifically those that have caused her personal conflict (jagged design in foreground).

GIFT AND CHALLENGE READING: The gift of this card is spiritual regeneration, cleansing, and renewal. It also directs her to follow her own inner star. The challenge of the card is to overcome pessimism and self-doubt and to find the inner meaning of past events.

POSITION 4, RECENT INFLUENCES: PAGE OF CUPS

NUMBERS AND SUIT KEYS READING: The Page represents an initiate, so whatever skills Sandra thinks she possesses, it's likely she still has a lot to learn about dealing with the emotions (Cups) that emerge from the shadow. The card also suggests that within the last six weeks or so, her shadow work or the impetus for it has intensified.

CARD MEANING READING: Sandra has recently begun an active phase of development (fish = emerging content from unconscious; the Self), but there's a chance that she may have made more of her recent experiences than was warranted. They could be no more than the tip of the iceberg. The Page's elaborate clothing, for example, may point to recent work that has been rather superficial. She needs to dig more deeply into the spiritual.

GIFT AND CHALLENGE READING: The gift of this card is skill in recognizing and expressing emotions. The challenge for Sandra is to not get too ego inflated about her past therapeutic work and think she is further along than she is.

POSITION 5, POTENTIAL: KING OF CUPS

NUMBERS AND SUIT KEYS READING: This card suggests that the potential to achieve mastery (the King) in shadow/emotional (Cups) work is there.

CARD MEANING READING: The potential exists for Sandra to delve deeply, confidently, and with some skill, into her shadow work. It is likely that the healing of some old emotional wounds will occur. Sandra may even become somewhat of an authority on shadow skills if she does not get caught up in ego inflation.

GIFT AND CHALLENGE READING: The gifts of this card are mastery and emotional sensitivity. The challenge it offers Sandra is related to self-centeredness. She could get so caught up in her own emotions that she fails to acknowledge those of others.

POSITION 6, OPTIONS: TEN OF CUPS

NUMBERS AND SUIT KEYS READING: Recognition of the emotions (Cups) that emerge from her shadow work possibly could connect Sandra more deeply with others and with the universe.

CARD MEANING READING: It is likely that Sandra's shadow work will not only increase her own happiness, but also enhance her love relationship—if she chooses to apply it there.

This is a card that speaks of the ending of old cycles and the beginning of new ones, so one of the options open to Sandra is to begin a new cycle.

GIFT AND CHALLENGE READING: The gifts of this card are recommitment to an ongoing purpose, or commitment to a new one. It highlights the value of family relationships. The challenge is to not engage in unrealistic hopes or dreams.

POSITION 7, SELF-IMAGE: SEVEN OF SWORDS

NUMBERS AND SUIT KEYS READING: As the coming together of the three and the four (3 + 4 = 7), this card is a definite message from Sandra's Self. It is calling upon her to go through this transformation (sevens), even though she can expect ordeals. Swords suggest that the Self is telling her either that she can use her intellect in the work, or not to rely too heavily on the intellect.

CARD MEANING READING: This card reminds Sandra that discipline is needed to achieve success. She will have to determine how the work applies to her without being unduly influenced by the work of others. The card is one of bravery, skill, and "derring-do." It also cautions her that her unconscious will be cunning and crafty, especially when she attempts to handle the situation logically or intellectually. There's a battle ahead.

GIFT AND CHALLENGE READING: The gift of this card is the ability to research and gather appropriate material. The challenge is to face and deal with the material she gathers.

POSITION 8, RESOURCES: ACE OF CUPS

NUMBERS AND SUIT KEYS READING: Sandra has the Ace's energy and inspiration to help her deal with her emerging emotions (Cups). She has all of her senses to rely on, as well as the power, focus, and endurance to handle whatever comes up.

CARD MEANING READING: "If you ask for it, it will come," Sandra said when this card was turned over. If she wants to express her spiritual ideals more fully and does the necessary work, her higher self will supply the information she seeks. It's likely that new influences, perhaps in the form of new teachers or teachings, will help her apply her work.

GIFT AND CHALLENGE READING: As with Signe, the gift of this card is the opportunity for Sandra to recognize and express her emotions. The challenge is to acknowledge resistance, especially toward negative feelings, hopes, or doubts.

POSITION 9, EXPECTATIONS: KING OF SWORDS

NUMBERS AND SUIT KEYS READING: Sandra expects to become a master (King) at shadow work, but she is still regarding it from a largely intellectual (Swords) perspective. The card could also be saying that Sandra expects her intelligence and knowledge to greatly aid her in shadow work.

CARD MEANING READING: Sandra expects to accomplish the shadow work and to be more powerful as a result of it. The card cautions her not to get too logical about it. In addition, she may already be shoring up her defenses, which is not a good sign.

GIFT AND CHALLENGE READING: The gift of this card is intellectual mastery and assertiveness. It challenges Sandra to be selective about how and with whom she shares her shadow material.

POSITION 10, NEW FOCUS: SEVEN OF RODS

NUMBERS AND SUIT KEYS READING: The seven suggests that Sandra will achieve unification and some resolution of the tension between masculine and feminine. Her new focus will be more on her own transformation rather than outer projects. There will definitely be a new spiritual (Rods/Wands) approach to her life.

CARD MEANING READING: Sandra can expect to achieve more comfort as a result of her shadow work. This is a card of self-accomplished success. Sevens show victory or accomplishment and its accompanying wisdom, but the card also reminds her that there may be some feelings of imbalance as she proceeds.

GIFT AND CHALLENGE READING: The gift of this card for Sandra is the courage and integrity to stand up for her beliefs or values. The challenge is to be realistic about the odds she faces and not get trapped.

SUMMARY: Sandra has three Major Arcana cards, including her personality card, all of which make this an important reading for her. She has one Rod/Wand, two Swords, and four Cups in the reading.

The four Cups show that this will be an emotional experience for her, as shadow work can only be. The two Swords (intellect and logic) both fall in positions that have to do with the way she thinks about herself and what she expects. At the time of the reading, she was quite cerebral about the shadow work. The one Rod (intuition), in the New Focus position, shows that as her work progresses, her focus will turn away from the intellect and more toward the intuitive, but probably not for six months or so.

Although Pentacles can sometimes refer to inner work, there are no Pentacles in the layout. We think this is because Sandra's question totally refers to inner work and not to physical work—unlike Signe's reading, which was focused on the connection of her physical work with her inner work and contained four Pentacles.

The first interrelationship we examine is that of Self-Image (Seven of Swords) and New Focus (Seven of Rods). They are both sevens, both mystical numbers, and this interrelationship shows that Sandra needs to consider the shadow work as part of her personal path, a necessary part of her growth.

In fact, Sandra has *four* sevens in her reading: The Chariot, The Tower (16 = 1 + 6 = 7), the Seven of Swords, and the Seven of Rods. They encourage her shadow work, yet also indicate that she will be sorely tested. Sandra will definitely be involved in creation and unification.

We can't resist the kind of visual puns the cards often make, so finally we consider the interrelationship between Here & Now (The Tower) and the Options (Ten of Cups). This combination says to us that even though the work is an upheaval, there is the possibility of a rainbow at the end of the storm.

17 ☀ Through the Looking Glass

It is our purpose in this chapter to present readings demonstrating the use of the five additional layouts presented in Chapter 14.

Micro-Cross Readings (2 cards)

As a result of some of Robert's meditative work, he decided he needed more personal information on the self-protective aspects of warriors. His question was "How can I be more of a self-protective warrior?"

Robert chose to work with the Morgan-Greer deck. The cards he drew appear in Figure 19.

POSITION 1, HERE & NOW: QUEEN OF RODS

This tells us that Robert needs to look for growth not destruction. He needs to get more in touch with his feminine side and learn to evaluate communication from a gentle and compassionate stance.

Because of her sensitivity, the Queen of Rods would know how to deflect attack. Robert needs to adopt her style. Is there any real need for him to defend himself? There are gentle warriors who have learned not to need swords. Robert has the capacity, if he will tune into it, to consider someone's expression of frustration and misunderstanding as poor communication, not necessarily as a challenge or personal attack.

Here & Now

Challenge

Figure 19
Robert's Micro-Cross Reading

POSITION 2, CHALLENGE: THREE OF RODS

Robert needs to consider options other than being wounded. There are several to choose from. Robert's "stance" as depicted in the card—his seeming disconnection from the surroundings and people present—may be a source of irritation to those he encounters in actual settings. Robert needs to evaluate and walk away, not stay and be hurt. His growth task is to avoid feeling attacked by considering what others' motivations might be.

*   *   *

Signe was anticipating a move from her earthquake-damaged condo. Her question was "How can I best facilitate my temporary move while my apartment is being repaired?"

Signe used the Aquarian deck. The cards she drew appear in Figure 20.

POSITION 1, HERE & NOW: FIVE OF CUPS

As the move comes about, Signe needs to stay focused on the positive rather than on the disorder and how put out she'll be feeling. A positive attitude will help her better organize herself.

Signe felt this card offered her confirmation of the position she has thought of taking. Dismayed by the mess that still needs to be taken care of, she responded to the card by saying, "There is a lot of stuff

Here & Now

Challenge

Figure 20
Signe's Micro-Cross Reading

I need to look through and discard. I'm not doing that and I need to start now.''

POSITION 2, CHALLENGE: QUEEN OF PENTACLES

Signe's challenge is to take charge and handle the situation in a practical way. Do the sorting. Move into her powerful feminine attitude and just do it.

Triad Reading (3 cards)

Robert was revising the material he used in his massage practice. Coinciding with that, he asked the question "How can I present myself to clients so they understand and connect with the talents I have to offer?"

He used the Rider-Waite deck. The cards he drew appear in Figure 21.

POSITION 1, PRESENT SITUATION: SEVEN OF WANDS

Sevens are numbers of creation, so it is appropriate to work on this matter at this time. Energy is building.

The Seven of Wands shows that Robert has achieved a level of

Past	Present	Future
Situation	**Attitude**	**Main Idea**
Body	**Mind**	**Spirit**

Figure 21
Robert's Triad Reading

mastery in his professional field, but may need to develop a way to succinctly explain his many areas of expertise without sounding like a know-it-all.

It is possible that when asked specific questions about his skills or how he would handle a situation, he gets a bit defensive. He may get caught up in trying to explain his work without having all the facts of another's situation, or without getting others to clarify their question.

Although the card refers to Robert's position, it also refers to the stance that his clients take, and he may not be explaining well enough how their "position" in the world affects their body, how the body can seem to be "in balance" and yet be "out of balance."

POSITION 2, ATTITUDE TOWARD SITUATION: KING OF CUPS

Robert's "I know this/I am in charge" attitude about his work may reduce his clients' feeling of power rather than build on it. He may be coming on too strong emotionally when a client needs other information or other needs met first. Robert could benefit if he were to slow down, stop giving his explanations so fast, and take time to get in touch with deeper feelings he has about how he approaches clients.

POSITION 3, MAIN THING TO KEEP IN MIND: TEN OF WANDS

The Ten of Wands suggests there's quite a different way to respond than Robert's typical way. His higher wisdom needs to connect with his clients' higher wisdom, which he may not be doing presently. He has to be careful not to let a lot of informational details get in the way of what a person is really requesting.

Daily Opportunity Reading (4 cards)

Sandra was experiencing a stressful day in which she felt a need to get away, but also thought she had an exceptional amount of work to accomplish. Using the Rider-Waite deck, she did a Daily Opportunity Reading, asking simply, "What's with me today?" Her cards are shown in Figure 22.

POSITION 1, INFLUENCE: KING OF PENTACLES

We can understand why this was a "run away" day. You see, unless the advantages of doing a particular task are patently clear to the King of Pentacles, he's not interested. Also the King has exceptionally high work principles. It's likely that those high standards were interfering with Sandra's enjoyment of the day's writing tasks.

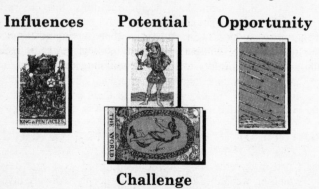

Influences   **Potential**   **Opportunity**

Challenge

Figure 22
Sandra's Daily Opportunity Reading

Position 2, Potential: Page of Cups

The Page of Cups doesn't always carry out his ideas in realistic terms, which may be quite true in this case, given the high standards and the demands/influence of the King of Pentacles.

Position 3, Challenge: The World (Major Arcana XXI)

The challenge or opportunity presented to Sandra is to get in touch with the unconscious material pushing to be expressed. It suggests that there are some active conflicts at work, which she has not identified and therefore cannot reconcile. If she can do this, she can take another step toward wholeness.

Position 4, Possibility: Eight of Wands

If Sandra can resolve the tension of the opposites, it is possible that she will experience a rush of ideas or energy. Things may be up in the air for a while, but she is moving forward toward the end of her course.

Summary

The presence of one Major Arcana and two court cards out of a total of four indicates this is an important reading, not to be ignored, especially the challenge to identify the conflicting opposites.

Fountain of Creation Reading (5 cards)

Robert had discovered some material on Druid work and its symbology, which he wanted to delve into more deeply. Already involved in two inner growth programs, he raised the question,

How will my study of Druid symbology
enhance my current studies?

Robert worked with the Morgan-Greer deck. The cards he drew are shown in Figure 23.

POSITION 1, SUPPORTIVE FORCES: JUDGEMENT (MAJOR ARCANA XX)

As a Major Arcana card, Judgement represents archetypal energy at work within Robert. Two (20 = 2 + 0 = 2) represents the need to balance or consider two positions, as well as the potential for combining them. At this time we presume those two positions refer to (1) already acquired information, and (2) the new information to be learned. Twos also represent new energy at work, ready to move into conscious awareness.

This card represents Robert's calling to be on a path, working toward the light. Where he is now is appropriate. A window is opening for him, or rather, he is in the process of entering a whole new realm. Being "on the path" calls for Robert to make different kinds of decisions about his daily life and how he will interact in the world.

That the three figures are so prominent suggests there is a harmony in the masculine, feminine, and inner child aspects. The work will touch all those energies. The cross shows an equal alignment between the vertical (spiritual) and the horizontal (mundane). The new work can help balance these two. There's a golden opportunity (gold water) for working with the emotions.

POSITION 2, DISTRACTING ENERGIES: FOUR OF SWORDS

Swords represent independence and logical thinking, while fours represent personal logic and the need for inner organization.

Robert is dealing with the death of old ideas and the birth of new ones. He needs to cut through the superficial and get to the essence of the material. This card cautions him not to rush through the new work, but to take the time to carefully integrate it into his present and continuing pursuits.

Mental constructs (armor) or preconceived ideas he has, based on his current studies, may distract him from looking to the heart—the spiritual principle—of Druidic symbolism.

POSITION 3, EGO ROLE: KING OF RODS

Wands is the suit of insight and represents Robert's spiritual journey. This card shows that Robert's "power of intuition" and his

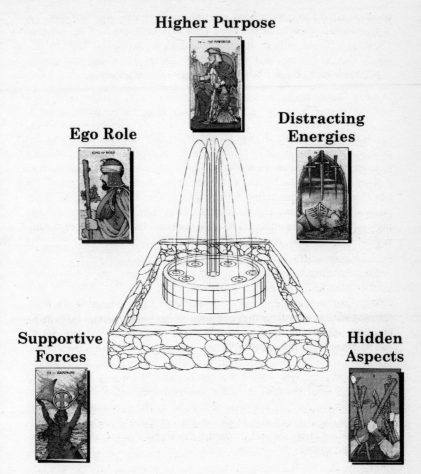

Figure 23
Robert's Fountain of Creation Reading

spiritual need have led to his current position. His maturity and his past spiritual work have prepared him to integrate all of his studies. They have fitted him to this time and have developed him to this point. The card shows that when Robert studies something thoroughly, it becomes part of his inner domain and he can act on it.

POSITION 4, HIDDEN ASPECTS: FIVE OF RODS

Once again Robert draws a card from the suit that indicates his intuition will be at work in his studies. Fives represent the opportunity to change direction or viewpoints.

This card involves Robert's putting things together in his mind. He has recently been pondering how to fit together all his interests, especially things that have equal importance for him. He has been balancing one against the other. The downside of the card is conflicting beliefs with no way to integrate them.

POSITION 5, HIGHER PURPOSE: THE EMPEROR (MAJOR ARCANA IV)

Powerful authoritative energy (Major Arcana) is available for Robert to draw upon to help him organize (fours) the material he will be learning and to fit it into its natural place in his other spiritual work.

The Emperor suggests that Robert is going to make his own rules; do it his way. He probably will not adopt anyone else's traditional way of studying. His work holds the possibility for him to know and understand what it's like to make powerful decisions.

The downside of this card is that it holds the potential for Robert to become rigid about the work, to get compulsive about making it fit with other ideas instead of seeing the Druidic work as an elaboration on the others.

SUMMARY

Robert has two Major Arcana cards and one court card, out of a total of five cards, making this a significant reading. The presence of two Rods cards suggests that this is an issue that directly relates to his intuitive skills and that they will benefit from the study of Druid symbology.

Knight writes that The Emperor can be considered an anthropomorphic symbol of nature as a divine aspect of God. The card aligns with the 28th Cabalistic path, which is reflected in nature worship, whether it be *Druidic* [emphasis ours], Celtic, or any other.[1]

Star Guides Readings (6 cards)

Lillian [not her real name] asks, "What are the pros and cons of my continuing to live with Harry or leaving him?" (See Figure 24)

POSITION 1, FACTS FIRST: FOUR OF PENTACLES

While there is a measure of financial stability in the present situation, Lillian is able to make her own living apart from Harry. The question is how leaving or staying will contribute to Lillian's growth, and this single card is ambiguous with respect to that. Can she use the break to grow, or will it cause her to have to concentrate on financial matters?

POSITION 2, SAGE ADVICE: TEN OF WANDS

Lillian feels weighed down with most of the day-to-day decision making and the responsibility for the interaction between herself and Harry. This card confirms her experience of this phase of her life and points out that there is more to be explored and lived "down the road."

POSITION 3, DRAGONS TO SLAY: FOUR OF SWORDS

Lillian needs time alone to reevaluate her life goals and, possibly, for spiritual pursuits. This may require a change from her present lifestyle, or may indicate allowing sufficient time to evaluate before making a decision.

POSITION 4, RIGHT USE OF TALENTS: ACE OF WANDS

This card carries the gift of inspiration and the ability to make a new beginning in her life, using her skills in a new direction for greater personal progress and fulfillment.

POSITION 5, MORE POSSIBILITIES: PAGE OF CUPS

Lillian can indeed further her emotional development when she is free to create new things or pursue a new path. The card's message is that she is only beginning to experience her full potential.

**Figure 24
Lillian's Star Guides Reading**

Position 6, Crucial Insight: Wheel of Fortune

Aha! Time for a change. Lillian has come into a new cycle, and it's time to make some practical adjustments. This does not necessarily mean leaving Harry, but if she stays, she will have to institute some definite changes in the relationship. Whether she can do that, what those changes would be, and how Harry would respond to them are unknown at this time.

Summary

This reading is a fairly balanced one in that at least one card from every Minor Arcana suit appears. There are two Wands, and both are cards that are outside the two-nine sequence. The Ace offers the gift of intuition, and the Ten promises a new vision. Whether or not Lillian leaves Harry, the cards suggest she should think more seriously about how a changed relationship will free her to rely on her intuition. The two fours (Pentacles and Swords) suggest a need for Lillian to organize her life and to put an end to internal chaos, possibly by setting some boundaries for Harry if she remains with him.

Charlene [not her real name] raises the question,

"How can I get started in my career in psychic counseling?" (See Figure 25)

Position 1, Facts First: Queen of Cups

This card represents skills that need to be honed for success in this field. Charlene has to develop through further study and practice the authority necessary to advise others. To become a better psychic counselor, she needs to become more aware of the role played by the unconscious, probably through work on herself.

Position 2, Sage Advice: The Chariot

This card indicates inner conflicts to be resolved. Charlene will need lots of discipline and to develop a deeper connection with her higher self. She must identify her inner conflicts related to psychic counseling and begin to resolve them before she can be successful.

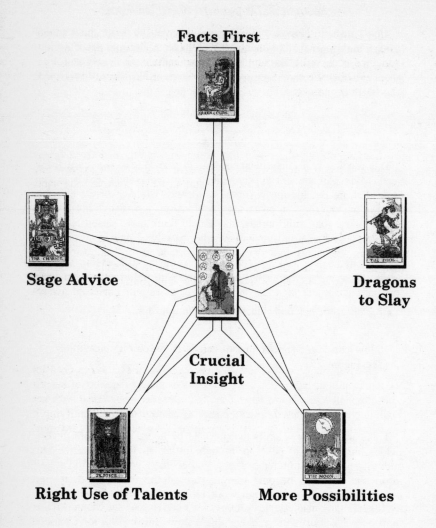

Figure 25
Charlene's Star Guides Reading

POSITION 3, DRAGONS TO SLAY: THE FOOL

Fools rush in. Naively thinking that this will be a fun, new adventure, Charlene may find that she will have to become more serious and focused about her intentions before making this a successful career. She may be unwilling to settle down and do the self-work that this reading indicates she will need to do.

POSITION 4, RIGHT USE OF TALENTS: JUSTICE

Charlene needs to consider the ethics of wanting to make a favorable impression with her clients. She must be willing to express any negativity she sees in the cards and not to make positive statements just for the sake of being positive.

POSITION 5, MORE POSSIBILITIES: THE MOON

Charlene needs to learn to live the symbolic life before she can show others the way. Studying symbolism, interpreting her own dreams, and understanding cycles will help, as will increased awareness of her own unconscious needs.

POSITION 6, CRUCIAL INSIGHT: THE SIX OF PENTACLES

Before becoming successful in this career, Charlene has to do a lot of work on herself. Specifically she needs to identify aspects of herself that she is not nurturing sufficiently. She must be able to deal with her own unconscious material well enough to be comfortable identifying it in herself and others. The "measuring out" aspect of this card indicates that at present her ability to give is limited.

SUMMARY

It is almost unbelievable that out of six cards, four are Major Arcana and one is a court card, making this a powerful reading for Charlene and suggesting significant issues that need to be considered.

Two Minor Arcana suits are represented, Cups and Pentacles. There are two theories regarding missing suits. The first is that the missing ones represent suits where no work is needed. This theory, then, would indicate that Charlene needs certain Cups and Pentacles experiences. However, because her Cup is a Queen and her Pentacle is a six (double completion), it is likely that the missing cards reflect that Charlene's inner work needs to come from Swords and Wands experiences.

Certainly you, or another Tarot reader, might interpret the readings we have included in Chapters 16 and 17 differently. Our purpose was to show you that whatever else a card may suggest, it also contains ideas regarding potential for personal or spiritual growth.

If we have succeeded, then you have begun to understand how using the Tarot can reflect and even cultivate psychological and spiritual awareness. Used in this way, each reading becomes another chapter in the ever-unfolding story of who we are, and another experience in nurturing the Self and in living what Thomas Moore calls the "soulful life."

Welcome to the path. *Bon voyage*, and look for us along the way. We'll be there.

☀ Appendix:
Journal Forms

Reproduce the appropriate forms in this appendix to use for your Tarot journal.

Tarot Journal - Micro-Cross

Date:_____ **Question:**_____

Here & Now

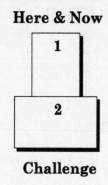

Challenge

Interpretation:

Tarot Journal - Triad

Date:_____ Question:_____

Past	Present	Future
Situation	Attitude	Main Idea
Body	Mind	Spirit

1	2	3

Interpretation:

Tarot Journal - Daily Opportunity

Date:_____ **Question:** _____

_____

Influences   **Potential**   **Opportunity**

| 1 | 2 | 4 |

| 3 |

Challenge

Interpretation:

Tarot Journal - Fountain of Creation

Date:_____ Question: _____

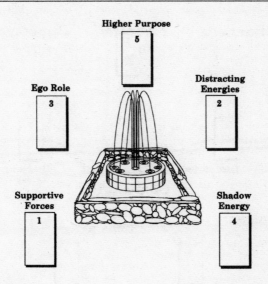

Higher Purpose
5

Ego Role
3

Distracting
Energies
2

Supportive
Forces
1

Shadow
Energy
4

Interpretation:

Tarot Journal - Star Guides

Date:_____ **Question:**_____

_____

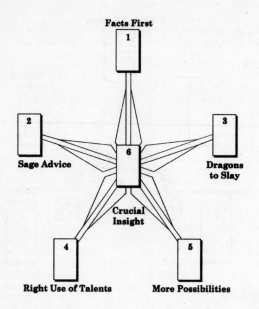

Interpretation:

Tarot Journal - Cross of Awareness

Date:_____ **Question:** _____

Options
6

New Focus
10

Recent
Influences
4

Here & Now
1

Potential
5

Expectations
9

Resources
8

2

Challenge

Past Experiences
3

Self-Image
7

Interpretation:

☀ Notes

1. What Is the Tarot?

1. Personal communication with Sandra Thomson, August 14, 1993.
2. Robert Mueller and Signe E. Echols, with Sandra A. Thomson, 1993, p. xiii.
3. William Irwin Thompson, 1976, p. 81.

2. What the Tarot Offers

1. Stuart Kaplan, 1978, p. 272.
2. Robert Wang, 1978, p. 31.
3. In metaphysics the Self is the One Will. Our understanding of the Will develops as we gradually reject the delusion that we are separate and recognize that we are the centers of the One Being or One Self.
4. John A. Sanford, "Parenting and Your Child's Shadow." In Jeremiah Abrams and Connie Zweig, eds., 1991, p. 59.
5. See A. E. Waite, 1989, p. 62. Waite says simply that the Tarot presents universal ideas by means of universal types and "it is in the combination of these types ... that it presents Secret Doctrine."
6. Robert Bly, "The Long Bag We Drag Behind Us." In Jeremiah Abrams and Connie Zweig, eds., 1991, pp. 6-12.
7. Sallie Nichols, 1982, Chapter 18, "The Devil: Dark Angel," pp. 250-281.

8. Individuation was expressed symbolically in ancient alchemy by the various stages necessary to transform base matter into gold, or the philosopher's stone.

3. Choosing a Deck and Using It

1. Manly P. Hall, 1975, p. CXXIX.

2. Stuart R. Kaplan, 1978, p. 1.

3. See A. E. Waite, 1989, p. 70. We and other Tarot authors attribute a higher message to the Minor Arcana scenes than did Waite himself, who described his Minor Arcana pictures as created to "respond to the divinatory meanings, which have been drawn from many sources." We cannot say what was the intent of later creators of Minor Arcana scenes, but we suspect from the scenes themselves that many of them relied on the Rider-Waite deck for inspiration.

4. We do not mean to imply that the use of pips is insignificant. Certainly the deck employed by the Hermetic Order of the Golden Dawn was one of the most symbolically meaningful decks of its time, and it used only designs and no figures for the Minor Arcana. See Robert Wang, 1978, p. 21, who writes that Waite's personification of the Minor Arcana is a "perversion of occult principle."

5. Steven Culbert, 1988.

6. Robert Wang, 1978, p. 15.

7. Serge Golowin (1988) advises the reader to sit slightly elevated and facing south (the direction of life, questions, and expectations), while the querent—the person with the question—faces north, which Golowin calls the direction of the earth and reality. Eileen Connolly (1979) suggests the same seating so the two people will be harmonious with "earth currents." She suggests the single reader face east because it is the direction of the rising sun and, therefore, symbolic of the first emanation from God.

8. Details of the "Spindrift" experiments are reported in Robert Owen, 1988, and in Larry Dossey, 1989, pp. 54-61.

9. See Larry Dossey, 1993, pp. 112-114; 120-121.

10. Both Aleister Crowley, author of the Thoth deck, and A. E. Waite, designer of the Rider-Waite deck, were members of the esoteric Hermetic Order of the Golden Dawn, which emphasized using the Tarot cards for inner growth and development. They did not, therefore, consider divinatory meanings as appropriate and did not ascribe specific "negative" meanings to reversed cards.

11. Rachel Pollock, 1983, p. 29.
12. Carol Bridges, 1989.
13. Gail Fairfield, 1985, p. 24.

4. The Tarot and . . .

1. Manly P. Hall, 1975, p. CXXIX.

5. Archetypal Mysteries

1. A. E. Waite, 1989, p. 152.
2. Linda Schierse Leonard, 1993, p. 227.
3. A. E. Waite, 1989, p. 152. Although our edition of Waite contains this description of the wallet, Knight quotes Waite as writing in the 1911 edition of the book that the wallet is inscribed with "dim signs to shew [sic] that many subconscious memories are stored up in the soul." See Knight, 1978, Vol. 2, p. 214.
4. A. E. Waite, 1989, p. 155.
5. Robert O'Neill, 1986, p. 309.
6. Paul Foster Case, 1985, p. 87.
7. Thomas Moore, 1994, p. 305.
8. Lao Tsu, 1972, Chapter 41.

6. Ten Archetypal Strengths and Resources

1. See Carl Japikse, 1989, p. 83. For Japikse, the V-shaped lines represent "God Immanent," and when inverted, represent "God Transcendent." In metaphysical work, the upward-pointing triangle represents Divine Immanence as expressed in material nature.
2. Barbara Walker, 1984, p. 68.

3. A. E. Waite, 1989, p. 79.
4. When earlier writers made the connection between card meanings and mythology, in an attempt to understand "higher" meanings of the cards, Waite reminded them that the Tarot was not of Roman or Greek mythology (Waite, 1989, p. 22).

   We do know that Waite's Major Arcana cards were a modified version of those in the Golden Dawn deck and that a full understanding of the latter relied on Egyptian mythology.

   In terms of archetypal meanings, which are similarly expressed even in different cultures, times, and artistic productions, the link is appropriate.

   See also Gareth Knight, 1978, Vol. 2, p. 235, where he states that Celtic mythology with its traces in the Arthurian cycle is the most fruitful source for correspondences with the Minor Arcana cards.
5. Barbara Walker, 1948, p. 71.
6. Madame Helena Blavatsky, founder of the Theosophical Society, believed that the 12 zodiacal signs represented the 12 initiatory rites through which a mystery school adept had to pass.
7. A. E. Waite, 1989, p. 83.
8. See Barbara Walker, 1988, p. 11. Traditionally the orb and the scepter acted as a model of the earth. The holding of the orb in the left hand represented a monarch's claim to dominion of the earth. Holding the scepter in the right hand represented the monarch and the sacred marriage between king and country.
9. Paul Foster Case, 1985, p. 194.
10. See Barbara Walker, 1988, p. 315, where she reminds us that before being adopted by Christianity, the "hand of blessing" was originally the "hand of the All-Goddess." The thumb stood for the child. The index and middle fingers, respectively, represented the goddess, the magic mother, and the god, the phallic father.
11. When any two complementary colors, or black and white, are mixed, they create gray, which has thus become a symbol for blending and the balance of opposites.
12. A. E. Waite, 1989, p. 91.
13. Personal communication, the Rev. Carl Yenetchi, Wayfarers Chapel, Rancho Palos Verdes, Calif.
14. A. E. Waite, 1989, p. 92.

15. According to Emanuel Swedenborg, seventeenth-century philosopher, mystic, and religious writer, women receive direct "influx" from God. Men receive indirect influx, so man's salvation is through marriage love, wherein two souls become one angel. Woman's soul is wisdom clothed in love. Man's soul is love clothed in wisdom. We thank the Rev. Carl Yenetchi, Swedenborgian minister associated with Wayfarers Chapel, Rancho Palos Verdes, for this information.

16. Before snakes took on the "evil" symbol of Christianity, they were ancient symbols of the divine feminine. Symbolically serpents/snakes have many seemingly conflicting meanings, but these need not be contradictory. For instance, in biblical symbology it was the serpent who tempted Eve. Yet serpents also represent healing (Asclepias's snakes) and transformation because they shed their skin.

    Since this is a card of opposites, we have assumed that the serpent has both of these qualities, i.e., the ability to create the delusion of opposites and then the ability to heal us when we use the kundalini energy to awaken our inner centers and overcome that delusion.

17. A. E. Waite, 1989, p. 96.

18. A. E. Waite, 1989, p. 96.

19. Barbara Walker, 1988, p. 110.

20. Rachel Pollock, 1980, p. 61.

21. See A. E. Waite, 1989, p. 100. Waite said she was closing the lion's mouth.

22. Paul Foster Case, 1985, p. 177.

23. Barbara Walker, 1988, p. 69.

24. See Carl Japikse, 1989, p. 176, where he calls this color a symbol of devotion. Metaphysically it is the color of sulfur, equated with the left pillar of the Cabalistic Tree of Life. Alchemically sulfur signifies the positive aspects of Divine Force.

25. C. G. Jung, 1953-1979, Vol. 10, paragraph 651.

26. See A. E. Waite, 1989, p. 21. Waite refers to these specific figures as an "invention in support of a hypothesis." Originally they were nondescript animal characters, Waite says, and that if more specific names of the figures are set aside, the grouping is "symbolically correct." Nevertheless, Waite identifies the snake as Typhon, one form of the Egyptian god Set and the son of the Greek goddess Hera, and the other figure as Hermanubis (Hermes/Anubis). Anubis is the Egyp-

tian god who presided over death and, as the "watcher of
the tomb," is associated with immortality and eternity.

27. Walker says that originally they represented the four pillars
(seasons) of the year. Barbara Walker, 1984, p. 97.

28. The feminine (Ida) and masculine (Pingula) kundalini energies rise from either side of the base chakra and intertwine
with one another along the spine through each chakra.

7. Ten Archetypal Tests and Dilemmas

1. Erich Neumann, 1973.
2. Marion Woodman, 1991.
3. Dorothy Norman, 1969.
4. See Barbara Walker, 1984, p. 76, who says this is the "Hermetic Four," traced on the heads and breasts of worshipers
of Hermes, and also the Nordic Cross of Odin, which later
became the Christian sign of the cross.
5. Sandra A. Thomson, 1994, p. 448.
6. Barbara Walker, 1984, 109.
7. See A. E. Waite, 1989, p. 124, who describes the figure as
a winged angel, neither male nor female, wearing the square
and triangle of the septenary. It therefore represents the multi-
tude of things that seven can symbolize.
8. Israel Regardie, 1984, Vol. 2, p. 17.
9. Mircea Eliade, 1959.
10. Gareth Knight, 1978, Vol. 2, p. 75.
11. See Barbara Walker, 1984, p. 114, where she suggests this
gesture, the "devil's pose," and his relationship to the two
figures may make this the shadow card to The Hierophant
(Major Arcana V).
12. Irene Gad, 1994, p. 246.
13. Sallie Nichols, 1982, p. 265.
14. Robert Johnson, 1991.
15. Gareth Knight, 1978, Vol. 1, pp. 59-68.
16. See Barbara Walker, 1984, p. 118, where she links this card
to the Carthaginian star goddess Astroarche, as well as other
star goddesses of Syria, Babylonia, Palestine, and northern
Europe, all of whom were accompanied by seven oracular
priestesses. They were associated with the seven pillars of
the Goddess of Wisdom mentioned in Proverbs 9:1.

17. Robert Mueller and Signe E. Echols, with Sandra A. Thomson, 1993, p. 121.
18. See Israel Regardie, 1984, Vol. 2, p. 15, where he writes that in the Golden Dawn Tarot the right tree represented the Tree of Life and the left one the Tree of Knowledge of Good and Evil. Thus the card represented the restored world.
19. Carl Japikse, 1989, p. 116.
20. Barbara G. Walker, 1988, p. 234.
21. Barbara G. Walker, 1983, p. 429.
22. A. E. Waite, 1989, 136.
23. Gareth Knight, 1978, Vol. 1, p. 28.
24. For a different opinion, see A. E. Waite, 1989, p. 140-141. According to Waite, the crayfish represents the nameless and hideous tendency which is lower than the savage beast and which comes from the deep. "Although it strives to attain manifestation, as a rule it sinks back whence it came" and thus never fully emerges. This certainly speaks of the shadow aspect of humankind.
    See Israel Regardie, 1989, Vol. 6, p. 139, where he describes the crayfish in the Golden Dawn deck as representing the scarab, the emblem of the sun below the horizon as it is when the moon is above.
25. Irene Gad, 1994, p. 277.
26. Erich Neumann, 1954, p. 85.
27. See A. E. Waite, 1989, p. 144, and Barbara Walker, 1984, p. 127. Waite called this the walled garden of the sensitive life, but Walker suggests that this symbol derived from the image of the child as being in the walled garden of Mother Night, "from whose 'enclosed garden' the children of the new creation must come."
28. Israel Regardie, 1984, Vol. 2, p. 14.
29. Barbara Walker, 1988, p. 435.
30. E. A. Waite, 1989, p. 144.
31. E. A. Waite, 1989, p. 148.
32. Traditionally these archangels are Tzaphquiel, archangel of Saturn, Tzadkiel, archangel of Jupiter, Kamael, archangel of Mars, Michael, archangel of the sun, Haniel, archangel of Venus, Raphael, archangel of Mercury, and Gabriel, archangel of the moon.
33. Barbara Walker, 1988, p. 53.

8. Achieving Unity

1. Paul Foster Case, 1985, p. 166.
2. See Paul Foster Case, 1985, p. 124, who writes that the four figures on the cards are the second, fifth, eleventh, and eighth signs of the zodiac. The numbers designating their positions total 26, the number of the name YHVH, Jehovah or Yahweh.
3. See Irene Gad, 1994, p. 310, who writes that wherever mandorlas are seen, it "always seems that something is beginning, is opening, is becoming."
4. Sandra A. Thomson, 1994, p. 231.
5. Barbara Walker, 1984, p. 132.
6. Barbara Walker, 1984, p. 13.
7. Irene Gad, 1994, p. 303.

9. Minor Arcana: Ten Growth Opportunities and Four Levels of Maturity

1. J. E. Cirlot, 1974, p. 230.
2. Mary K. Greer, 1984, p. 221.
3. Sandra A. Thomson, 1994, p. 511.
4. Clarissa Pinkola Estés, 1992, p. 402.
5. Carl Japikse, 1989, p. 166.
6. Mary K. Greer, 1984, p. 223.
7. Rose Gwain, 1994, pp. 36-37.
8. Irene Gad, 1994, p. 34.
9. See Gareth Knight, 1978, Vol. 1, p. 73, who suggests still a third combination, which switches the functions of Swords and Wands: Swords = intuition; Wands = thinking; Cups = feeling; Pentacles = sensing.
10. Juliet Sharman-Burke and Liz Greene, 1986, p. 84.
11. Mary K. Greer, 1987, p. 182.
12. Mary K. Greer, 1984, p. 237.
13. Mary K. Greer, 1987, p. 182.
14. Rachel Pollock, 1983, p. 30.
15. Juliet Sharman-Burke and Liz Greene, 1986, p. 85.
16. Mary K. Greer, 1987, p. 183.
17. Mary K. Greer, 1984, p. 234.

18. Rachel Pollock, 1983, p. 50.
19. Janet Sharman-Burke and Liz Greene, 1986, p. 85.
20. Mary K. Greer, 1987, p. 183.
21. Mary K. Greer, 1984, p. 233.

10. Pentacles: Grounding the Psyche

1. Robert Wang, 1978, p. 35.
2. For metaphysical students, the white lily symbolizes the mystic path to enlightenment, which seeks union with the soul, or God, through the heart. The red rose represents the occult path, union through knowledge or the mind.
3. Thomas Moore, 1994, p. 177.
4. Rachel Pollock, 1983, p. 117.
5. Carl Japikse, 1989, p. 170.
6. Craig Junjulus, 1985, p. 91.
7. Rachel Pollock, 1983, p. 110.
8. Clarissa Pinkola Estés, 1992, p. 419.
9. A. E. Waite, 1989, p. 268.
10. Mary K. Greer, 1987, p. 113.
11. Susan Gerulskis-Estes, 1981, p. 81.
12. Rachel Pollock, 1983, p. 103.
13. Craig Junjulus, 1985, p. 93.
14. Rachel Pollock, 1983, p. 100.
15. Craig Junjulus, 1985, p. 95.
16. Thomas Moore, 1994, p. 183.

11. Swords: Fighting Illusion

1. Robert Wang, 1978, pp. 34-35.
2. Angeles Arrien, 1987, pp. 200-204.
3. Rachel Pollock, 1983, p. 74.
4. See A. E. Waite, 1989, p. 250. We'd like to make more of the use of this term, but in fact, *hoodwink* was a nineteenth-century term for a blindfold or an actual hood placed over the head of a criminal about to be hanged or an initiate into a secret society. When used in initiation, it represents the darkness of the material mind.
5. Carl Japikse, 1989, p. 166.

6. See Rachel Pollock, 1983, p. 88, where she says it is Christ giving the blessing.
7. These ideas were presented by Dr. Walter Bonime, in his invited address on "The Myth of Masochism," delivered at the 1993 meetings of the Association for the Study of Dreams in Santa Fe, New Mexico.
8. Clarissa Pinkola Estés, 1992, p. 70.
9. Rachel Pollock, 1983, p. 85.
10. Richard Prosapio, 1990, p. 49.
11. See Carl Japikse, 1989, p. 177, where he refers to this boatman as a magician, a wise sage, the higher self.
12. Rose Gwain, 1994, p. 161.
13. Rachel Pollock, 1983, p. 11.
14. Lynn Buess, 1973, p. 183.
15. See Carl Japikse, 1989, p. 180, where he says that the figure has such a clear understanding of the meaning of spiritual success that he doesn't mind taking on the appearance of failure or even humiliation if it lets him reach his spiritual goal.
16. Rachel Pollock, 1983, p. 82.
17. Mary K. Greer, 1987, p. 122.
18. Robert Mueller and Signe E. Echols with Sandra A. Thomson, 1993, p. 81.
19. Carl Japikse, 1989, p. 193.
20. Carl Japikse, 1989, p. 193.

12. Cups: Feeling Your Way

1. Robert Wang, 1978, p. 34.
2. This is one of the first mysteries in the artistic rendering of cards in the suit of Cups. In A. E. Waite, 1989, p. 224, Waite describes the card as having *four* streams of water pouring from it. Is this merely a typo, was his intent something else, or, as Mary K. Greer has suggested to us, was it a lack of interest on Waite's part in the Minor Arcana, leaving their artistic rendering and symbolism largely to Pamela Colman Smith?
3. Carl Japikse, 1989, p. 160.
4. Rachel Pollock, 1983, p. 62.
5. Sandra A. Thomson, 1994, p. 252 and p. 557.

6. J. E. Cirlot, 1971, p. 68.

7. Angeles Arrien, 1987, p. 170.

8. Carl Japikse, 1989, p. 179.

9. Marie-Louise von Franz, 1993, p. 133.

10. Clarissa Pinkola Estés, 1992, p. 138.

11. Carl Japikse, 1989, p. 183.

12. A. E. Waite, 1979, p. 208.

13. Gareth Knight, 1978, Vol. 2, p. 266, identifies the garment as a lily-embroidered coat. This is another mystery in the understanding of the artistic rendering of the suit.

14. Carl Japikse, 1989, p. 136.

15. A. E. Waite, 1989, p. 204.

16. Irene Gad, 1994, p. 156.

17. Barbara Walker, 1988, p. 429.

13. Wands: The Spirit Soars

1. Juliet Sharman-Burke and Liz Greene, 1987, p. 87.

2. Robert Wang, 1978, p. 34.

3. Paul Foster Case (1981, p. 107) defines intuition as the "personal recollection of some aspect of truth that the Universal Mind has never forgotten."

4. Barbara Walker, 1983, p. 624.

5. Barbara Walker, 1988, p. 462.

6. Richard Prosapio, 1990, p. 38.

7. Rachel Pollock, 1983, p. 46.

8. Juliet Sharman-Burke and Liz Greene (1986, p. 126) call it the "public validation of a creative vision which began amidst anxiety and uncertainty."

9. Carl Japikse, 1989, p. 184.

10. A. E. Waite, 1989, p. 182.

11. Mary K. Greer, 1987, p. 121.

12. Carl Japikse, 1989, p. 192.

13. Rachel Pollock, 1983, p. 34.

14. Hans Biederman, 1994, p. 293.

15. Craig Junjulas, 1985, p. 70.

16. Angeles Arrien, 1987, p. 129.

17. A. E. Waite, 1989, p. 170.

14. Learning the Lay of the Land

1. This idea is presented in Rachel Pollock, 1983, pp. 140-141.
2. Juliet Sharman-Burke and Liz Greene, 1986, p. 204.
3. Mary K. Greer, 1984, p. 33.
4. Gail Fairfield, 1985, p. 141.
5. Mary K. Greer, 1984, pp. 31-33.

15. What Do I Consider?

1. Rose Gwain, 1994, p. 110.
2. Personal communication to Robert E. Mueller.
3. We are indebted to Mary K. Greer, one of the most innovative Tarot readers and teachers working today, for giving us the idea that once you dispense with the notion of reading the cards for divination only, there are a variety of styles of reading the cards available to you. Each can give you different information.

See Greer, 1988, pp. 33-44, where she talks about four methods of reading—analytic, psychic, therapeutic, magical—and four dimensions of meaning for the cards: literal, allegorical, moral, and spiritual.
4. Personal communication to Sandra A. Thomson, February 25, 1995.
5. Richard Prosapio, 1990, pp 71-73.
6. Irene Gad, 1994, p. 349.
7. Gail Fairfield, 1985, p. 134.

17. Through the Looking Glass

1. Gareth Knight, 1978, Vol. 1, p. 43.

❀ Bibliography

Abrams, Jeremiah, and Zweig, Connie, eds. *Meeting the Shadow*. New York: A Jeremy P. Tarcher/Putnam Book, 1991.

Arrien, Angeles. *The Tarot Handbook*. Sonoma, Calif.: Arcus Publishing Co., 1987.

Bidermann, Hans. *Dictionary of Symbolism*. New York: A Meridian Book, 1994.

Braun, Lilian Jackson. *The Cat Who Went Into the Closet*. New York: Jove Books, 1993.

Bridges, Carol. *Medicine Woman Tarot*. Stamford, Conn.: U.S. Games Systems, Inc., 1989.

Buess, Lynn M. *The Tarot and Transformation*. Marina del Rey, Calif.: DeVorss & Co., 1973.

Case, Paul Foster. *The True and Invisible Rosicrucian Order*. York Beach, Maine: Samuel Weiser, Inc., 1985.

Cirlot, J. E. *A Dictionary of Symbols*, 2d. ed. New York: Philosophical Library, 1971.

Connolly, Eileen. *Tarot. A New Handbook for the Journeyman*. North Hollywood, Calif.: Newcastle Publishing Co., Inc., 1979.

Cooper, J. C. *An Illustrated Encyclopedia of Traditional Symbols*. London: Thames and Hudson, 1978.

Culbert, Steven. *Reveal the Secrets of the Sacred Rose*. London and New York: W. Foulsham & Co., Ltd., 1988.

D'Agostino, Joseph D. *Tarot. The Royal Path to Wisdom*. York Beach, Maine: Samuel Weiser, Inc., 1985.

Davies, Ann. *Inspirational Thoughts on the Tarot*. Burbank, Calif.: Candlelight Press, 1983.

Dossey, Larry, M.D. *Healing Words: The Power of Prayer and the Practice of Medicine*. San Francisco: HarperSanFrancisco, 1993.

Dossey, Larry, M.D. *Recovering the Soul. A Scientific and Spiritual Search.* New York: Bantam Books, 1989.

Edinger, Edward. *Anatomy of the Psyche: Alchemical Symbolism in Psychotherapy.* La Salle, Ill.: Open Court, 1985.

Eliade, Mircea. *The Sacred and the Profane.* New York: Harcourt, Brace, Javonovich, Inc., 1959.

Estés, Clarissa Pinkola. *Women Who Run With the Wolves.* New York: Ballantine Books, 1992.

Fairfield, Gail. *Choice Centered Tarot.* North Hollywood, Calif.: Newcastle Publishing Co., 1985.

Gad, Irene. *Tarot and Individuation.* York Beach, Maine: Nicolas-Hays, Inc., 1994.

Gerulskis-Estes, Susan. *The Book of Tarot.* Dobbs Ferry, N.Y.: Morgan & Morgan, 1981.

Golowin, Sergius. *The World of the Tarot.* York Beach, Maine: Samuel Weiser, Inc., 1988.

Greene, Liz. *Relating. An Astrological Guide to Living with Others on a Small Planet.* York Beach, Maine: Samuel Weiser, Inc., 1978.

Greer, Mary K. *Tarot Constellations. Patterns of Personal Destiny.* North Hollywood, Calif.: Newcastle Publishing Co., Inc., 1987.

Greer, Mary K. *Tarot for Yourself. A Workbook for Personal Transformation.* North Hollywood, Calif.: Newcastle Publishing Co., Inc., 1984.

Greer, Mary K. *Tarot Mirrors. Reflections of Personal Meaning.* North Hollywood, Calif.: Newcastle Publishing Co., Inc., 1988.

Guthrie, Al. *Murder by Tarot.* New York: Zebra Books, 1992.

Gwain, Rose. *Discovering Your Self Through the Tarot.* Rochester, Vt.: Destiny Books, 1994.

Hall, James. *Dictionary of Subjects and Symbols in Art.* London: John Murray, 1974.

Hall, Manly P. *The Secret Teachings of All Ages*, Golden Anniversary Edition. Los Angeles: The Philosophical Research Society, Inc., 1975.

Heline, Corinne. *The Bible and the Tarot.* Oceanside, Calif.: New Age Press, Inc., 1969.

Japikse, Carl. *Exploring the Tarot.* Columbus, Ohio: Ariel Press, 1989.

Johnson, Robert. *Owing Your Own Shadow. Understanding the Dark Side of the Psyche.* San Francisco: HarperSanFrancisco, 1991.

Jung, C. G. *The Collected Works.* Trans. by R. F. C. Hall, ed. Princeton, N.J.: Princeton University Press, 1953-1979.

Junjulas, Craig. *Psychic Tarot.* Dobbs Ferry, N.Y.: Morgan & Morgan, 1985.

Kaplan, Stuart R. *The Encyclopedia of Tarot*, Vol. I. New York: U.S. Games Systems, Inc., 1978.

Knight, Gareth. *A Practical Guide to Qabalistic Symbolism*, two volumes in one. Vol. 1, *On the Spheres of the Tree of Life*; Vol. 2, *On the Paths and the Tarot*. York Beach, Maine: Samuel Weiser, Inc., 1978.

Konraad, Sandor. *Numerology. Key to the Tarot*. Rockport, Mass.: Para Research, 1983.

Lao Tsu. *Tao Te Ching*. Feng, G. F., and English, J., eds. New York: Vintage Books, 1972.

Leonard, Linda Schierse. *Meeting the Madwoman*. New York: Bantam Books, 1993.

Matthews, Boris, trans. *The Herder Symbol Dictionary*. Wilmette, Ill.: Chiron Publications, 1986.

Moore, Thomas. *Care of the Soul*. New York: HarperPerennial, 1994.

Mueller, Robert, and Echols, Signe E., with Sandra A. Thomson. *The Lovers' Tarot*. New York: Avon Books, 1993.

Neumann, Erich. "On the Moon and Matriarchal Consciousness." Spring, 1954, 83-100.

Neumann, Erich. *The Origins and History of Consciousness*. Princeton, N.J.: Princeton University Press, 1973.

Nichols, Sallie. *Jung and Tarot. An Archetypal Journey*. York Beach, Maine: Samuel Weiser, Inc., 1982.

Norman, Dorothy. *The Hero: Myth/Image/Symbol*. New York and Cleveland: World, 1969.

Odajnyk, V. Walter. *Gathering the Light. A Psychology of Meditation*. Boston & London: Shambhala, 1993.

O'Neill, Robert V. *Tarot Symbolism*. Lima, Ohio: Fairway Press, 1986.

Owen, Robert. *Qualitative Research, the Early Years*. Salem, Oreg.: Grayhaven Books, 1988.

Peach, Emily. *The Tarot Workbook*. Wellingborough, Northamptonshire: The Aquarian Press Limited, 1984.

Pollock, Rachel. *Seventy-Eight Degrees of Wisdom. Part I: The Major Arcana*. Wellingborough, Northhamptonshire: The Aquarian Press Limited, 1980.

Pollock, Rachel. *Seventy-Eight Degrees of Wisdom. Part 2: The Minor Arcana and Readings*. Wellingborough, Northhamptonshire: The Aquarian Press Limited, 1983.

Prosapio, Richard. *Intuitive Tarot*. Dobbs Ferry, N.Y.: Morgan & Morgan, 1990.

Regardie, Israel. *The Complete Golden Dawn System of Magic*, ten volumes in one. Phoenix, Ariz.: Falcon Press, 1984.

Sharman-Burke, Juliet, and Greene, Liz. *The Mythic Tarot*. New York: Simon & Schuster, Inc., 1986.

Thierens, A. E. *Astrology & the Tarot*. North Hollywood, Calif.: Newscastle Publishing Co., Inc., 1975.

Thompson, William Irwin. *Evil and World Order*. New York: Harper & Row, 1976.

Thomson, Sandra A. *Cloud Nine: A Dreamer's Dictionary*. New York: Avon Books, 1994.

Tichenell, Elsa-Brita. *The Masks of Odin. Wisdom of the Ancient Norse*. Pasadena, Calif.: Theosophical University Press, 1985.

von Franz, Marie-Louise. *Alchemy. An Introduction to the Symbolism and the Psychology*. Toronto: Inner City Books, 1980.

von Franz, Marie-Louise. *The Feminine in Fairy Tales*, rev. ed. Boston & London: Shambhala, 1993.

Waite, Arthur Edward. *The Pictorial Key to the Tarot*. York Beach, Maine: Samuel Weiser, Inc., 1989.

Walker, Barbara G. *The Secrets of the Tarot*. San Francisco: Harper & Row, Publishers, 1984.

Walker, Barbara G. *The Woman's Dictionary of Symbols and Sacred Objects*. San Francisco: HarperSanFrancisco, 1988.

Walker, Barbara G. *The Woman's Encyclopedia of Myths and Secrets*. San Francisco: Harper & Row, Publishers, 1983.

Wang, Robert. *An Introduction to the Golden Dawn Tarot*. York Beach, Maine: Samuel Weiser, Inc., 1978.

Wang, Robert. *The Qabalistic Tarot*. York Beach, Maine: Samuel Weiser, Inc., 1983.

Woodman, Marion. *Holding the Tension of the Opposites*, audiocassete tape no. A-138; 1991. Available from Sounds True Recordings, 735 Walnut Street, Boulder, CO, 80302.

☀ Index

FASCINATING BOOKS
OF SPIRITUALITY
AND PSYCHIC DIVINATION

CLOUD NINE: A DREAMER'S DICTIONARY
by Sandra A. Thomson
77384-8/$6.99 US/$7.99 Can

SECRETS OF SHAMANISM:
TAPPING THE SPIRIT POWER
WITHIN YOU
by Jose Stevens, Ph.D. and Lena S. Stevens
75607-2/$6.50 US/$8.50 Can

THE LOVERS' TAROT
*by Robert Mueller, Ph.D., and Signe E. Echols, M.S.,
with Sandra A. Thomson*
76886-0/$11.00 US/$13.00 Can

REASON TO BELIEVE: A PRACTICAL
GUIDE TO PSYCHIC PHENOMENA
by Michael Clark
78474-2/$5.99 US/$7.99 Can

SPIRITUAL TAROT: SEVENTY-EIGHT
PATHS TO PERSONAL DEVELOPMENT
*by Signe E. Echols, M.S., Robert Mueller, Ph.D.,
and Sandra A. Thomson*
78206-5/$12.00 US/$16.00 Can